TERRORISTS AMONG US
The Militia Threat

Also by Captain Robert L. Snow

The Complete Guide to Personal and Home Safety

Family Abuse: Tough Solutions to Stop the Violence

Looking for Carroll Beckwith: The True Story of a Detective's Search for His Past Life

Stopping a Stalker: A Cop's Guide to Making the System Work for You

SWAT Teams: Explosive Face-Offs with America's Deadliest Enemies

TERRORISTS AMONG US
The Militia Threat

Captain **Robert L. Snow**

PERSEUS
PUBLISHING
A Member of the Perseus Books Group

The hardcover edition of this book was published as *The Militia Threat: Terrorists Among Us*

Cataloging-in-Publication data for this book is available from the Library of Congress.
ISBN 0–7382–0766–7

Perseus Publishing is a Member of the Perseus Books Group.
Find us on the World Wide Web at http://www.perseuspublishing.com

Perseus Publishing books are available at special discounts for bulk purchases in the U.S. by corporations, institutions, and other organizations. For more information, please contact the Special Markets Department at the Perseus Books Group, 11 Cambridge Center, Cambridge, MA 02142, or call (800) 255–1514 or (617) 252–5298, or e-mail j.mccrary@perseusbooks.com.

First paperback printing, September 2002
1 2 3 4 5 6 7 8 9 10—06 05 04 03

For Martha, Paul, Frances, Hugh, and Stella.
With love.

CONTENTS

PREFACE

Being a police captain in a large city, and the militia movement confined mostly to small cities and rural areas, I had never knowingly met a militia member until I began the research for this book. However, like many people, I did have a preconceived idea of what constituted the militia movement in our country. I imagined small groups of military wannabes. I pictured gatherings of men who wished they had gone to Vietnam or had served in the Persian Gulf War, but had not. I envisioned groups of men who daydreamed about how heroic they would have been.

But, my preconceived idea continued, these men were not real war veterans. They were, in fact, military wannabes who outfitted themselves at Army surplus stores and played out their fantasy war games in the woods every weekend. And while I knew that the militia movement could be dangerous, as Timothy McVeigh proved to America, I suspected he was an aberration, an isolated radical fringe member, rather than a widespread danger.

However, as we shall see throughout this book, my image of the militia was wrong—dead wrong. My research brought me into contact with many militia members and groups, and I found that Timothy McVeigh was not quite the aberration I had believed him to be. Frighteningly, he is only one of many radical militia members in this country who hate the federal government with a burning intensity. In several of the incidents we shall discuss, we will see that only skillful, painstaking work by law enforcement agents has prevented other radical militia members from committing other devastating tragedies such as we saw in Oklahoma City.

Yet even more than the danger from the radical fringe of the militia movement, we will see that the militia movement as a whole presents a very clear and present danger to every American citizen. This danger, which is often unknown to urban dwellers, is the major reason for the existence of this book. Only a knowledgeable public, I felt, could insist that the government confront the immense danger posed by the militia movement, and only a knowledgeable public could insist that the government enforce the law and disband these illegal paramilitary groups. This must become a public mandate, because, as we will see throughout this book, the militia movement presents a very real and imminent threat to everyone.

Acknowledgment

I want to extend my thanks to Detective Ernie Hann for his help in the research of this book.

❖ ❖ ❖ ❖ ❖ ❖ ❖ ❖ 1

THE BIRTH OF THE MODERN MILITIA MOVEMENT

O ften, seemingly insignificant events can become watersheds in history. On 11 October 1989, one such event occurred.

On that day, in an obscure area of Idaho, an undercover informant for the Bureau of Alcohol, Tobacco, and Firearms (ATF) met with a man named Randy Weaver. From this insignificant meeting, a major social phenomenon would be born: the militia movement. This social phenomenon would grow and expand rapidly during the 1990s and bring with it the deaths of many innocent American citizens and the commission of an untold number of crimes.

The results of this seemingly insignificant meeting between Weaver and the informant would also eventually bring accusations against the federal government of a ruthlessness so severe that it would mobilize thousands of Americans in angry opposition. Yet the event that spawned all of this began simply as a typical police operation.

American law enforcement officers use undercover informants thousands of times every day. Police agencies utilize informants because these individuals are more suited than police officers to surreptitiously infiltrate criminal organizations and gain evidence concerning illegal activities. However, as any police officer who has worked with undercover informants knows, "snitches" must be closely monitored, since they are often criminals who are working for the police in order to have a criminal charge against them reduced or dismissed. Unfortunately, it appears that in the Randy Weaver case, the informant was not as closely monitored as he should have been. This can be a crucial mistake in any criminal investigation, because law enforcement officials find that occasionally, informants, in hopes of making their work appear more significant, may attribute much more importance to a target than should be given, may exaggerate a target's criminal background or propensity for violence, and may entrap a target into committing a crime. Unfortunately, all three of these apparently occurred in the Randy Weaver case.

Weaver and the informant were not strangers when they met to talk on 11 October 1989. They had come to know each other through their mutual attendance at various Aryan Nations events. The Aryan Nations is a white supremacist organization based in the Pacific Northwest, with its headquarters at Hayden Lake, Idaho. ATF had infiltrated the Aryan Nations with an undercover informant because they suspected that the organization had been involved in several bombings in northern Idaho.

The Aryan Nations' creed, according to their Internet website, is "We believe in the preservation of our Race, individually and collectively, as a people as demanded and directed by Yahweh (Aryan Nations members do not call the supreme being God because God is dog spelled backwards). . . . We believe that Adam, man of Genesis, is the placing of the White Race upon this earth. Not all races descend from Adam. Adam is the father of the White Race only. . . . We believe that the Cananite [sic] Jew is the natural enemy of our Aryan (White) Race. . . . The Jew is like a destroying virus that attacks our racial body to destroy our Aryan culture and the purity of our Race . . ."

Besides Jews, Aryan Nations members also hold an intense hatred for the other non-Caucasian races. Their creed continues: ". . . the White workingman curse[s] over his beer about the latest boatload of mud-creatures (all races other than Caucasian) dumped on our shores to be given job preference over the White citizens who built this land." The Aryan Nations' Internet website also contains a photo of the present leader of the organization, Richard G. Butler, posing in a Nazi salute from the pulpit.[1]

Randy Weaver, however, when interviewed by Secret Service agents in 1985 concerning threats he had reportedly made against the President of the United States and the Governor of Idaho, denied both making these threats and having any affiliation with the Aryan Nations. He and his wife, Vicki, eventually filed an affidavit with the county clerk's office, claiming that individuals were making false statements about his alleged threats against public figures and his relationship with the Aryan Nations. Weaver also later denied any belief in the Aryan Nations' philosophy.

"I attended a couple of their picnics during the summer, but I never joined them," Weaver said of the Aryan Nations. "Their beliefs were different than mine."[2] Yet, while denying any belief in their philosophy, Weaver still became well-known enough at Aryan Nations events to be targeted by the undercover informant.

Interestingly, and eventually a crucial point in the case, in all of the informant's previous encounters with Weaver at various Aryan Nations' events, he had always worn a hidden tape recorder, and in none of these encounters had Weaver ever made any mention of his predisposition to commit an illegal act. At the meeting on 11 October 1989, however, the meeting at which the informant claimed that Weaver did offer to commit a crime, the informant wore no hidden tape recorder, and so the only evidence of what was said became the informant's word.

According to later testimony by the informant concerning the unrecorded meeting, Weaver reportedly asked the informant, who had earlier bragged he was in the business of supplying guns to motorcycle gang members, how his business was going. The informant replied that it was going great, so great in fact that he had sold all of his products. Weaver then, according to the informant, told him he wanted to work for him, that he could supply the informant with all of the sawed-off shotguns he wanted, and that the weapons would have "no paper," meaning they would have no registration documents. Sawed-off shotguns are weapons that, at close range, do enormous damage to a victim, ripping huge holes in body cavities or shearing off limbs. Consequently, they are often the favorite weapon of criminal gangs. For this reason, sawed-off shotguns are illegal to manufacture or possess.

On 24 October 1989, the informant, this time wearing a hidden tape recorder, met again with Randy Weaver. At this meeting, Weaver gave the informant two sawed-off shotguns. The informant paid Weaver $300 for the weapons, and then asked Weaver if he could supply more of them, which Weaver agreed to do. The two men met again in November 1989 and discussed the delivery of more sawed-off shotguns, but no more were delivered because ATF officials advised the informant to have no more contact with Weaver.

For an unexplained reason, ATF agents waited until mid-1990 before continuing their investigation of Weaver's illegal manufacture and sale of the shotguns. In June 1990, ATF agents met with Weaver at a motel in Sandpoint, Idaho. The agents showed Weaver photographs of the sawed-off shotguns he had sold to the informant and told him they had a tape recording of the transaction, which Weaver declined to hear. The ATF agents then offered Weaver the opportunity to work for them, which they said would help him in his own criminal case. The agents wanted Weaver to become an undercover informant for them and report on illegal activities within the Aryan Nations. While this may sound to some like Hollywood screenwriting, recruiting informants—individuals already involved with and known to a closed organization—is a common law enforcement tactic. Without informants, law enforcement personnel could never infiltrate many tight-knit criminal organizations, which often watch new members closely, looking for government infiltrators. Weaver, however, steadfastly refused the offer, saying he would not become a "snitch."

Again for an unexplained reason, the federal government waited until December 1990 before seeking an indictment against Weaver for "manufacturing and possessing an unregistered firearm." The ATF agents who would serve the warrant, however, felt certain that this would not be just a routine arrest. They suspected that taking Weaver into custody would likely be a dangerous assignment. When several ATF agents had earlier visited the Weaver home on Ruby Ridge, near Naples, in northern Idaho, they found that all of the Weaver family members, including the women, carried firearms, and so they decided that, for safety reasons, they would use a ruse and arrest Randy Weaver while away from his home.

On 17 January 1991, two ATF agents stopped a camper on a bridge near where Weaver lived. They raised the hood and pretended to have engine problems, while inside the camper, more ATF agents and the local sheriff waited. When Randy Weaver and his wife, Vicki, stopped to help the apparently stranded motorists, officers leaped out of the camper and placed Randy under arrest. Randy reportedly told the agents, "Nice trick; you'll never do that again."[3] The agents found that both of the Weavers were armed.

At Weaver's initial hearing on the sawed-off shotgun charge, a judge released Randy on personal recognizance. This means that the accused person is released simply on his word that he will return for court, and no bail bond is required. Although Randy Weaver gave this promise to show up for court, he never did return.

There has been considerable speculation that the reason Randy Weaver did not return for court was because he had been given an incorrect date on which to appear. The court apparently first told him he had to return on 19 February 1991. However, two weeks later, the court clerk notified him that the date had been changed to 20 February 1991. Soon afterward, though, Weaver received a letter from the U.S. Probation Office that mistakenly said his court date was 20 March 1991. Regardless of the mix-up, however, Randy Weaver did not return for any of the dates.

On 14 March 1991, a federal grand jury indicted Randy Weaver for failure to appear in court as required on 20 February 1991. An eventual Justice Department investigation of the Weaver incident, however, would charge the U.S. Attorney's Office with being "unnecessarily rigid" in its rushing forward and seeking an indictment against Randy Weaver before the erroneous 20 March 1991 date given by the U.S. Probation Office.[4]

The task of arresting Randy Weaver for his failure to appear in court fell to the federal court's officers, the U.S. Marshal's Service. Yet, because Randy Weaver had threatened that the police would never pull another ruse on him, and he and his wife had both been armed during the initial arrest, careful plans had to be made for Randy Weaver's rearrest. During their planning, federal authorities discovered that Randy Weaver had reportedly been making statements that he would violently oppose being taken into custody again by the authorities. Vicki even sent a letter to the authorities, which she addressed to "The servants of the Queen of Babylon." In the letter, Vicki said, ". . . the tyrant's blood will flow . . ." and ". . . whether we live or die, we will not bow to your evil commandments."[5] Randy Weaver had also filed an affidavit with the county clerk saying that he believed he would eventually be forced to defend himself and his family from physical attack by the FBI. Apparently, both Randy and Vicki Weaver shared a "paranoid fantasy" that the federal government was out to get them. Ironically, it turned out not to be a fantasy after all.

Most of the officers concerned with the arrest planning felt that since Randy Weaver had apparently affiliated himself with the Aryan Nations, was an ex-Green Beret, reportedly kept a large stockpile of weapons at his home, and his cabin on Ruby Ridge would be difficult to approach without being detected, that to apprehend him safely would require an undercover operation. In preparation for this operation, the Marshal's Service began a surveillance of the Weaver home on Ruby Ridge, which included aerial reconnaissance and the installation of a solar-powered video camera.

On 21 August 1992, several federal marshals in camouflage outfits were conducting this surveillance near the Weaver home. Suddenly, one of the Weaver's dogs, a golden retriever named Striker, began barking and then charged at the men. The officers retreated. Hearing the dog's bark and thinking he was chasing game, Randy Weaver, his fourteen-year-old son Sammy, and a friend living with the Weaver family, Kevin

Harris, grabbed their guns and followed the dog as he chased the marshals up a trail in the thick woods. The Weavers lived a very rugged existence on Ruby Ridge, and hunting provided a large part of their sustenance. They did not detect anything out of the ordinary.

At a spot called the "Y," where the trail split into two, the Weavers and Kevin Harris caught up with the federal marshals but did not immediately see them because of their camouflage outfits. Striker did see them, however, and one of the marshals stepped forward and shot and killed the dog. Sammy, apparently both outraged at seeing his dog killed and in fear since he did not know who the camouflaged men were, fired at the marshal who had killed his dog. Sammy then turned and tried to flee back toward the Weaver house, but before he could, one of the marshals reportedly shot him in the back and killed him. Kevin Harris, in defense of Sammy, he would later claim, allegedly fired his weapon at the marshals, striking one of them in the chest and killing him. Harris and Randy Weaver then fled back to the Weaver house.

Once the shooting stopped, two of the marshals raced to a nearby house and called 911, telling the Boundary County Sheriff's Office that they had an officer dead, the others pinned down, and that they needed help. Considerable controversy would later arise from the use of the phrase "pinned down," since Sammy Weaver was dead and Randy Weaver and Kevin Harris had apparently fled back to the Weaver house. Also, at some point during the time the marshals were "pinned down," Randy Weaver and Kevin Harris returned to the "Y," apparently without the marshals knowing it, and collected Sammy's body, which they laid out in a shed behind the house. It would not be until days later, when federal officials were demolishing the buildings around the Weaver house, that they would discover Sammy had been killed.

The marshals who had called 911 also called the Marshal's Service Headquarters in Washington, D.C. and reported their situation. The officials there activated the Marshal's Service Crisis Center and, in addition, ordered deployment of the Marshal's Service Special Operations Group. Other law enforcement agencies also dispatched officers to assist the marshals, including deputies from the Boundary County Sheriff's Office, officers from the U.S. Border Patrol, and troopers from the Idaho State Police.

Because none of the officers arriving at the scene knew where the Weavers or Harris had gone, and they feared that the men could be hiding with their weapons in the thick woods, it would be some time before they would feel safe enough to remove the slain marshal's body and relieve the other marshals from the area of the "Y." Eventually, however, law enforcement officials from several agencies arrived in a large enough force to secure the area and set up a command post.

The command post personnel immediately established a perimeter around the Weaver cabin, where they now suspected the men had fled to, and began gathering more intelligence about the situation. Convinced that it would be extremely dangerous to both law enforcement personnel and the Weaver women and children to assault the Weaver's Ruby Ridge home, the officers at the scene made the decision to call in the FBI's Hostage Rescue Team (HRT) to resolve the situation. The FBI had formed the HRT as an elite, full-time tactical team, whose task was to handle sensitive, high-risk situations such as this.

At this point in the Weaver incident, however, a number of poor decisions by the FBI turned what was already a tragedy into a colossal blunder that would both tarnish the FBI's reputation and further galvanize America's politically far-right in their paranoia with regard to the federal government. Because of Weaver's military background, his affiliation with a radical group, and the fact that all members of his family carried firearms, FBI officials concluded that this would be an "extremely high-risk operation, possibly the highest risk situation [they] could encounter."[6]

Apparently, because of this appraisal, FBI officials illegally changed the agency's "rules of engagement" for Ruby Ridge. Rules of engagement lay down the guidelines for when deadly force can be used by a law enforcement agency. Until this point, the rules of engagement for all federal agencies stated that deadly force could be used only to protect oneself or another person in imminent danger of death or serious bodily injury. For this incident, however, supervisors instructed the FBI agents that lethal force "can and should" be used against any male seen on the Weaver property carrying a firearm.[7] This unwritten, on-the-scene change not only violated the FBI's own regulations, but also is patently illegal and in violation of the Fourth Amendment to the Constitution. Even local and state police agencies, whose deadly force policies are more relaxed than federal agencies, must still follow the guidelines laid down by the Supreme Court's 1985 decision in *Garner v. Tennessee*. This decision states that police officers can only use deadly force to defend themselves from death or serious bodily injury, to defend another person from death or serious bodily injury, or to stop a fleeing person who has committed a forcible felony (meaning a crime during which someone was killed or seriously injured, or threatened with death or serious injury). This on-the-scene change, which apparently applied only to the Ruby Ridge incident, obviously went far beyond the guidelines of *Garner v. Tennessee.*

This sudden modification of their deadly force policy did not sit well with some of the FBI agents at Ruby Ridge. Several agents refused to follow it.

"My reaction was 'you've got to be kidding,'" FBI agent Donald Kusulas told a Senate panel that eventually investigated the Ruby Ridge incident.

FBI agent Peter King told the senators that his reaction was "that's crazy; that's ridiculous."[8]

Unfortunately, not all of the agents decided to ignore the new, relaxed rules of engagement. On 22 August 1992, Randy Weaver, Kevin Harris, and Randy's sixteen-year-old daughter Sara left the Weaver cabin to go look at the body of Sammy, which Randy Weaver had placed in a shed behind their house. An HRT sniper, Lon Horiuchi, later said he thought Randy Weaver and Harris intended to shoot at an FBI helicopter that was overhead. Consequently, Horiuchi fired a shot at Kevin Harris but missed and instead wounded Randy Weaver in the shoulder, who, along with Harris and Sara, reacted by running as fast as they could back to the cabin, where Vicki and two other daughters waited. As Randy and Sara raced through the door and into the safety of their home, the sniper fired again at Harris, the last person through the door. However, the bullet missed its target, smashed through a window in the door, and hit Vicki Weaver, who stood just inside the cabin holding her ten-month-old daughter Alisheba in her arms. The high-powered bullet struck Vicki in the face, shredding away huge pieces of bone and flesh, instantly killing her. Harris, as he raced through the door, was hit by fragments of the bullet that struck Vicki, along with bone shrapnel from Vicki's face, and was seriously injured. The infant tumbled to the floor, fortunately suffering no injury.

After this, no one left the cabin again, and with both Randy and Kevin injured and Vicki lying dead on the floor, the standoff went on for well over a week. The Weavers' cabin had no air-conditioning, and so, as the standoff continued day after day in the August temperatures, Vicki's body, placed under a table in the kitchen, began to decompose.

In an attempt to bring the standoff to an end, FBI agents decided to try to negotiate, and they delivered a telephone to the front of the cabin (the Weavers had no telephone). After receiving no response from inside, the FBI finally warned the cabin's occupants over a loudspeaker that if everyone did not come out and surrender, they would start demolishing the buildings around the cabin. When the authorities still received no response from the people inside, they began tearing down the out buildings. It was during this demolition that they discovered Sammy Weaver's dead body. Until this point, no one outside the cabin knew that Sammy had been killed.

The authorities later discovered that the reason the Weavers or Harris would not pick up the telephone offered by the FBI was because it had been delivered to the Weaver cabin by a robot. This robot, along with carrying the telephone, also carried a shotgun, and, considering what had happened so far, no one inside the cabin felt safe stepping outside to get the telephone (the FBI would later insist that the robot's weapon was not loaded). On 26 August 1992, after the standoff had continued for five days, the FBI commander, apparently beginning to feel uneasy about what had happened so far, rescinded the new rules of engagement and reinstated the FBI's long-standing policy on deadly force.

To support the continuing siege of the Weaver property, the federal government brought in dozens of federal agents and massive amounts of equipment and supplies. As the standoff continued throughout the last days of August 1992, dozens of protestors began gathering at the police lines around the Weaver property. Some of the protestors were neighbors of the Weavers; others had traveled long distances to visit the remote site. The protestors often verbally challenged the law enforcement officers and National Guardsmen about their justification for being there, and several of the protestors carried signs that said "Death to ZOG." ZOG stands for Zionist Occupational Government, which is a conspiracy theory held by many in the Pacific Northwest that claims the legitimate government of the United States has been secretly taken over and replaced by a Jewish cabal. Many of the protestors felt that ZOG was behind the siege of the Weaver family.

Finally, as the standoff at Ruby Ridge continued to wear on with no resolution in sight, the FBI allowed former Green Beret Colonel Bo Gritz, a Populist Party presidential candidate, who had also run a presidential campaign with former Ku Klux Klan member David Duke, to approach the cabin and talk with Weaver and Harris. The first few times Gritz went to the cabin, though, the occupants would not let him in, but would only speak to him through the door. Finally, taking along with him a female neighbor the Weavers knew and trusted, Gritz persuaded the cabin's occupants to let them come inside. Following this face-to-face meeting with the cabin's occupants, Gritz asked the FBI for a body container and brought

Vicki Weaver's now-decomposed body out of the cabin, then convinced the people inside to surrender, finally ending the eleven-day standoff.

The federal government immediately filed murder charges against both Randy Weaver and Kevin Harris for the killing of the federal marshal, and asked for the death penalty. However, on 8 July 1993, a jury found both Weaver and Harris innocent, believing that the government had provoked the entire incident by killing the Weaver dog, Striker. A jury also found Weaver innocent of the original charge that started the incident in the first place: his sale of the two sawed-off shotguns to the ATF informant. In his winning effort against this charge, Weaver's attorney used the defense of entrapment. To successfully use this defense, an accused person must show that he was not predisposed to commit the crime, but rather that his reluctance to commit the crime was overcome by repeated requests for the act by a government agent. The jury members obviously felt troubled by the fact that while so many of the meetings between Weaver and the ATF informant had been secretly taped, the crucial meeting in which the idea for the crime was born had not.

The eventual Department of Justice investigation into the Ruby Ridge incident also saw this as a problem. The report of this investigation said: "We are troubled by the lack of firsthand information before the first weapon sale. . . . the crucial meeting was not recorded. . . . the only account of the meeting comes from [the informant]."[9]

An unwritten, but ironclad, rule exists in law enforcement that the ATF agents violated in the Randy Weaver case: Never trust an informant! Law enforcement officers have instituted this rule because they know that informants are not always trustworthy, honest people. Most are criminals who will lie, cheat, steal, and do just about anything they can get away with in order to help themselves. Many police officers who have not followed this rule have been embarrassed later in court upon discovering that their informants have lied to them.

Despite Randy Weaver's other acquittals, a jury found him guilty of not showing up for his 20 February 1991 court date and for committing an offense while on personal recognizance release. A court sentenced him to eighteen months in prison, but credited him with the time already spent in jail awaiting trial, which meant that Randy Weaver had only a few more months to serve.

However, unlike Weaver and Harris, the federal government did not appear guiltless. Following the Ruby Ridge incident, the federal government found itself facing serious public censure for its killing of a fourteen-year-old boy and a woman holding an infant in her arms. These deaths appeared even more abhorrent when it became clear that the original charge against Weaver, which had started the entire incident, was bogus. It is common in law enforcement that when something such as this occurs, no one will ever step forward and accept blame, but rather, those involved usually begin pointing fingers at each other. That is exactly what happened in this case.

The FBI official in charge at Ruby Ridge, Special Agent Eugene F. Glenn, insisted that senior FBI officials in Washington, D.C. had approved the changed rules of engagement. Senior FBI officials, however, including FBI Deputy-Director Larry Potts, insisted that they had not seen or approved the new rules, and that they were the total responsibility of Agent Glenn, the on-scene commander. Agent Glenn responded by charging in a letter to the Office of Responsibility at the United States Justice Department that the FBI's internal review of the Ruby Ridge incident was incomplete, inaccurate, and undercut by flaws that "reveal a purpose to create scapegoats and false impressions."[10]

Unfortunately, we will likely never know the truth, because senior FBI official Michael Kahoe, chief of the FBI's violent crimes and major offenders section, and the man in charge of conducting the FBI's internal review of the Ruby Ridge incident, destroyed documents collected during the investigation that were apparently highly damaging to the FBI. He destroyed every copy of the FBI's "After-Action Critique" of the Ruby Ridge incident. Many observers believe that the documents he destroyed contained the names of FBI higher-ups who had approved the changed rules of engagement. In December 1996, Kahoe pled guilty to a charge of obstruction of justice, and in October 1997, a court sentenced him to eighteen months in prison.

And as if the federal government did not already look bad enough, it seemed that blunders and misbehavior would continue to follow this case. The U.S. Attorney's Office entered into an agreement with Kevin Harris, saying that if he would not object to their requested continuance of his preliminary hearing, the government would allow Harris to have a complete preliminary hearing before they proceeded further against him (during a preliminary hearing, a judge can dismiss the charges if he or she feels the government does not have a valid case against the defendant). Harris agreed to this continuance, but then the U.S. Attorney's Office, despite the agreement, quickly indicted Harris before he could have the promised preliminary hearing.

In addition, the U.S. Attorney's Office also attempted to seek the death penalty against Weaver and Harris (which can often enflame jurors against defendants) even though the alleged crimes very obviously did not merit the death penalty. This made the government appear to have a vendetta against Weaver and Harris. Also, during the trial, even though ordered to do so by the court, the FBI continually delayed providing evidence for both the prosecution and defense, at one time sending documents by fourth-class mail so they would take several weeks to arrive. Because of this misbehavior by the FBI, the judge in the trial ordered the agency to pay for the defense costs of the delay. Considering all these actions by the government, it is not surprising that the jury sided with Weaver and Harris. Most people probably would have.

This incident did not end, however, with the sentencing of FBI agent Kahoe and the not-guilty verdicts for Weaver and Harris. In August 1997, five years after the incident, and just hours before the statute of limitations was set to expire, Boundary County (Idaho) Prosecutor Denise Woodbury filed first-degree murder charges against Kevin Harris and involuntary manslaughter charges against FBI sniper Lon Horiuchi. A judge, however, threw out the charge against Harris, ruling that trying him again would be double jeopardy. Horiuchi sought and succeeded in having his case moved from state to federal court, where on 12 January 1998 he entered a not-guilty plea.

On 14 May 1998, U.S. District Judge Edward Lodge dismissed the charges against Horiuchi. "The actions of Mr. Horiuchi had tragic results," Judge Lodge said in his eighteen-page decision. "However, Mr. Horiuchi did no more than was 'necessary and proper' for him to carry out his duties under the totality of the circumstances."

Not everyone agreed with this decision, however. Attorney Chuck Peterson, who assisted in the defense of Weaver and Harris, said, "That seems absurd. This clearly isn't a vindication of Horiuchi. It's like the Simpson verdict: We all know he did it, there's just nothing we can do about it."[11]

After an extensive investigation of the Ruby Ridge incident, the Department of Justice found that the FBI had overreacted to the threat Randy Weaver presented and had instituted a "shoot-on-sight" policy that violated the Fourth Amendment to the Constitution. The investigation of this incident also found that the FBI's handling of the Ruby Ridge incident fell short in other areas of proper law enforcement procedure: the agency had not properly utilized negotiating personnel; it had not secured the site correctly; it had conducted a poor and disorganized search of the scene; and the HRT had not interviewed the marshals involved in the shooting until the following day, and then only in a cursory manner.

As an endnote, the Justice Department eventually agreed to pay Randy Weaver and his three surviving daughters $3.1 million. The Justice Department, though, said this payment was not an admission of any wrongdoing. However, FBI Director Louis Freeh, in 1995, said, "Ruby Ridge was a series of terribly flawed law-enforcement operations [in which] the FBI did not perform at the level which the American people expect or deserve."[12]

This incident, which resulted from the insignificant act of an ATF undercover informant apparently trying to recruit Randy Weaver to commit a crime, quickly became a pivotal event for those on the far right of America's political scene and also became a watershed in history. The events at Ruby Ridge served as the catalyst for the emergence of the modern militia movement in America.

Most far-right groups and individuals in 1992, already highly suspicious of the federal government, saw the Weaver incident as indisputable proof that the government, in its desire to disarm Americans and strike down those with unpopular beliefs, would no longer respect anyone's rights. (Unfortunately, what most of these far-right individuals and groups said about the federal government was, in this case, believed by the American public to be true.) The Weaver incident was seen as an atrocious example of overreaction to a perceived threat and a blatant violation of the Weaver family's constitutional rights. And though, before the Weaver incident, far-right groups in America often had little to do with each other, this case brought them together and united them in their opposition to the federal government. Far-right individuals and groups concerned about the growing strength of the federal government now had a concrete example of its abuse of power and violation of constitutional rights.

According to Morris Dees, chief trial attorney for the Southern Poverty Law Center, in his book *Gathering Storm*, following the Weaver incident, leaders of some of America's most violent and racist right-wing organizations met in Estes Park, Colorado, to discuss what they should do now that the federal government had so openly displayed what they felt was its true colors. Dees claimed that the leaders of these groups decided that the time was ripe to recruit people of more moderate leanings into far right-wing organizations. But to accomplish this, the leaders agreed they would have to tone down the racism and extreme violence in their rhetoric, and instead use the Weaver incident, gun control, and other issues as their rallying call. If they could do this, they could begin recruiting and mobilizing citizens with moderate right-leaning political beliefs into armed civilian militias, which could then be used to prevent another Ruby Ridge from occurring.[13]

An article in *Law Enforcement Technology* concerning the militia movement said: "According to most observers, there is a distinction to be made between rank and file militia members and long-time extremists. Average militia members tend to be lower to middle-income white men worried about economic security as well as government excesses and what they believe are their Second Amendment gun ownership rights. Long-time extremists appear to be encouraging the militia movement in furtherance of their own radical, and often violent, aims."[14]

Supporting this, most observers of the modern militia movement find that, in stark contrast to the usually unemployed and often sociopathic individuals who make up America's most virulent hate groups, many members of the armed civilian militias hold jobs, have families, and have never been in trouble with the law. Yet, these "average Americans" often unknowingly allow themselves to be led by racist individuals who have no proven leadership skills, but, as we shall see throughout this book, many times have criminal tendencies.

Although throughout American history various militia groups have sprung up and then died away, the modern militia movement is actually very young. With the idea for the militias sparked at Estes Park in just 1992, the Militia of Montana and the Michigan Militia were both formed only a few years ago, in 1994. These two organizations became the first modern militias to attract the attention of the news media. The Michigan Militia in particular received extensive coverage because its members made their first public appearance, in fatigues and carrying weapons, on a children's playground in Pelliston, Michigan, much to the chagrin of the residents, who did not appreciate the militia's choice of mustering areas.

What exactly is a militia? The militias are the militant arm of the patriot movement, which includes such groups as the John Birch Society, the Liberty Lobby, tax resisters, and others. Basically, militias are private armies run by self-appointed "generals." Militias are groups of individuals who have formed into paramilitary organizations that stockpile and carry assault-type, military weapons, wear military uniforms, practice military maneuvers, and yet are not part of the military. Nor are they part of any government entity. Actually, most militia members hold the government in disdain, believing that the government has gotten too large and has attempted to regulate too much. Most militias oppose the federal government because they believe it is slowly attempting to take away its citizens' constitutionally guaranteed rights, and that the first step in doing this is the disarming of the American public.

In addition, militias are groups of individuals who steadfastly believe that the reference made to the militia in the Second Amendment to the Constitution authorizes them both to own and to carry whatever firearms they wish, and also authorizes them to form into these paramilitary groups. This belief comes from the fact that, at one time, the militia was an integral part of our country's defense. The government in colonial times considered every male between the ages of eighteen and forty-five to be a member of the militia, and many localities during this time also demanded that every male between these ages have a firearm. However, the colonial militias that the Second Amendment refers to were not the private armies that many of the modern militias groups are, private armies that answer to no one but their own self-appointed leaders. The colonial militias were under the control of the government, and these units either fought alongside regular army soldiers or provided community security. The original colonial militias were an essential supplement to our country's defense when the Constitution was written, because at that time there was no large standing army. Militias were also needed in colonial America because a community had to be ready at any moment to fight against an Indian attack or an invasion by French or Spanish soldiers. Help was seldom close by and readily available. Today, however, we no longer fear Indian attacks or invasions by foreign armies. And, while in colonial times it could take days or weeks to summon help, in today's society, help is only minutes away, through dialing 911. Therefore, while a reference to the militia may have made sense to the framers of the Constitution, its existence is no longer necessary as the founding fathers envisioned it.

The members of modern-day militias, however, see it otherwise. According to Dave Delaney in an article in *Modern Militiaman*: "The militia is a 'grass roots' tool of the people, designed to check the abuse of its own internal government, and to defend against the incursions of a foreign enemy."[15]

In a prepared statement given before the Senate subcommittee on Terrorism, Technology, and Government Information, Militia of Montana founder John E. Trochmann said, "At the present time we view the militia movement as a giant neighborhood watch. The movement is made up of a cross section of Americans from all walks of life, with one singular mandate which is public and overt: the return to the Constitution of the United States, as your oath implies."[16]

Even more frightening than the idea that there are now private armies existing in the United States that answer to no one but themselves is the fact that these heavily armed, private armies almost all subscribe to one or more (often many more) conspiracy theories, such as ZOG. These conspiracy theories are many times so far-fetched and unbelievable that it makes one wonder why the group subscribes to them. Most of the conspiracies militia groups believe in involve some evil and secret group plotting to take over our country and enslave the citizenry. The armed civilian militias believe that one of the major reasons for their existence is to save our country from these evil cabals.

In addition to believing in various conspiracy theories, many militia members also believe that the present government is corrupt and ruthless beyond redemption. Martin Lindstedt, managing editor of *Modern Militiaman,* said, "The current ruling criminal regime is destroying the foundations of civilization, and after the current civilization has reached its deserved fate, a new civilization must be allowed to emerge and flourish, free from the parasitic rulers of the past."[17]

This hatred and rejection of the government underlines one of the real dangers of the militias: They are not under the control of the government but, rather, under the control of untested and often untrained individuals who decide for the members who is good and who is bad, and when to fight. Even though the leaders of these militias have many times given themselves impressive titles, their leadership abilities and often their true motives are completely unknown. In the regular military, individuals must pass entrance exams, receive extensive training, and then slowly work their way up the rank structure. During this time, they are tested, graded, and evaluated before they reach the stage where they can give orders that might cause a loss of life or property damage. Yet militia leaders often initially appoint themselves as majors, colonels, or generals, many times with no training or military experience at all.

This is not to say that everyone who joins or leads a militia is a dangerous person. Quite the contrary, many people who join the militias have no intent other than to ensure that the government respects everyone's constitutional rights. Often these people have never even had any thoughts about committing a crime or using violence. Yet crime and violence are often the end result of the militias' actions. With their military uniforms, impressive titles, stockpiles of weapons and explosives, and their shared belief in various conspiracy theories, militias attract not only the good, honest people mentioned earlier, but also a radical fringe, individuals who often harbor no inhibitions against using violence.

"People in these movements are part of a lunatic fringe," said an article in the *Jewish Bulletin of Northern California*. "We laughed when they were tax protesters. But since they've shown a propensity for violence, we can't dismiss them that easily."[18]

FBI agent Tom Smith adds, "I see danger from individuals within the militia who are troubled and take anti-government sentiment too seriously, and who then do something drastic about it."

In addition to attracting a radical fringe, the rhetoric of hatred of the government that most militias espouse also bestows a sense of legitimacy upon the beliefs of this radical fringe and makes their acts of violence appear to be a reasonable response to government actions. In other words, this radical fringe insists that, through their violent acts, they are only striking out at an evil entity that thousands of militia members hate, not at innocent citizens. It was the militia mentality that attracted Terry Nichols and Timothy McVeigh—the two men convicted of the Oklahoma City bombing—to militia meetings. McVeigh, in particular, considered himself to be a militia-type thinker long before it became popular. And, as we shall see throughout this book, besides McVeigh and Nichols, militias have attracted many other criminals and sociopaths, people who have committed hundreds of crimes under the guise of militia patriotism.

Given that they can be a serious threat, the first questions that arise are where are these armed civilian militias located, and how big are they? "Militias are probably everywhere," said an article in *Law Enforcement Technology*. "[T]here are chapters of different groups like this in every state in the nation, including the District of Columbia."[19]

Mark Koernke of Michigan, one of the most recognized leaders in the modern militia movement, told me after a talk he gave at a preparedness/survival expo in Atlanta, "The militias are everywhere. We have them in every state."

According to the Klanwatch Division of the Southern Poverty Law Center, in 1997, they were monitoring 523 patriot groups, 221 of which were armed civilian militia groups.[20] However, the actual number of people in America who belong to these militias is an area of much conjecture, particularly since most militias keep their membership rolls secret. Because a mistrust of the government was the basis of their birth, most militias feel compelled not to advertise who belongs to their organization for fear of retribution by the government. Still, there have been estimates of militia membership ranging from 10,000 all the way up to the millions. Most experts believe that the number of truly dedicated militia members is more likely at the lower end of this estimate, but that the number of people who feel some type of sympathy for the militia movement is certainly much higher.

"Fifty percent of the people in the United States have the same sort of values that are motivating the militias," said Professor Craig R. Cauley of Bryn Mawr College.[21]

Coupled with the problem of the militias keeping their membership rolls secret is the fact that the numbers tend to fluctuate, making it difficult to establish the true number of militia members in America. The militia movement tends to be very fluid. After an incident occurs that inflames far-right sensibilities, new groups will form and old groups will suddenly gain large numbers of new members. But when events calm down, groups quietly disappear or shrink in size, leaving only the hardcore members. Every week, it seems, new militia groups are born and old groups die.

But what drives a person to become a member of an armed civilian militia? Chip Berlet of Political Research Associates in Cambridge, Massachusetts, said, "We need to remember that the growth of the militias is a social by-product, coming on the heels both of economic hardship and the partial erosion of traditional structures of white male heterosexual privilege."[22] In other words, many members of the militias are white males who have been downsized out of jobs or are stuck in low-paying jobs and unable to obtain the position they want because of affirmative action or some other government-implemented social program. These individuals feel frustrated and powerless in what they see as a society that does not care about them any longer and instead caters to minorities and other underprivileged groups. The militia movement helps these frustrated individuals manage their feelings of resentment and anger, because joining a militia unites them with others who have the same problems and fears. There is comfort in knowing they are not alone. Although the Ruby Ridge incident in 1992 may have been the starting point of the modern militia movement, Mr. Berlet sees a large part of the desire to join the militias as a backlash to the social revolution of the 1960s and 1970s.

"Among militia members, there is a great sense of anger over unresolved grievances, over the sense that no one is listening, and the anger has shifted to bitter frustration," said Chip Berlet. "The government is perceived to be the enemy because it is the agency by which the economy is governed, and by which equal rights for previously disenfranchised groups are being protected."[23]

While for these angry, bitter militia members the incident at Ruby Ridge may have been the impetus that started the modern militia movement, it was the federal government's blunders the following year at Waco, Texas, that truly solidified the concept. In my book *SWAT Teams* (Plenum, 1996), I extensively cover the serious and deadly mistakes ATF made during its raid at the Branch Davidian compound in Waco, Texas, known as Mount Carmel. Briefly, what happened is that ATF had properly followed up on complaints that David Koresh, leader of the Branch Davidians, and his followers at their Mount Carmel compound were amassing large amounts of illegal firearms and explosives, which indeed they were. The Branch Davidians believed that an apocalyptic end to civilization was approaching, and consequently, they were arming themselves in order to survive it. The ATF agents applied for and received warrants against Koresh for various criminal violations involving these illegal firearms and explosives. Following this, they then formulated a complex plan for serving the warrants at the Branch Davidian compound, a plan whose success depended totally on the warrant service being a surprise. The ATF agents rehearsed the plan for months at nearby Fort Hood, where they had constructed a replica of Mount Carmel. In the days preceding the ATF raid, federal officers expended thousands of dollars and hundreds of man hours in amassing equipment and acquiring and coordinating the hundreds of police officers and support personnel needed for the raid.

The morning of the raid, however, through an unfortunate incident in which a television news cameraman told a postal worker, who happened to be a Branch Davidian, that a raid at Mount Carmel was imminent, David Koresh became aware of the warrant service. Soon afterward, the ATF supervisors in charge discovered that their secret had been compromised. Yet despite this, they allowed the warrant service to go ahead, even though the keystone of their plan was that it would be a surprise and they would catch the Branch Davidians unprepared. Of course, the

Branch Davidians were not unprepared, but armed and ready, waiting for the agents' "surprise attack." The raid failed miserably, resulting in the deaths of four ATF agents and six Branch Davidians.

Once the raid failed, ATF pulled back and the FBI's Hostage Rescue Team (HRT), the same group that had mishandled the Ruby Ridge situation, moved in and took over the incident scene. For the next fifty-one days, the standoff between the federal authorities and the Branch Davidians continued. During this time, the HRT succeeded in persuading a small number of people to come out of the Branch Davidian compound and surrender but could not budge the bulk of the people still held up inside. During the fifty-one days, the HRT tried both negotiation and psychological pressure in their attempt to force David Koresh and the other Branch Davidians to surrender, but to no avail.

Finally, on 19 April 1993, with approval from Attorney General Janet Reno, the HRT stopped negotiating and decided to use force in order to make the people held up inside come out and surrender. HRT agents began pumping tear gas into the Mount Carmel compound. However, the tear gas did not force the people out as expected. Instead, a fire, reportedly started by the Branch Davidians (though this is an assertion vehemently contested by some people), eventually burned down the compound, killing all of the people inside, including twenty-five children. The federal government suddenly found itself with another disaster of unbelievable proportions on its hands.

While to most citizens this incident appeared to be a terribly unfortunate tragedy, to America's politically far right it became absolute, 100 percent proof that the federal government was now aggressively attacking anyone who disagreed with it or held unpopular views. They saw this as confirmation that the federal government would now seek out and kill anyone who opposed gun control, because, while the Branch Davidians were certainly amassing illegal weapons, many people do not see this as a crime.

In an article in *The New Republic*, Larry McMurtry asked: "What were the Davidians doing to provoke [the raid]? Probably they were converting semiautomatic rifles to full auto. That is certainly a crime; even possessing the capability to convert them is a crime. But down here in the Fifty Caliber Belt this particular crime is usually treated about as seriously as spitting on the sidewalk."[24]

Like the deadly incident at Ruby Ridge, many critics of the federal government saw the Waco incident as another example of government bumbling and overreaction. And indeed, as at Ruby Ridge, mistakes were certainly made at Waco. Besides the ineptness of the ATF leadership that caused the initial raid to fail, the FBI's HRT demonstrated again that it was much less than the top-notch outfit the FBI likes to boast it is. Critics complained that HRT officials would not listen to experts who could have given them advice on how to end the standoff, and that if the HRT officials had listened to these experts, they would have known that the aggressive actions they took were very likely going to produce the exact outcome they did.

David Koresh, while inside Mount Carmel, was looked upon and treated as a god by his followers. However, only if he stayed safely inside the compound would he remain so. If he allowed the FBI to take him out by force, not only would he not appear to be god-like any longer, he also would become just another prisoner in the local jail. For someone with delusions as grandiose as David Koresh, this was something he simply could not face.

Another thing the FBI did not recognize was that the siege of Mount Carmel by the federal government did not intimidate Koresh's followers as much as simply confirm for them Koresh's predictions about the coming apocalypse: dozens of armed men, tanks, helicopters, and the attempts at psychological pressure through the use of loudspeakers that blasted chants, rock music, and the screams of animals being slaughtered. Rather than frightening them, this only hardened their resistance. In addition, the FBI contributed to the tragedy at Waco by not being prepared for the possibility of fire when using chemical weapons. Regardless of how the fire started, preparing for such an possibility should have been standard procedure. Chemical weapons often start fires. But since they were not prepared, once the fire started, there was no firefighting equipment nearby to put out the flames and perhaps prevent some of the deaths.

All of these blunders, however, were not seen as grave errors by many on the far right, but rather as a deliberate extermination of the Branch Davidians. The government's actions at Waco solidified the rise of the modern militia movement in America. According to the article "The State of the Militia, April 19, 1997" in the 19 April 1997 issue of *Modern Militiaman:* "The movement was conceived at Ruby Ridge in 1992, [and] given birth on April 19, 1993 at Waco."

The phrase "Remember Ruby Ridge and Waco" has become as potent a call to battle as "Remember the Alamo." At several of the preparedness/survival expos I visited while researching this book, a number of the people wore T-shirts or sweatshirts that said: "Forget the Alamo—Remember Waco."

And yet, as if these two events did not do enough to solidify the fear many people with far-right leanings had concerning the federal government's determination to discard the Constitution, the final blows were the passage of the Brady Bill in 1993 and the subsequent passage of the Omnibus Safe Streets Act of 1994, which outlawed many types of assault rifles. All of these events have made some people come to see the federal government as a large, unfeeling entity that intends to eventually take away all constitutional rights, particularly the Second Amendment right to own and bear firearms. These events have made some people come to see the federal government as a dark, evil force that will eliminate anyone who opposes it.

"I emphasize the need to understand what motivates them," said Dr. Ted Daniels, director of the Millennium Watch Institute, "which is fear and a sense of powerlessness and helplessness in the face of the government."[25]

The militia's fear of the federal government is not just some unsubstantiated paranoia. There are some logical reasons behind it. Both Ruby Ridge and Waco are examples of law enforcement officials running amok. But there is more. As with its law enforcement agencies, there is also unquestionably a certain amount of abuse of power within other agencies of the federal government. For example, during Congressional hearings in 1997 and 1998, members of Congress heard horror story after horror story from individuals harassed and hounded by the Internal Revenue Service. In addition, anyone who has ever dealt with a federal agency that disburses money knows the incredible amount of red tape and overregulation that is involved.

However, not only abuses of power but also betrayals of trust by the federal government have added to the paranoia many people feel. For example, during the 1980s, the federal government encouraged farmers to borrow heavily and expand their operations. They needed to do this, the government claimed, so they could plant their fields from "fence to fence" in anticipation of bountiful returns from the Soviet grain deal. The Soviet Union, government officials promised, would buy all of the grain U.S. farmers could grow. Upon this encouragement, many farmers went heavily into debt. However, when the Soviet grain deal fell through, and grain prices tumbled, farmers found that the same bureaucrats who had been encouraging them to borrow money were now foreclosing on their farms.

Yet, although the incidents in this chapter certainly might explain a person's mistrust of the federal government and shed some light on a person's decision to join a militia, they do not quite explain what leads these armed civilian militias to commit acts of violence and other crimes. Yet as we will discuss in the following chapters, incidents of violence and crime are exactly what have occurred. While many people may join militias for what they believe are honorable and just reasons, too many others join militias solely with the idea of committing crimes and acts of violence.

"Although most militia members may be law-abiding citizens," said Morris Dees of the Southern Poverty Law Center, "militia groups attract those with a propensity for violence and act as a springboard for their activities. After a while, angry loners are likely to grow bored roaming the woods and shooting at paper targets."[26]

As we will see throughout this book, the armed civilian militia movement in America presents a very real threat to our country. It is a movement with a lethal recipe for tragedy and death.

THE BELIEFS AND PHILOSOPHIES OF MILITIAS

"We need to do four or five [buildings] to create problems for the government," a man reportedly suggested at the August 1995 meeting of the Tri-State Militia in Gregory County, South Dakota. "God won't be mad at us if we drop four or five buildings. He will probably reward us."[1]

A federal criminal complaint filed several months later claimed that this conversation, overheard by an undercover informant who reported it to the FBI, involved the plotting of a campaign of terror, which included the proposed bombing of four or five buildings by members of the militia. The conversation, led by several people, including self-proclaimed antigovernment prophet Ray Lampley, eventually moved on to deciding which locations should be targets for the bombings. After considerable discussion, the agreed-upon sites of the bombings became the Houston office of the Anti-Defamation League of B'nai B'rith, another Anti-Defamation League office, and the Southern Poverty Law Center in Montgomery, Alabama. What were the reasons behind these selections? Both of these organizations maintain task forces that investigate and track militias and other groups.

Later, at another militia meeting, Ray Lampley and his wife, Cecilia, suggested more targets for bombing. They added abortion clinics, welfare offices, and homosexual hangouts. Cecilia reportedly offered the suggestion that they use bombs with timers in order that any children could be evacuated from welfare offices before the bombs exploded.

Fortunately, the FBI acted before the actual bombings could take place. On Saturday, 11 November 1995, FBI agents arrested Ray and Cecilia at their home in Vernon, Oklahoma, and charged them with conspiring to manufacture and possess bombs. The FBI also arrested John Baird at the Lampley home and charged him with conspiracy in the case. On 25 April 1996, a federal jury found the three defendants guilty of conspiracy to manufacture bombs.

Anyone sympathetic to the militia movement will likely want to jump up and cry out that the above incident is not typical of all militia members, but only of a fringe element, who apparently took over the Tri-State Militia meetings. While admittedly this may be true, this is also one of the greatest dangers of the militia movement: it attracts a radical fringe, that, depending on its persuasiveness and charisma, can convince other less criminal and violence-prone militia members either to take part in violent acts or at least not object to them.

"The real threat of the militia could be huge," said ATF agent George Stoll, who has retired from the ATF since I first interviewed him, and now teaches courses on the threat of violent antigovernment groups. "It depends on how many of the lunatic fringe listen to the rhetoric, join up, and then decide to do something."

But why, readers may ask, would ordinarily law-abiding members of the militia movement allow themselves to be persuaded by this radical fringe into taking part in these kinds of acts, or, at best, quietly not opposing them? The answer lies in the beliefs and philosophies of the militia movement. Most members of the modern militia movement share certain common tenets, and so, violence-prone individuals, working on these shared beliefs, can make violent actions seem, if not perhaps legal and proper, at least effective in carrying out the beliefs and philosophies of the militia. These violence-prone individuals can convincingly make the other militia members look past the detrimental effects the proposed actions may have on innocent people, and instead see only the end result, which is a powerful statement against the government.

What are these beliefs and philosophies that drive modern militia members? According to *American Militias* by Richard Abanes: "The glue binding them together is a noxious compound of four ingredients: (1) an obsessive suspicion of the government; (2) a belief in anti-government conspiracy theories; (3) a deep-seated hatred of government officials; and (4) a feeling that the United States Constitution, for all intents and purposes, has been discarded by Washington bureaucrats."[2]

As can be seen, the militia movement's philosophy centers largely around a mistrust and even hatred of the government. The Lampleys used these beliefs to persuade the members of the militia to go along with their plan, because they argued that bombing buildings could create severe problems for the government. Since most militia members dislike the government, this reasoning made the Lampley's proposed actions seem not like a criminal act, but simply a way to strike back at a corrupt and unfeeling government.

But just how corrupt and unfeeling do militia members believe their government is? The Internet web page of the 7th Missouri Militia states: "The 7th Missouri Militia is dedicated to fighting the true enemies of the Patriot movement—the federal and state governments and their degenerate quisling lackeys."[3] Harold Sheil, a militia member, said, "One of the things that people really fear from the government is the idea [that] the government can ruin your life, totally destroy your life. I don't mean kill you. But they can totally destroy your life, split your family up, do the whole thing and walk off like you're a discarded banana peel, and with a ho-hum attitude."[4]

Ex-ATF agent Steve Wortham, who now runs a company called Intellicon, which gives seminars and other training on topics such as militia groups, said, "In my 29 years of law enforcement, the militia movement has the possibility of developing into the greatest threat to the United States I've seen. It is driven by emotion and a disenchantment with an institution that has never, in the history of the United States, changed in any way that decreases control and intrusiveness in the lives of the citizens."

As Wortham says, and as we saw in the last chapter, the belief that the government is abusive and does not care any longer about the welfare of ordinary citizens is not always unjustified. It occasionally can be supported by real-life abuse or neglect from the government. Yet, this does not in any way excuse wholesale violence such as the bombing proposal of the Lampleys. Regardless, many militia members still hold a deep-seated hatred of their government that makes these types of acts more likely to occur. Why do militia members have this feeling about their government?

According to Richard Abanes, author of *American Militias:* "When patriots are asked why they hate their government, four answers regularly surface in varying combinations: (1) declining economic conditions; (2) unwanted social change; (3) imposition of federal authority over states' rights; and (4) environmental legislation that imposes strict regulations on what land owners can do with their property."[5] In other words, many members of the militia movement see their lifestyles declining and believe that the government, who should be helping them, really does not care about them any longer, but instead now caters only to minority groups and special interests.

It must be remembered that for many, many years in this country, the white male held an exalted position. Even without strong skills or education, white males could still obtain jobs in manufacturing that paid a very good wage. But today, all of that has changed. Many of the formerly high-pay, low-skill jobs are now gone or work is being sent out of the country, where labor is cheaper. The better-paying jobs that remain usually require considerable training and education. In addition, militia members see affirmative action programs suddenly allowing a large number of minorities to attain and hold on to many of the jobs previously held exclusively by white males. All of this makes many right-wing .militant, white males feel that they have been discarded and abandoned by their government, who should be looking out for their welfare.

Because many future militia members are white men who see themselves as abandoned by the government, and also, because of certain minority social programs, see their lifestyles being threatened, they will often, for reassurance and security, seek out others in the same situation and consequently join a militia. Interestingly, after a period of bonding and reinforcement of each others' views, the modern day militia members do not see themselves as untrained and undereducated individuals who, because of their lack of life preparation, must settle for low-paying, dead-end jobs. Instead, their reasoning has gone completely in the other direction. They see themselves as akin to the Revolutionary Era heroes who also found themselves abandoned by their government and economically threatened, but who successfully fought against it.

As a consequence of their belief in this close similarity to Revolutionary Era heroes, many of these modern-day militia members spend all of their free time studying the Revolutionary Era and its resulting documents, studying so intensely that they eventually merge their personalities with the heroic personalities of the American Revolution. And like the past heroes, modern-day militia members want to change their situation. So, in response to their alleged grievances, modern-day militia members many times follow the example of their historical idols, who often became involved in violent acts, such as the Boston Tea Party, Lexington and Concord, and so on, actions that, while illegal under the laws at that time, eventually led to a positive social change.

The perceived legality of these actions, of course, depended on which side of the American Revolution a person stood. While those sympathetic to the Revolution applauded the acts, those sympathetic to the British Crown saw them as simply vandalism, terrorism, and treason. The same is true today. Many militia members have come to believe that their acts, such as the Lampley bombing proposals, though perhaps criminal in the eyes of some, are actually in the interest of the common good. Many modern-day militia members believe their actions are as heroic as those of the Revolutionary Era heroes, and most see the present government as oppressive to the citizenry as many people in the late 1700s saw the British Crown.

Just how close do the modern-day militia members believe their purpose is to that of the Founding Fathers? From the Michigan Militia Corps Internet web page: "Therefore, it is to us, the inheritors of the task begun more than two centuries ago, to seek and to secure these same ideals in the face of the same threats expressed by Patrick Henry. To wit, that the organized government, having removed itself from the citizens, inter se, had intended to dissolve the rights and liberties of free people."[6]

The Internet web page for the Stark County Unit of the Ohio Unorganized Militia states: "We are a state-wide group of patriots following the advice and laws of our forefathers to guard and protect our liberty."[7] The Internet web page for the 52nd Missouri Militia states: "The 52nd Missouri Militia is being formed in response to a clear need. The age in which we live all but surpass [sic] what our founding fathers went through before the American Revolution."[8]

In support of the belief that they are simply carrying on the tradition of the American Revolution, almost every militia Internet web page, and there are literally dozens of them, is filled with pictures of Revolutionary Era soldiers and heroes, and packed with quotes from the founding fathers. The militias fill their web pages with these images even though many leaders during the early history of our country did not hold the militia in high regard, particularly after the militia revolted against the government during Shay's Rebellion in 1786 and the Whiskey Rebellion of 1794.

The various militia Internet web pages and newsletters also like to quote heavily from the Declaration of Independence, the Constitution, and the Bill of Rights, particularly the Second Amendment. The Second Amendment to the Constitution, which talks about owning and carrying firearms, has become almost holy writ to the militias, which believe it says that any gun-control law is unconstitutional. Consequently, most modern-day militias hold strongly to the belief that any type of gun-control law is simply an illegal, unconstitutional government plot to disarm the citizenry. For example, one of the reasons for the formation of the South Carolina Militia Corps, according to their Internet web page, is as follows: "The Right To Keep and Bear Arms was given to us by our Founding Fathers for many reasons. But the 'last resort' reason (as Thomas Jefferson explained) was to help the people resist tyrannical government."[9]

As a result of this holding of the Second Amendment as near holy writ, almost all militias oppose any restrictions on gun ownership and sales, and particularly oppose waiting periods and background checks. This is true even though, according to the Bureau of Justice Statistics' report *Presale Handgun Checks, 1996,* presale handgun checks in 1996 prevented the sale of firearms to over 70,000 individuals who were under a felony indictment, had a criminal record, or had a drug addiction or mental illness history.[10]

Unfortunately, their opposition to any form of gun control, their hatred and rejection of the government, and their belief in their almost divine mission as exemplified by our Founding Fathers can many times bring modern-day militia members into dangerous conflict with law enforcement personnel. The following incident clearly shows this danger.

On 29 January 1996, fifty-three-year-old Larry Martz, while reportedly returning home from a militia meeting, stopped his pickup truck when an Ohio state trooper pulled him over for a minor turn-signal violation, so minor that the trooper later said he had not even planned on writing Martz a ticket for it. He would have just let him go with a warning. The problems began, though, when the trooper asked Martz to step out of his vehicle. Later, in court, both Martz and the trooper agreed what happened next, which was that Martz grabbed the trooper from behind in a bear hug, forcing the two men to wrestle a bit before the trooper finally managed to get free. The trooper said he feared that Martz was trying to grab his gun. Once free, the trooper arrested Martz for assaulting him, and, after securing Martz in the police car, he searched the cab of Martz's pickup truck. Inside, he found two assault rifles, a shotgun, and a .45 caliber handgun, along with 1,337 rounds of ammunition. In the bed of the truck, the trooper discovered six more firearms and another 3,800 rounds of ammunition. The trooper then also arrested Martz for firearms violations.

In court, Martz, who was voted as the "Most Likely To Succeed" by his 1959 high school class, decided to act as his own attorney (something many militia members do, which accounts for their extraordinarily high conviction rate). At first, however, before the court proceedings had even begun, Martz caused a scene by steadfastly refusing to leave the specta-tor's section of the courtroom. His reason, he told the judge, was because the flag in the courtroom had a gold fringe on it. This, according to Martz, made it a military flag, and he believed that if he took part in the court's proceedings, he would actually be taking part in a military tribunal, and as a consequence he would forfeit his constitutional rights. The judge, not amused or swayed by this argument, ordered the court bailiffs to forcibly seat Martz at the defense table.

Following this, according to an article in *The New York Times*, Martz repeatedly told the judge that the court had no jurisdiction over him, and that, like the militiamen at Bunker Hill, "I am a man of action." During his defense, Martz did not deny grabbing the trooper in a bear hug but said he only did it because he feared the trooper was about to draw his gun and shoot him. (Several months earlier, there had been a shooting of a militia member by an Ohio law enforcement officer, which Martz claimed he had witnessed. Although a grand jury cleared the officer in this shoot-ing, militia members still contend it was murder.)

In his closing argument, Martz likened himself to a late 1700s min-uteman and spoke to the jury about the tremendous sacrifices the Revolu-tionary Era militia members had made. While waiting for the jury's decision, he reportedly said, "I want them to think, 'How would you vote if George Washington was standing up there instead of me?'"

The jury obviously did not feel sympathetic to Martz's arguments. They deliberated for only three and a half hours before finding him guilty of both felony charges. The judge then sentenced Martz to two years in prison.

In his closing argument before the jury, the prosecutor in the case said, "He's [Martz] out here to protect us. From whom? I submit that we need to be protected from him."[11]

The prosecutor posed an excellent question. Just what exactly do the modern militias believe their role is in society? From what and whom do they believe they are protecting society? According to the February 1996

newsletter of the Tennessee Volunteer Militia: "The Unregulated Militia is to defend the Constitution of the people of the States, and subdivisions thereof from all Foreign and Domestic enemies; be they Officials or Employees serving in State or Local government; or Criminals within the general populace of the State. Both acts being an insurrection against the Constitution, We the People, and the Laws of the Union. Additionally, the Unregulated Militia is to repel invasions, which concerning Foreign enemies might well be the defending of the State borders. Domestically, however, it would include the unlawful search and seizure of our persons, houses, papers, and effects, without due process of law."[12]

From what is the Tennessee Volunteer Militia protecting us? Apparently from government officials and agencies not performing properly in the eyes of the militia. As can be seen through the statement of purpose of the Tennessee Volunteer Militia, this self-appointed organization feels that it is entitled to take armed action if it believes that a government employee or agency is not performing according to its standards. This is an extraordinarily dangerous idea, because what some people may think is poor performance, others may not. Yet the militias have set themselves up as judge, jury, and often executioner of government employees. Many militia leaders like to talk about hanging government employees that they believe are corrupt. In the videotape *America in Peril*, Michigan militia leader Mark Koernke plainly states the militia's intention to execute the present government leaders by hanging.

But who is to decide if a government official is corrupt and needs to be hung? Apparently, the militia. And who is to decide if a search or seizure is illegal? Again, apparently, the militia. This is also extremely risky, because, many times, militias see any attempt by the Internal Revenue Service or a financial institution to foreclose on or repossess a piece of property as a wrongful act. This is particularly true if the property is owned by a militia member, which happens quite often because, many times, a person's membership in the militia is a reaction to poor finances, something militia members also usually want to blame on the government. As should be obvious, all of these beliefs can be extraordinarily perilous to government officials and to the public at large, because militia members, as shown earlier in the Martz case, often tend to be heavily armed and hold unusual views about the law and their rights. A shootout on a public highway, for example, with a person as heavily armed as Martz could very easily result in injury or death not only to law enforcement personnel but also to any innocent citizens passing by.

Most militias, along with believing the government to be corrupt and neglectful, also hold to the belief that the government has become too intrusive in the everyday life of its citizens. According to an article in the *San Antonio Express-News:* "[John] Zimmerman, a leader in the Bexar County, Texas, Constitutional Militia, said his group wants a less intrusive government with fewer restrictions on gun ownership and on the use of such things as freon, a regulated refrigerant, in car air-conditioners, for example."[13]

This belief of too much government interference in its citizens' lives is not just some far-right paranoia, however. The government does exert considerable influence upon the lives of its citizens. For example, in 1992, the federal government passed 1,397 new federal laws and generated 62,928 pages of new regulations.[14] In 1995, a *Times-Mirror* poll found that 69 percent of Americans felt the government "controls too much of our daily lives."[15] A Gallup poll the same year found that 39 percent of Americans think the federal government "poses an immediate threat to the rights and freedoms of ordinary Americans."[16]

Yet what would happen if the government left citizens entirely on their own, with no regulations, no rules, no restrictions? The following incident shows very clearly what could happen.

Ken Medenbach, a member of the Oregon Militia, owns five acres of property near the town of La Pine in central Oregon. On this piece of property, Medenbach is in the process of building his dream home. However, while doing so, he has had a number of confrontations with county officials concerning building codes. The reason? He is building the house out of discarded refrigerators, water heaters, and other such material. The county building code enforcement officer states that the property is really little more than a junkyard, and, as a consequence, Medenbach has been cited a number of times for code violations, to which he refuses to respond.

"A 'code' is only a suggestion," Medenbach explains. "It's not a law." He subscribes to the legal theory that the courts have no authority over him because all judges belong to the state bar association, which he believes is unconstitutional. The courts, however, have disagreed with his theory, and, as a consequence, Medenbach has spent considerable time in jail, yet he refuses to stop work on his dream home.

"I'm willing to pay the price for my convictions," Medenbach said. "Someday, when the laws become too stringent, people will start waking up." Like many militia members, Medenbach sees himself as a modern-day replica of the Revolutionary Era minutemen. "Two hundred and twenty years ago they saw the corruption," he said. "They had the right to revolution, and we have the right to revolution."[17]

Most militia members, as well as believing they are modern-day minutemen, as Martz and Medenbach do, also feel they must be the guardians of the Constitution, because they hold strongly to the belief that the present government is out of control and attempting to discard the Constitution. The Michigan Militia Corps mission statement says: "To defend the Constitution of the State of Michigan and the Constitution of the United States of America. To uphold and defend the Bill of Rights, seen as unalienable, given by God to free men that they remain free." Later, on the Internet web page, it states: "The Michigan Militia Corps' goal is to restore the Federal and state governments to their historical, limited, and constitutional function. Every day government is getting larger and more intrusive on individual rights. We are here to try and curb this frightening phenomenon."[18]

The belief that the government has run amok, has discarded the Constitution, and is attempting to control every part of its citizens' lives is a widespread belief of the modern militia movement. According to "Militia—History and Law FAQ" from the Militia Watchdog Internet web page: "The belief system of the new militiaman believes that (1) less government is better; (2) strong government tends to interfere with concerns more properly belonging to the province of the private citizen; (3) strong government tends to be socialistic in nature; and (4) individual liberties are best protected by individuals."

The web page continues: "Two additional glues cement these concerns together. The first is probably psychological as much as philosophical: a strong desire to own firearms . . . that firearms are necessary to protect individual liberties. . . . The second glue is a strong sense of paranoia coupled with pessimism. Members of the new militia movement sincerely believe that society is disintegrating rapidly."[19]

However, in addition to believing themselves to be a continuation of the Revolutionary Era minutemen and the present-day guardians of the

Constitution, some militias also see themselves as a part of law enforcement. The mission statement of the U.S. Militia includes the following task: "Execute the laws of the United States, the respective States, and local jurisdictions."[20] This is an extremely dangerous belief for any heavily armed and self-appointed group to hold, particularly when few or none of its members have any formal understanding of the law or law enforcement techniques. One can only imagine the possible outcome of confrontations with individuals the militia members believe are law violators. This is particularly true when considering the U.S. Militia's "vision statement," which says: "Insofar as social arrangements are determined by naked force and not mutual consent, the Militia must always be the ultimate and final arbiter of American liberty and public security."[21]

Not all of the beliefs and philosophies of the modern-day militia groups, however, center around just government corruption, government interference with citizens' rights, and the militia's role as the guardian of society. Militias also usually espouse strong conservative and religious family values, and often their mission statements refer to God and Christian people. We will discuss this further in a later chapter, but suffice it to say that people who hold strongly to these beliefs often show little tolerance for those who do not believe as they do.

While the modern militia movement is very conservative in nature, it is not so conservative as to exclude women from the movement. Rather, a number of the militias encourage women to join. According to an article in the *Washington Post* about women in the militia, the author states: "Some are merely following their husbands into militia service; others say they are getting involved because of their own beliefs that constitutional abuses must be curbed. They also identify with the emphasis many of the groups place on conservative family values, including their opposition to abortion, gay rights, and the feminist movement, and their advocacy of home schooling."[22]

Yet while many militias do contain women members, information about them and their roles is elusive and very hard to find. Hundreds of articles have been written about the militia movement, but only a handful discuss women in the militias. From the contacts I have had with militia groups, women tend to play mainly supporting roles to the men, but not always. If women militia members want, they can occasionally play much more extensive roles. We will discuss this further in a later chapter.

Unfortunately, however, even with their conservative and religious family values, many militia members still cling tightly to their fear and hatred of the present government, and because of this, many also believe that violence and bloodshed between the militia and the government is inevitable. According to the article "Always Use a Tool Which Works or the Myth of Non-Violence," by Martin Lindstedt, editor of *Modern Militiaman:* "Sane people should be able to work out their differences without the need for bloodshed, express or implied. However, a policy of non-violence seldom, if ever, works. . . . For good people to eschew violence merely assures that evil people will seek, then gain, an unobstructed monopoly on violence. Once these evil people have a monopoly on violence they will use it to enslave more docile human beings and kill anyone who threatens to get in their way."[23]

Mr. Lindstedt continues this line of thought in his article "A Second Interview with the Editor Concerning the Militia Movement," when he says, "The ruling criminals are not going to peacefully hand themselves over to our justice. So we will have to drag them out and exterminate them the hard way, along with anyone who would protect them from the consequences of justice."[24]

Does this mean that anyone who does not go along with a militia group's actions will be considered an enemy? Yes, it does. Many militias hold strongly to the "you're either with us or against us" philosophy. According to *The Pennsylvania Minuteman:* "Anyone that opposes the constituted and mandated militia is by description a domestic foreign enemy."[25] Is all of this saying that militia members would act against a person just because their leaders have designated him or her as the enemy? Yes, it is. The U.S. Militia Internet website states: "Every militia member must be prepared mentally to fight, to risk his life for liberty, to take a life for freedom."[26] According to the Missouri 51st Militia Internet website: "Only in self-defense will a militia member discharge his weapon, *except when ordered to do so* [emphasis added]." The website then continues: "It shall also be the right of each militia member to appeal to authority within the direct chain-of-command regarding grievances. In every case however, the militia member shall follow the order or directive first, and make his appeal afterward. If a militia member for conscience sake, feels impelled to disobey, he should immediately withdraw from the militia without prejudice."[27]

What this means is that militia members must follow the orders of their leaders, whether these orders appear legal and humane or not. In other words, militia members must follow orders to arrest, and perhaps even fire on, those designated as enemies by militia leaders. This then begs the question: What kind of leaders does the militia have?

Interestingly, in many of the modern-day militia groups, the membership elects the leaders, which means the most popular, not necessarily the most competent, militia leaders are chosen. From the Michigan Militia Corps' Internet web page: "Militia leadership is democratically elected at a series of levels beginning at the Brigade, or county unit, where a Commander is elected who in turn votes for a multi-county Division Commander. The general membership votes for a State or Theater Commander. A Commander may serve until he or she leaves the position or until the membership votes for a new Commander."[28]

As might be imagined, this can be an extraordinarily sloppy and dangerous way to select leaders in any heavily armed organization that can order its members to use violence. With this method, those with the most charisma take over the leadership, regardless of their leadership ability, and regardless of their lack of experience or training. Unfortunately, many examples in history have shown that evil people can have great charisma. Adolph Hitler and Jim Jones are two examples that immediately come to mind.

Many of the beliefs and philosophies of the modern militia movement, as we have witnessed throughout this chapter, seem to put them on a collision course with the present government. And unfortunately, this collision course can very easily lead to violence and criminal acts. In addition to the the militias' philosophies, however, their belief in wildly improbable conspiracy theories, as we shall see in the next chapter, is also a road map for dangerous confrontations, not only with government employees, but also, unfortunately, with private citizens.

❖ ❖ ❖ ❖ ❖ ❖ ❖ ❖ 3

NATIONAL AND WORLDWIDE CONSPIRACIES

"This has got to be some kind of mistake," Fred said as he steered the Avis rental car down a narrow, two-lane road that ran alongside a beautifully maintained golf course.

"I think you're right," I agreed, watching the golfers skimming across the greens in their golf carts, a few hearty souls walking across the grass with their golf bags slung over their shoulders. Late autumn in southern Nevada meant sunny days in the high 70s and low 80s, and the golfers obviously meant to enjoy the fine weather.

My brother Fred and I were looking for a reported underground concentration camp that a militia Internet posting claimed had been secretly built somewhere on this golf course. According to the posting, this internment camp, along with others across the United States, had been clandestinely built to hold dissidents, meaning militia members, when United Nations troops invaded the United States, overthrew and replaced our national government with a tyrannical dictatorship, and reduced the citizens of the former United States of America to slavery status.

The golf course, located in the midst of a very upscale housing development (the lots starting at $100,000 and the homes at $400,000), looked to me just like what it was supposed to be: a very well-manicured and expensive golf course. As I glanced around, I wondered how anyone could believe, even accepting the very dubious theory that there were conspirators presently in league with the United Nations to take over the United States, that these conspirators would try to hide something like a concentration camp at such a site.

"The report says that the concentration camp is supposed to be buried under the golf course," I said, reading from the Internet posting. I looked out the window and shook my head. "Don't you think the people around here would probably notice something like that?"

"Yeah, you'd think so," my brother answered. "You know—whoa, hold on a second!" Fred slowed the car down, then pulled off the road and stopped, staring at something out the window. I stretched my neck to see what he was staring at and found myself looking at something that appeared completely out of place. On the side of the road opposite the golf course, but several hundred yards off of the road, was a fenced-in compound that held a square, concrete block building about thirty feet on a side. I could see one door going into the building, but no windows. A radio antenna soared about fifty feet above the building, while a twenty-five-foot-high earthen revetment (a sloped wall of dirt) surrounded the facility. Inside the earthen revetment, an eight-foot-high chain-link fence enclosed the area. It looked very much like a facility the owners did not want anyone trespassing on, and, because of the earthen revetment, even looking into. However, because we sat on high ground, we could see down into the installation. Near where we parked, I saw the entrance to a one-lane, gravel road that ran to the area we were staring at, but we could not use it because a padlocked chain across the road blocked any vehicle access.

This looked much too interesting to let a little padlock and chain stop us. "Come on," I said, scrambling out of the car, "let's go take a look."

Until this moment I had considered the possibility of a secret prison facility sitting in the midst of such an upscale neighborhood as so unlikely as to be ludicrous. I figured the report had simply been invented or, giving the author the benefit of the doubt, a mistake had been made concerning the location of the site. However, my assessment of the report began to change radically as we walked along the narrow gravel road leading to the fenced area. At regular intervals, I saw what appeared to be air vents sticking up out of the ground, showing that indeed something certainly was buried underground at this location.

A few minutes earlier, while we were driving through the area, Fred had laughed as I read the Internet report to him, but now, like me, he had a puzzled look on his face as we approached the earthen revetment around the facility, which, at close range, completely hid the building. When we climbed to the top of the revetment, however, the mystery appeared solved. We stood looking down onto a natural gas regulator station.

Before becoming a police officer, I had spent four years in the Air Force as an intelligence specialist during the Vietnam War. My job during those four years had been studying both aerial and satellite photography, looking for and analyzing possible military targets. So I knew what a natural gas regulator station looked like. A regulator station reduces the pressure of natural gas from the high pressure needed to transfer the natural gas from storage to the lower pressure needed for home use.

Suddenly, what had appeared mysterious from the road now looked very explainable. The concrete building obviously contained the control apparatus for the regulator facility, and the microwave radio antenna made remote control of the regulator station possible. Nearby sat a large odorizer tank. Natural gas has no odor, and so, in order to detect leaks, gas companies add a distinctive odor. The air vents we had seen while approaching the facility, I now knew, were necessary to regulate the pressure within the gas lines, given the high temperature variations of southern Nevada. The earthen revetment also now became very explainable. The builders had constructed it for aesthetic reasons. While these types of facilities have to exist, even in expensive neighborhoods, they are not aesthetically pleasing, and so the earthen wall hid the facility from view.

"Well, it looks like this mystery's solved," I said, after explaining to Fred what the facility was. I felt certain that whoever had reported that this was an underground concentration camp had simply misinterpreted the "evidence" he or she had seen: the earthen revetment, the radio antenna, the air vents around the facility, and the windowless building (which had been built that way to make entry and any vandalism, which could be extremely dangerous, much more difficult). However, Fred played the devil's advocate to my explanation, and by doing so, he gave me a very good lesson in the difficulty of disproving conspiracy theories.

"But how do we know that this place really is just a gas regulator station?" Fred asked.

"What do you mean, 'really is'?"

"Well sure, it looks like a gas regulator station," Fred explained, "but how do we know for sure it's not all just camouflage? How do we know for sure that all of this stuff isn't just fake equipment put here to make it look like a gas regulator station, when in reality, it actually is an underground concentration camp?"

"But you can see that all of the stuff here is real," I argued, waving my arm at the facility.

"It looks real from here, sure, but how can we be positive since the fence is locked?"

A section of some heavy metal piping lay on the ground just inside the fence at the bottom of the revetment, apparently either a piece of pipe replaced or left over from the construction. We walked down to it and I showed Fred that it was a real piece of heavy, metal, gas pipeline.

Fred shrugged. "Yeah, but how do you know they didn't just put that here so that anyone who came snooping around would think everything else was real?"

We walked over to the gate that led into the facility. I pointed to a sign that said the facility belonged to a local utility company.

Fred shrugged again. "Anybody can put a sign up. What does that prove?"

I found that no matter what proof I tried to offer Fred, he could quite easily twist the proof into being part of the conspiracy cover-up. After several more fruitless attempts to convince him that this was not a secret concentration camp, but simply a natural gas regulator station, it occurred to me that to anyone who truly believed in a conspiracy, any proof offered against it could simply be dismissed as the work of the people involved in the conspiracy. As we made our way back along the gravel road to our car, I realized that once a person had totally embraced belief in a conspiracy, and had the concept firmly fixed in his or her mind, how extremely difficult, and maybe even impossible, it would be to dislodge it. For the truly conspiracy-minded, along with their ability to dismiss any evidence contrary to the conspiracy, they can also dismiss anyone who does not agree with the conspiracy, or tries to argue against it, as simply being part of the conspiracy. In this way, a conspiracy can never be disproved. Even if the conspiracy believer should find what appears to be indisputable proof contrary to the conspiracy, he or she can point to this as only more proof of how far the conspirators will go to hide the conspiracy.

However, there was one thing that happened, or rather did not happen, that convinced me this facility was simply what it appeared to be: a natural gas regulator station. An Internet posting about other supposedly hidden concentration camps around the United States had said: "Citizens are reportedly detained because of their discovery of an internment camp."[1] This part of the posting seemed logical, even if likely imagined. If this natural gas regulator station had actually been a secret underground concentration camp as reported, I'm certain Fred and I would not have been allowed to walk around and inspect it as we had. And we certainly would not have been allowed to return later and photograph the facility. A secret this large and important would need constant watching to make certain it remained a secret. If this location had actually been a secret underground concentration camp, we would very likely have been approached by someone as we neared the site, probably politely asked what we were doing there, and then ushered away from the property.

After reading about the above investigation, most readers are likely thinking: What? A concentration camp? United Nations invasion? What is he talking about?

While all of this may sound like something out of a B-movie, the belief that there is a conspiracy involving the United Nations, which is secretly controlled by a clandestine group of powerful men and women, to invade the United States, disarm the citizens, overthrow the established government, install a tyrannical dictatorship, and reduce much of the American public to slavery is almost universally accepted in the militia movement. The secret organization behind this plot, the organization covertly controlling the United Nations, is known in militia circles as the New World Order, called this because militia members believe that in addition to taking over the United States, the conspirators' goal is total world domination. The name New World Order has become a rallying call for modern militia members. The primary mission of almost every militia in the country is to thwart the impending New World Order takeover.

The Militia of Georgia Handbook, which I picked up while attending a preparedness/survival expo in Atlanta, states: "We believe that America is under siege from forces seeking the overthrow of our dejure (legal) system of government. Under the auspices of the United Nations, the New World Order, Liberalism and other innocuous sounding names, a fringe element seeks to change our form of government and put petty tyrants into power."[2]

According to the conspiracy theory popular among militia members, the United States, under the reign of the New World Order, will be divided into eleven regions, each governed by a henchman of the new regime. Where did the idea for this part of the conspiracy come from? Unbelievably, particularly since militia members insist that the map they have of these eleven regions is absolute proof of the conspiracy, the information came from the back of a 1993 box of Kix cereal. The colorful map had been intended to teach children about the eleven geographical regions of the United States. The map shows the important sites and points of interest for each of the eleven regions. Conspiracy spinners, however, insist the map is actually part of the plan for the New World Order.

While attending a preparedness/survival expo, I stopped at a booth that displayed the Kix cereal map. The woman manning the booth explained to me that while the map looks harmless and educational, in reality, it is an attempt by the henchmen of the New World Order to indoctrinate children into their way of thinking. She pointed out the disturbing fact that the map denoted the location of the United Nations, but not of Washington, D.C. Even though this "proof" of a cereal box map may seem ridiculous to nonmilitia members, the belief in the New World Order is so entrenched in the militia mentality that those who do not believe it, militia members maintain, are either trusting fools or in league with the conspirators.

According to the conspiracy spinners, the New World Order will not only mobilize United Nations troops in the takeover of the United States, but has also recruited two Los Angeles street gangs, the Crips and the Bloods, to help expedite the invasion. Some militia members claim that the gangs have signed secret agreements with the New World Order and are now being trained and equipped to be a large part of the muscle of the takeover. They will execute many of the home invasions, gun seizures, and arrests of citizens who resist the takeover. Some conspiracy spinners also claim that, along with street gangs, the New World Order has 100,000 Hong Kong police and a large number of Nepalese Gurkhas hidden throughout the United States (in salt mines in Utah according to one version of the conspiracy, and in the wilderness of Montana in another), just waiting for the call to begin the takeover of the United States.

John Trochmann, one of the founders of the Militia of Montana, and one of the most influential figures in the modern militia movement, said in an interview with freelance writer David Neiwert, "It just so happens that the New World Order has that answer—it's called Force 2000. The melding together of law enforcement and the military, which is what we see today all over America—they're training together. They're working hard on their house to house search and seizure."[3] Many militia members believe that the year 2000 is the target date for the installation of the New World Order. "When the troops come in, they'll come in such force it'll be incredible!" Trochmann said in an article in *The New Yorker*. "In forty-eight hours, they can have one hundred million troops here. They'll come out of the ground! They'll come from submarines! They'll come from air drops! They'll come from everywhere!"[4]

Another influential leader of the modern militia movement, Mark Koernke, said, "You'd better be armed. The juggernaut we face is the New World Order."[5]

Where did this conspiracy theory about the United Nations and the New World Order originate? Many of the modern militia movement's beliefs about the New World Order began in 1991, when Pat Robertson, a television evangelist and host of the *700 Club*, wrote a book entitled *The New World Order*. This best-seller, though short on proof, tells of an alleged conspiracy by the New World Order, using United Nations troops, to take over the United States.

The origin of the term New World Order, however, comes from an unexpected source. Although used by militia members to denote an ominous group of conspirators bent on world domination, the phrase "New World Order" was actually innocently and unintentionally coined by President George Bush. He used it during a speech made before a joint session of Congress on 11 September 1990, though he did not mean the phrase as most militia members choose to interpret it. "We stand today at a unique and extraordinary moment," President Bush said. "Out of troubled times . . . a new world order can emerge; a new era— freer from the threat of terror, stronger in the pursuit of justice, and more secure in the quest for peace, an era in which the nations of the world, East and West, North and South, can prosper and live in harmony."[6] President Bush's words referred to the condition of the world since the Cold War had ended, about the new opportunities for peace and prosperity, but many people mistook his words as an ominous threat of global domination.

Regardless of President Bush's intentions, the New World Order conspiracy is now firmly entrenched in the militia belief system. It has become as important to militia members as the issue of gun control. Members feel it is their duty to fight against both of these issues because they believe gun control laws are actually a New World Order plot to facilitate the takeover of the United States. The henchmen of the New World Order, according to the conspiracy theory, do not expect all American citizens to surrender meekly. Some will fight back. Most militia members believe that because of their membership in the militia, and their belief in owning firearms, they have already been identified by the New World Order as likely to be resistant to this takeover. Therefore, according to the most widely held version of this conspiracy theory, militia members expect that they will be the first people forcibly disarmed and rounded up, then sent to one of the forty-three secret concentration camps that have been constructed around the United States. What happens after this internment depends on the particular version of the conspiracy a person believes in. One version states that the concentration camp prisoners will be forced to perform slave labor for their new masters in sweatshop type factories, while another claims they will be exterminated.

In tandem with this belief that the New World Order will soon begin its plot to take over the world is the belief that one of the first things the new rulers will do is implant a biochip in every person's body. This biochip will allow the new rulers to track a person's whereabouts, can be used to positively identify the person, and will be necessary to carry on any type of commerce in the new society. Some versions of this conspiracy also believe that the biochip, when activated, can turn people into mindless zombies who will do whatever their new masters want. There are dozens of variations on the New World Order conspiracy. One states that the New World Order plans to reduce the world's population by 50 percent by the year 2000; another, that the New World Order is actually part of the "End Times" told about in the Book of Revelations, and on and on.

For most readers, the immediate question that arises is why would any person, much less thousands of people, believe in such a conspiracy simply on someone else's word and with no proof? Some believers in this conspiracy insist there is proof. Many militia members claim to have seen black, unmarked helicopters passing overhead, which they believe are the vanguard of the impending invasion. According to militia reports, these helicopters, operating in violation of all state and federal aviation laws, swoop down around militia locations, follow militia member's cars, hover over their homes, and follow anyone known to oppose the New World Order.

Not everyone, however, believes that the black helicopter stories are proof. "[T]he Black Helicopter Syndrome," explains the publisher of *Soldier of Fortune* magazine Bob Brown. "It's this paranoid view that there is a New World Order plot to have U.N. troops take over the United States, that large numbers of U.N. troops are conducting operations in the United States, with swarms of black helicopters swooping through the skies. What these people do is take certain pieces of information, selectively interpret them, put them together, and the whole becomes much greater than the sum."[7] Most observers of the militia movement believe that any black helicopters reportedly seen by militia members were actually dark green National Guard helicopters, which were probably assisting law enforcement in spotting illegal marijuana crops, looking for forest fires, or conducting training flights.

Other militia members insist that they have seen foreign troops massing at various secret locations across the United States, just waiting for the word to begin the invasion. In support of this, I recently pulled a report from the Internet that claimed to have proof of foreign troops amassing in the United States. Accompanying this report, which claimed that militia members had witnessed foreign troops drilling in the DeSoto National Forest in the southeastern part of Mississippi, was a fuzzy picture of what the author claimed was a Scud missile. Another report on the Internet claimed that witnesses had seen two Russian helicopters at Fort Polk, Louisiana. Even giving these authors the benefit of the doubt and assuming their reports are true, none of this is proof of a conspiracy. A number of these weapons and vehicles were captured during the Persian Gulf War, and American troops use them for training in order to be acquainted with what they could possibly face in the future.

Some believers in the New World Order conspiracy, however, will point to the colored stickers on the back of certain road signs as proof of an impending invasion. They claim the stickers have been put there to guide invading foreign troops who may not be able to read English. (State road personnel explain that the stickers are there to tell when the sign was installed and when it should be replaced.) Also, many believers in the New World Order conspiracy claim they have proof that the incident at Waco between the federal government and the Branch Davidians was actually just a dry run in order for the conspirators to practice disarming the citizenry. All of this "proof" is, of course, easy to disprove, but only to nonbelievers. To true believers in a conspiracy, any disproving evidence only shows how adamantly the conspirators want to hide their plans, and how far they will go to plant this disproving evidence.

When looking for a explanation as to why so many rank-and-file militia members would believe in conspiracies that are based on such flimsy or nonexistent proof, it should be pointed out that many militia leaders do not discourage this belief system, but actually encourage it. Conspiracy belief by the rank-and-file members is beneficial to militia leaders. Believing in conspiracies demands that the believers take some kind of action to prevent them. So as long as there are evil conspirators everywhere, the militia must stay intact and vigilant. And, of course, the leaders will then always have groups over which they can exert power and remain leaders. Most of the talks I have heard given by militia leaders concentrate almost exclusively on the various conspiracies afloat and the necessity of the militia to stop them.

"Although the specific allegations about the plots and plans by the alleged conspirators frequently are complex and Byzantine," said Chip

Berlet of Political Research Associates, "the ultimate goal is still simple: the good people must expose and stop the bad people, and then conflict will end and grievances will be resolved. Conspiracism is thus an action-oriented worldview which holds out to believers the possibility of change."[8]

In addition, proving that evidence of the conspiracies held by militia members was actually just mistakes, misjudgments, or coincidences can also be near impossible, because for those in the militia movement who believe in these various conspiracies, mistakes, misjudgments, and coincidences simply do not occur. They are actually proof of the conspirators at work. The incidents were just made to appear to be mistakes, misjudgments, or coincidences. Also, conspiracy-minded militia members will thoroughly and minutely scrutinize all new government regulations to determine how they could in any way be part of the plot, and anytime the rich or the powerful meet, it is never seen as anything but an event meant to help further the plan of the New World Order takeover. The fact that the meeting occurred is considered as absolute proof of the conspiracy. Actually, anytime conspiracy spinners find any fact or event that could even remotely fit into the conspiracy theory, no matter how far they have to stretch it, they use it as proof of the New World Order's intentions.

Dennis Johnson, a clinical psychologist at Behavior Analysts & Consultants, said, "There is almost always a kernel of truth to the false beliefs that groups hold to." Richard Abanes, author of *American Militias*, adds, "Unfortunately, when a kernel of truth is planted in the fields of paranoia, the crop that springs forth bears little resemblance to reality."[9]

Given that a large number of militia members believe in the conspiracy of the New World Order, who do they believe are the evil instigators of this grand plan to take over the world, the ones who control the United Nations and the others involved in the takeover? Actually, it depends on who you listen to and which version of the conspiracy you believe. One version of the conspiracy claims the group is an organization called the Illuminati. This was a secret society founded in 1776 by Adam Weishaupt, a professor at the University of Ingolstadt in Bavaria, and disbanded by the Bavarian government in 1786. However, conspiracy believers insist that the group did not disband, but only went underground. This group's ultimate purpose, they say, is to take over the world. The Illuminati have been blamed for the French Revolution, the writing of the *Communist Manifesto*, the War of 1812, and various insurrections and government overthrows in the last two hundred years.

Another group often accused of being the behind-the-scenes instigators of the New World Order is the Council on Foreign Relations. According to the conspiracy believers, this organization, founded in 1921 and headquartered at the Harold Pratt House in New York City, contains hundreds of the most powerful and influential people in the United States, including former U.S. presidents and other highly placed government officials. Their purpose, however, is not the well-meaning explanation given in their charter—to assist in maintaining friendly international relations—but, instead, dominance of the world.

Other variations of the conspiracy say that the group behind the New World Order is the Trilateral Commission (an organization of prominent individuals from North America, Western Europe, and the Far East) or the Bilderbergers (a group of international leaders named for the hotel in Holland where the group first met). The Bilderbergers' charter states that the intent of the organization is to strengthen understanding between nations. Not so, say the conspiracy spinners.

One of the underlying elements in each of the last three groups, and something that brands them as conspirators in the eyes of the militia, is that these groups do contain many influential and powerful individuals who control governments and international industry. For conspiracy spinners, no matter how benevolent these groups may appear or claim to be, their real purpose is world domination and enslavement of the earth's people.

No matter which conspiracy variation a militia member believes in, however, a common factor is that all of these groups will use the United Nations as the main force of the invasion and takeover of the world. A skeptical person might wonder why conspiracy spinners would pick the United Nations as the evil force selected to spearhead the takeover of the world, especially considering this organization's history of military ineptness and the fact that the United Nations is always on the brink of insolvency and consumed by infighting. Part of the explanation comes from the fact that the Cold War has ended. With the collapse of the Soviet Union, and with that the end of the threat of communist domination, conspiracy spinners have been forced to look for other evil empires or cabals set on world domination. Many have settled on the United Nations. Some, however, have found groups closer to home.

Not all conspiracies involve global domination. A number of conspiracy beliefs popular with militia members involve the corruption of our national government into a dictatorship worthy of Hitler-era Germany.

Militia members believe that gun control is the first step in this coming dictatorship. The government must disarm the citizens in order to lessen the chances of any organized or sizable resistance to the establishment of the dictatorship. Interestingly, many conspiracy believers see the Federal Emergency Management Agency (FEMA) as the lead organization in this takeover and change to a dictatorship. Formed in 1978 by President Carter, FEMA began with the stated purpose of assisting in emergencies—natural and man-made. When first formed, this agency's primary task was to prepare to assist the country to survive a nuclear war. But since the end of the Cold War, it has now turned instead to assisting in natural disaster relief. However, the fact that this agency, which was formed as a backup for the government in the event of a nuclear war, still exists has spread fear throughout the militia movement. They see it as a shadow government that will take over and rule the United States once the dictatorship begins. According to this conspiracy theory, there are a number of Executive Orders already signed that give FEMA absolute authority over all of the nation's communications facilities, power supplies, food supplies, transportation facilities, civilian labor force, and health and education facilities. Conspiracy theory also says that FEMA is the agency responsible for the construction of the secret concentration camps.

One time, soon after I had been named the Indianapolis Police Department's Executive Officer, I attended a school given by FEMA at their headquarters in Maryland. If this is the shadow government of a coming dictatorship, they certainly hide their real purpose well. During my time there, and I toured the entire facility, I saw only an agency whose job it is to assist in large emergencies.

At this point, many readers might ask the obvious question of why militia members see so many conspiracies. And believe me, they do see conspiracies, dozens of them, by every agency and organization possible. Conspiracy theories, both national and worldwide, pervade the militia movement. They have become almost as important as gun control, because, like gun control, conspiracies have become the nexus of the militia's reason for existing. Members join together to prevent the various conspirators from carrying out their evil plots. But more important, truly believing there are national or worldwide conspiracies afoot that must be thwarted gives each militia member a sense of purpose and fulfilment.

"[Militia members] find satisfaction in embracing conspiracies that offer explanations for problems in their own lives or in society as a whole," said James DeFronzo, a University of Connecticut professor of sociology who lectures on militia psychology. "There is a certain psychological fulfillment to thinking you've latched onto some larger truth that better-educated or wealthier people don't understand. For someone who doesn't have a whole lot going on in their life, it's a feeling of being a part of something elite and important."[10]

Embracing conspiracy theories also keeps people from having to accept blame for, or even examine their own contribution to, their present financial and/or social condition. A person's failure to obtain or hold on to a well-paying job has nothing to do with the fact that the person never finished his or her education or has had attendance or conduct problems on past jobs. If one believes that a group of conspirators is responsible for all of the woes of the country, that then also becomes the reason behind the individual's situation. Also, many people are attracted to the militia movement because they feel powerless in their lives. Believing in and preparing to fight against conspiracies gives these people a renewed feeling of power and purpose.

However, to continue this sense of power and purpose, new twists and elements of the conspiracies must constantly appear. And they do. Many militia members, for example, believe that Francisco Duran, the man who sprayed the White House with assault rifle fire, had been brainwashed and programmed, probably by the CIA, to do this. According to some militia members, the government did this so they could use the incident as an impetus to speed up gun control. Conspiracy spinners also dreamed up the same type of brainwashing plot to explain the attempted bank holdup in Los Angeles in February 1997, in which two would-be robbers, after a failed holdup, walked nonchalantly down the street firing high-powered assault weapons at both police and civilians, seemingly unconcerned about being shot. The police eventually killed both of the robbers, but not before ten police officers and five civilians were injured. While many people may question the idea that these two individuals were brainwashed, it is quite possible, actually likely, that they were under the influence of drugs.

Of course, it is important to point out that militia members are not the only people in America who see conspiracies behind practically everything that happens. Actually, a large percentage of the American public does this. A national poll found that 49 percent of Americans believe the CIA was involved in the murder of President John Kennedy, and 9 percent believe that the manned moon landings were a hoax.[11] As ridiculous as it sounds, because of conspiracy claims, Lee Harvey Oswald's corpse had to be dug up to prove that he actually did die. When TWA Flight 800 crashed off of Long Island, New York, in July 1996, conspiracy theories immediately sprang up, insisting that the aircraft had been taken down by a missile, a bomb on board, and so forth. Even after officials from the FBI and the National Transportation Safety Board finally concluded that an accidental explosion in a fuel tank aboard the aircraft had caused the crash, some people wondered if this was just a fabrication to cover up the real cause of the crash.

In his book *The Paranoid Style in American Politics*, Richard Hofstadter claims that America is full of people who see history as "a vast and sinister conspiracy, a gigantic and yet subtle machinery of influence set in motion to undermine and destroy a way of life."[12]

However, the difference between militia members and the general public is that while many ordinary citizens do believe in conspiracies, they do not make them the controlling force in their lives, the major reason for their existence, as do many militia members. I recently witnessed just how seriously militia members take conspiracies and how easily they are passed along. At a preparedness/survival expo, I stopped by a booth that sold mainly conspiracy items, including reports on foreign troops massing inside the United States, secret foreign-run military bases inside our borders, and the concentration camps being built on American soil. They also sold newsletters on the latest efforts of the New World Order to topple the various world governments, videotapes that claimed to show the many conspiracies in action, and books and magazines devoted entirely to conspiracies. As I stood at the table looking at the information offered, I listened in on the conversation of three individuals who were talking with the woman staffing the booth. They talked for perhaps ten minutes, each one expounding on some aspect of a conspiracy. It seemed to me that the conversation was actually a game of one-upmanship, each person trying to top the last person who spoke. But what I found really interesting was that never, not once, did anyone talk about proof or verification. Each person accepted the others' stories as absolute truth.

Chip Berlet of Political Research Associates and freelance writer Matthew Lyons said, "Attending a Patriot meeting is like having your cable-access channel video of a PTA meeting crossed with the audio from an old Twilight Zone rerun. The people seem so sane and regular. They are not clinically deranged, but their discourse is paranoid, and they are awash with the crudest conspiracy theories."[13]

How can this many people share a delusion without someone expressing doubt or demanding proof? Psychologists say it is because militias become closed societies, where everyone reinforces everyone else's beliefs. Also, because militias are closed societies, members gradually have less contact with nonmembers who could offer alternative explanations or theories. Militia members eventually insulate themselves from any logical alternatives to the conspiracy theories.

"It's all bull," said Bob Brown, editor and publisher of *Soldier of Fortune* magazine, talking about conspiracy theories. "But they don't want reasonable explanations because they don't fit their preconceived notions."[14]

This conspiracy spinning by militia members, however, can be carried to outlandish levels. For example, two of the founders of the Michigan Militia, Norman Olson and Ray Southwell, were forced to resign their positions of leadership in the militia when they issued statements claiming that the bombing in Oklahoma City was the work of the Japanese government, who did it in retaliation for the American government's involvement in the poison gas attack in a Tokyo subway. The two men said their information came from a woman they spoke with on the telephone, who claimed she had contacts in the intelligence community. Interestingly, neither man knew the woman but simply accepted her claims with no corroboration. This example alone should explain how many of the conspiracy theories begin and spread.

And yet, as silly as this conspiracy theory about the Japanese government sounds, it is tame compared to some of the conspiracies put forth. For example, according to the *Patriot Report*, scientists working with the New World Order are in regular contact with four types of aliens from other planets, two types of gray aliens with large heads and almond-shaped eyes, a reptilian-type alien, and one that appears human. In return for allowing these aliens to kidnap hundreds of thousands of humans every year for genetic experiments and other uses, the New World Order receives high-level technology from the aliens, which it apparently plans to use in its takeover of the world.[15]

Another conspiracy alleges the government has satellites in orbit that can control the weather. Apparently, this technology can cause weather disturbances such as cyclones, tornados, and so on. Militia members have also proposed a conspiracy theory that alleges the cameras posted along busy highways, supposedly there to monitor traffic conditions, are actually there to spy on people and track their movement. Finally, a number of our national parks have been forced to go so far as to print in their brochures that they are not controlled by the United Nations, which a number of militia publications have alleged, since these parks were selected as World Heritage Sites by the United Nations. Other locations named World Heritage Sites include Pompeii, the birthplace of Buddha, and the stone temples at Angkor Wat, Cambodia. This selection is simply an honorary designation that makes the sites eligible for UNESCO funding, and that is all. It gives the United Nations no authority over them. However, no matter what the United Nations does, no matter how benign, militia members see it as somehow connected to their plot to take over the world.

As might be imagined, for most of the conspiracy theories put forth by militia groups and members, just a little investigation will show them to be misinterpretations or intentional misrepresentations of the facts. Former Green Beret Colonel Bo Gritz, while attempting to end the standoff at the Weaver cabin in Ruby Ridge, Idaho, said he received reports that 30,000 United Nations Cambodian soldiers were swarming toward them. He sent several associates out to investigate, and they found that indeed the forests were swarming with Asians. They were there picking the mushrooms that sprout up in the area just after the fire season—mushrooms that are extremely popular in oriental groceries across the United States.

Yet, as I said earlier, even despite the ability to debunk conspiracies, this often only reinforces many militia members' belief in the conspiracy. And so, given that many people simply will not give up their belief in these hidden plots, how dangerous can militia members believing in them be? Extremely dangerous. In 1995, a former member of the Michigan Militia told the police about an alleged militia plot to blow up Camp Grayling, a National Guard base in northern Michigan. Apparently, photographs had been taken that showed open railroad cars delivering Russian tanks to this camp. For most militia members, this became absolute confirmation that the New World Order plot was underway, that the conspirators were amassing troops and equipment for the takeover of the United States. According to the former militia member, the militia's strategy included not only blowing up the camp, but also killing anyone who tried to stop them. Fortunately, this plot never got under way. Interestingly however, part of the conspiracy beliefs turned out to be true. The photographs really did show Russian tanks. However, rather than equipment for the New World Order takeover, this was captured equipment that the military uses, and has used for years, to train soldiers to combat foreign tanks and equipment. A spokesman for Camp Grayling said that they had purposely used open, uncovered rail cars "to avoid precisely the kind of suspicions voiced by paramilitary groups.[16]

As we have seen throughout this chapter, although many Americans love to believe in conspiracies, almost all militia members subscribe to them. Most militia members truly believe there is an evil cabal that intends to invade the United States and overthrow the government. While there is nothing illegal or wrong about holding this belief, the militia movement tends to attract a radical fringe that harbors no inhibitions against using violence. Consequently, these fringe militia members often want to do more than just talk about and pass along the knowledge of the conspiracy. As demonstrated earlier in the case involving Camp Grayling, these fringe militia members often feel absolutely justified in taking armed action against whomever they believe is involved in a conspiracy.

While this radical fringe element is undeniably dangerous, it actually makes up only a small percentage of militia membership. As we shall see in the next chapter, many other types of people also belong to the militias.

❖ ❖ ❖ ❖ ❖ ❖ ❖ ❖   4

WHO BELONGS TO MILITIAS?

The roll call room suddenly went silent as the dozen police officers abruptly stopped talking and jerked their heads toward the television. As the news anchor began reading the video prompter, a half dozen mouths fell open in shock. Even though hardened by years of witnessing people commit just about every act imaginable, the officers still could not believe what they were seeing. Every few seconds during the broadcast, for just a moment, one of the officers would pull his or her eyes away from the screen and glance around nervously at the other officers, as if not sure what the correct reaction should be, then look back unbelieving at the television.

The news broadcast, scratchy and in black and white because it had been taken with a concealed video camera smuggled in by a local television news team, showed Indianapolis police sergeant James Heath, in full police uniform, addressing a secret meeting of the civilian militia group known as the Sovereign Patriots, of which, the stunned officers discovered during the report, he was the leader. As the hidden video camera panned around the room, none of the officers watching the broadcast or even the lieutenant in charge of roll call knew what to say. It had only been two weeks since the bombing of the Alfred P. Murrah Federal Building in Oklahoma City, and every officer in the room knew that the men charged in that bombing had been linked in the press to the Michigan Militia. While most officers did not view every person who joined the militia as a dangerous fanatic, they still realized that these organizations—essentially private armies answerable to no one—held the potential of being extremely dangerous.

57

"We've seen power corrupt, abuse of power with kings and queens, mayors," Sergeant Heath said on the television screen. "Mayor Goldsmith [the mayor of Indianapolis]. What do we call him? I better not say it, ah, we call him Goldstein."[1]

Sergeant Heath, a twenty-nine-year police veteran, also talked to the members of the Sovereign Patriots about Jesus Christ and assault rifles. "If He were here today, with the weaponry we have today, He would say, 'Sell your garments and buy an assault rifle because that is going to reach out, whereas 70 percent do survive handguns.'"[2] Sergeant Heath also told the group that, as a police officer, he would not enforce some laws because he found them unconstitutional.

The unexpected exposure of Sergeant Heath as the leader of the Sovereign Patriots naturally aroused immediate and serious concern both inside and outside of the police department. Many of the citizens who watched the broadcast, stunned by what they saw and heard, demanded action by the police department. Responding to the public uproar, Indianapolis Police Chief James Toler suspended Heath for thirty days without pay and demoted him from the rank of sergeant to patrol officer.

"In my opinion, Sergeant Heath has eliminated himself from being the effective example-setting supervisor our officers are accustomed to and deserve," said Chief Toler.[3]

However, despite the chief's actions, many members of the Indianapolis Jewish community felt the chief did not go far enough in punishing Heath because of the harm caused by his anti-Semitic comments. "If you were Jewish, would you want him to stop you?" asked Michael Maurer, chairman of the Jewish Community Relations Council. "I'm disappointed that the action didn't go far enough. This man does not belong on our police force."[4]

Heath, on the other hand, felt his comments had been taken out of context. He called the mayor's office the day after the tape had played on the local news to apologize. "I meant it as a compliment," he said of his comments about the mayor, "because of the job he did cutting unnecessary expenses and trimming down and saving the city of Indianapolis money. We all recognize the fact that Jewish businessmen are probably some of the sharpest in the world. I didn't even know he was Jewish."[5]

The former police sergeant, and now patrol officer, was not as cordial when speaking about the news media coverage of his secret talk to the gathering of the Sovereign Patriots. "The hatchet job that they did on the things that I said, without the qualifiers before the statements I made, is disgusting. It was taken totally out of context." He also said that when he told the members of the Sovereign Patriots he would not enforce certain laws he found unconstitutional, he had meant only "unpopular" laws, such as the seatbelt and motorcycle helmet laws.[6]

Six months later, the Civilian Police Merit Board, a six-member civilian board that oversees and must approve all serious discipline within the Indianapolis Police Department, held a two-and-a-half hour hearing that eventually upheld the chief's suspension and demotion of Heath. "His remarks were derogatory and personally disparaging toward Mayor Goldsmith and his religious beliefs," the Merit Board said. "The religious slur undermines that trust and confidence (of the community) and impedes the effective performance of the department's public services."[7]

Heath appealed the Civilian Police Merit Board's decision to the Marion County Superior Court. In August 1996, Marion County Superior Court Judge Gerald Zore overruled the Civilian Police Merit Board and ordered the police department to restore Heath's rank and pay him for the thirty days he had been suspended. "Officer Heath's statement," said Judge Zore, "while perhaps inappropriate and even offensive to some members of the community, was protected speech under the First Amendment of the Constitution of the United States."[8]

On 19 November 1997, however, the Indiana Court of Appeals overturned Judge Zore's ruling and held that the demotion of Heath was proper. The court felt that while Heath had the right of free speech, the city's interest in fostering trust between the community and the police department outweighed Heath's rights.

"There was evidence that Heath's comment had a detrimental effect in the community, especially the Jewish community," the court said.[9]

Heath retired from the Indianapolis Police Department in January 1998 and is reportedly still active in the militia movement.

Unfortunately, even though the revelation that a police officer commanded a civilian militia group shocked most members of the Indianapolis Police Department, this is by no means an isolated incident. Two weeks before the bombing in Oklahoma City, the FBI sent a memo out to its field offices warning its agents to use caution, because it had received information that a number of local police officers had joined the ranks of civilian militias that held antigovernment views. The memo said that agents "should note that the FBI has received information, corroborated by investigation, which indicates that law enforcement officers are also involved with militia groups."[10]

"It's definitely a conflict of interest," said FBI agent Tom Smith, talking about police officers belonging to militias. "It makes the officer vulnerable to being used by them. It also puts the police department administration in a bad light."

Mark Koernke, however, a prominent militia leader from Michigan, after a talk he gave at a preparedness/survival expo in Atlanta, told me, "We have members in almost all small police departments. Maybe not the command people, but we have the officers. Mostly we have them in police departments under 100 people."

Jack McLamb, a retired Phoenix police officer, who likes to wear his old police uniform at gatherings of the militia, wrote a seventy-five-page booklet titled *Operation Vampire Killer 2000*, a rambling account in which he claims that a global conspiracy exists to unite the entire world under the rule of the United Nations. The plot, he says, will begin in the year 2000 and be accomplished by the year 2001. His primary mission, however, is not to write booklets. It is to recruit police officers into the various civilian militias. In fact, a large part of *Operation Vampire Killer 2000* is a recruiting pitch for police officers. McLamb travels the country every year in pursuit of his goal.

McLamb also believes there is a conspiracy among law enforcement leadership to erode constitutional rights and that police officers must join militias in order to fight this. "We're being taught that the Constitution gets in the way of law enforcement . . . and how to get around reading people their rights," preaches McLamb. "That belief system is causing America to decline at a very fast rate."[11] As proof of his belief about the state of American law enforcement, McLamb claims that more than 6,000 police officers and soldiers presently belong to his organization: Police Against the New World Order.

Brian Levin, a former police officer and now assistant professor at Richard Stockton College, believes militias try to recruit public safety officials because these individuals have access to information vital to the survival of the militias. Law enforcement officers, for example, have access to local, state, and federal crime computers, to intelligence gathered on militia groups, and they are often involved in joint state–federal law enforcement operations. "They want them because of their utility," said Professor Levin. "They view law enforcement as a very solid potential enemy or a very helpful potential friend."[12]

Occasionally, public safety officials not only become members of civilian militias, but also are deeply committed to their cause. The Michigan Militia, for example, reported that it recently had to expel two deputy sheriffs who were just too radical. The militia did not give details about what the deputies wanted to do, but it can be assumed that they wanted the militia to take forceful actions that made the other members feel uncomfortable. "There are groups out there that are just plain off the wall," said the commander of the Michigan Militia, Lynn Van Hurzen, a veteran wounded in combat in Vietnam, "and we won't have anything to do with them."[13]

As substantiation of this claim that a large number of public safety officials belong to or are sympathetic to militia groups, employees of government agencies operating in areas of the country where civilian militias have large memberships report often being stopped from performing their duties by local law enforcement personnel who support the militias. This is particularly true for government employees whose jobs involve restricting land use. A home video shown at a militia meeting in Montana featured a local sheriff encouraging membership in the group and telling the viewers that he would never enforce the Brady Bill. "I would never register my guns," the sheriff says in the video. "How could I ask you to register yours?"[14]

It is not only local law enforcement officials, however, who occasionally support the militias. The FBI, though usually an agency vehemently opposed by most militas, is not immune from having members sympathetic to civilian militias. At a militia conference held in Palm Springs, California, former Los Angeles FBI chief Ted Gunderson claimed that the United States government detonated the bomb that destroyed the Alfred P. Murrah Federal Building in Oklahoma City. The government's purpose in this, he states, is "to further erode our liberties and destroy constitutional rights." Gunderson said he believes the bombing was perpetrated by "an element within the government, a demonic element from within the government, but I don't know who it is. . . . Somebody in the government—Army, whatever—somebody in the system was responsible."[15]

Some public safety officials, though, can go far beyond just supporting or even joining civilian militias. Some, as in the incident below, take an active role in the crimes committed by militias.

A federal court recently convicted Lieutenant James R. Rodgers, a nineteen-year veteran firefighter in Clarksburg, West Virginia, under a new federal antiterrorist law. Rodgers, a major in the West Virginia Mountaineer Militia, reportedly slipped into the basement of the fire department and photographed thirty-four blueprints the fire department had on file of the federal government's new $200 million Criminal Justice Information Services Facility, located in Clarksburg. The fire department maintained these blueprints in their files in case of emergencies at the facility. The Criminal Justice Information Services Facility, operated by the FBI, houses huge computers that store millions of fingerprints that have been electronically coded. However, the leader of the West Virginia Mountaineer Militia, Ray L. Looker, believed that the facility was actually an intelligence center for the New World Order. He was convinced that the facility would be able to track and watch anyone anywhere in America. Therefore, it had to be destroyed. It was Looker who convinced Rodgers to photograph the blueprints and then provide this information to the militia.

After receiving these photographs, Looker then tried to sell the information to an undercover police officer posing as a representative of a Middle East terrorist group. What Looker and the others did not know was that the chief of security for the West Virginia Mountaineer Militia was an undercover informant for the FBI, and had told the FBI about the passing of the blueprints to the militia. The FBI moved in and made several arrests, including Rodgers and Looker, who were both eventually convicted in the case. In March 1998, a court sentenced Looker to eighteen years in prison.

A court also convicted Edward F. Moore in this case. A member of the high-IQ group Mensa and a colonel in the Mountaineer Militia, Moore demonstrated during a training session for militia members how to make a bomb out of fertilizer and racing fuel. He received a sentence of two years in prison.

According to court documents, the West Virginia Mountaineer Militia, in addition to targeting the FBI's Criminal Justice Information Services Facility, had also talked about waging a "holy war" against the government. Part of this holy war included plots to assassinate Senator Jay Rockefeller and Federal Reserve Chairman Alan Greenspan.

In another incident involving law enforcement officers and the militia, in August 1997, a federal grand jury indicted a Storey County (Nevada)

sheriff's deputy and a reserve deputy. The grand jury charged the men, who belonged to an unnamed militia group, with conspiracy, possession of illegal machine guns, and possession of pipe bombs and hand grenades. The men allegedly planned to use the weapons and explosives in attacks on the federal government. An undercover FBI agent said one of the men talked about shooting "blue-helmeted, jack-booted thugs."[16]

Regardless, however, of the number of public safety officials involved with militias, most readers, when they see reports about the militia, likely visualize the members as angry, young, out-of-work, white males, and quite often they are right. Many members of militia groups are unemployed or marginally employed, young, white males, because the high-pay, low-tech industrial jobs that these individuals used to be able to obtain have now mostly disappeared. These men instead see high technology, for which they have no training, taking over American industries, and this frightens them. They fear that their lives will be spent in low-paying, meaningless jobs. They fear what an article by the Political Research Associates says many of their futures appear to be: "Flip burgers or die!"[17]

These angry, young, white males, finding themselves unable to capture the American Dream because they lack the job skills necessary to obtain well-paying jobs, often look for someone (other than themselves) to blame for their problems. Also, veterans, which many militia members are, and particularly those who have served in combat, many times feel that their country owes them a good living because of their service and become angry and frustrated when this does not occur. They, too, then look for someone to blame for their plight. The militias give them someone to blame.

Brent L. Smith, chairman of the department of Criminal Justice at the University of Alabama, Birmingham, and author of *Terrorism in America,* explains that "worker bees in the movement tend to be much lower-educated than the general population." And with jobs for unskilled workers drying up, "they are unlikely to attain middle-class status—or much of a stake in the status quo."[18]

With their philosophy that all of the troubles in the country come from big government and its programs, such as welfare and affirmative action, and with their belief that there is a conspiracy of corrupt bankers to control the economy, civilian militias give prospective members scapegoats for their problems. They tell new members that their present economic predicament does not come from a lack of job training or skills.

They tell them that their present problems are not their fault at all; they are the fault of uncaring bureaucrats and money-hungry bankers.

"These people simply want to understand why they can no longer maintain a comfortable standard of living," said Richard Abanes in his book *American Militias.* "Their financial security has somehow disappeared overnight, along with any hope of enjoying the reward that every red-blooded American envisions: twilight years of bliss and contentment earned by a life of honest, hard work."[19]

However, once prospective members accept the belief that their predicament is not their fault, but the result of a conspiracy by the federal government and an evil cabal of international bankers, joining the militia seems an obvious decision. They see membership in the militia as their chance to fight against these groups and bring back the good life they deserve but are missing.

Militias also recruit new members by using such emotional social issues as gun control, taxation and IRS abuse, abortion, welfare, gay rights, affirmative action, and illegal immigration. Many of the angry, young, white males that the militias attempt to recruit feel strongly opposed to these issues, and the militias play on this emotion.

Jerry Franks, a teacher of government and philosophy at Midland College, said that the militia movement is populated "for the most part with people who are not adjusting well to modernity, to change, to modern society, to the changing racial balance in the country, the new roles of women."[20]

However, it is a mistake to believe that the civilian militias in our country consist only of angry, unemployed, young, white males. Militias are also attracting many new recruits that few would suspect could be drawn to such groups. Many new recruits are older people who have lost family farms, executives who have been downsized out of their jobs, individuals who have seen their long-held jobs go to foreign countries, or small businessmen who have been put out of business (at least in their minds) by agencies of the federal government, usually by the IRS, but occasionally by other federal agencies, such as the U.S. Forestry Service in the logging areas of the Pacific Northwest. These individuals, thrust into unemployment late in life, feel confused, angry, and frightened, and look for someone to blame. The militas give them someone to blame. An article in the *Idaho Press-Tribune* describes a typical militia recruit from this group: "[He] lost his job and his marriage in a single year and calls himself overeducated and underemployed. And he didn't trust the federal government."[21]

For all of these reasons, the membership lists of the various civilian militias in our country now cut across all of America's socioeconomic classes. They include ministers, real estate developers, veterinarians, police officers, attorneys, gun dealers, war heroes, and even family members of the wealthy. James Allen Monaghan, for example, brother of Domino's Pizza magnate Thomas Monaghan, belongs to the Michigan Militia.

Interestingly, however, while the militia movement may appear to be a white movement, since a number of the militias are simply outgrowths of white supremacy groups, this is not entirely so. There exists a number of minority militia members. J. J. Johnson, an African American, was one of the founders of the Ohio Unorganized Militia, a mostly white organization. Like many businesses that want minorities in key spots in order to show how nondiscriminatory they are, militias also want to appear, at least on the surface, as though they are representing all Americans. In 1997, however, Johnson turned up in Las Vegas, saying he had severed all ties with the militia and was considering running for Clark County (Nevada) sheriff. Clifford Brookins II, another African American, is the commander of the Detroit Constitutional Militia, an African American militia group, the only one I found any information on. However, his group is actually more a collection of community activists than militia members. They do not wear uniforms, march in the woods, or carry guns. They are concerned with urban issues such as jobs, housing, crime, drugs, and education. They call themselves a militia, he said, "because it scares the government."[22]

In an attempt to attract a broader base of members and shed their white supremacy roots, many militia groups across the United States now look to recruit minority members. "Maybe there is some racism," Brookins said of many militia groups' white supremacy backgrounds. "If all they know is what they see about black people in the media, how can they help it? Once we sit down at the table, we'll work it out."[23] As we will talk about in a later chapter, however, the militia movement in America is basically a white movement, with many of the groups having strong racist or anti-Semitic views.

As mentioned in an earlier chapter, women have become a small, but increasing, block of the militia membership. Hate-group watchdog organizations say that women presently make up between 10 and 20 percent of the militia membership in the United States. "My biggest worry is that my son will not have the freedom to pursue what he wants the way we did," said forty-three-year-old Wendy Dalton, who joined a militia in

1993. "The government has grown too large; it does not realize that it is a servant and not a master."[24]

While most women militia members hold supporting roles, in a few cases, women have taken over the leadership of their groups. Stephanie Birmingham, a disc jockey, is commander of the Chattanooga (Tennessee) cell of the Gadsden Minutemen. Another woman, Indianapolis attorney Linda Thompson, heads the Unorganized Militia of the United States of America.

Both women and men in the armed forces are especially sought after as recruits by civilian militias. As claimed earlier by former Phoenix police officer Jack McLamb, many members of the armed forces have already joined civilian militias. This is not only troublesome to our military leaders, since some militias are only thinly veiled hate groups, but also dangerous to everyone, because military personnel often have the tactical training militias want and access to weaponry and explosives, which militias also want.

"We're not going to be outgunned by the Government because everything they've got is ours," said M. J. Beckman, a militia leader in Montana. "We have tremendous numbers of people inside the National Guard, Navy, Army, Marines who would turn on the Government if they start something."[25]

Civilian militias especially want to recruit military personnel because, since most militias readily accept one or more of the various national and global conspiracies concerning a takeover of the United States, they often devote themselves to stockpiling weapons and explosives to prevent this. This makes military personnel, because of their access to weapons and explosives, very attractive as recruits. And unfortunately, there are some military personnel very willing to give or sell these weapons and explosives to fringe groups. In 1994, the Army charged five soldiers at Fort Benning, Georgia, with conspiracy to steal explosives and parts to convert rifles to fully automatic weapons. The soldiers were reportedly going to funnel these items to white supremacy groups, which often have contacts with or are a part of the militias. In another case, four times in three months, soldiers at Fort Bragg, North Carolina, sold land mines, rockets, grenades, explosives, and small arms to undercover police officers.

"Hate groups 'target' active-duty soldiers for recruitment for several reasons, including gaining access to arms," said Laurie Wood, a field researcher for the Klanwatch Project in Montgomery, Alabama. "Groups that can boast soldiers as members also are more attractive to new civilian recruits."[26]

A report released by the Pentagon in March 1996, said senior commanders believe that members of the Green Berets and other elite military units have been targeted by militant militias for recruitment. The report recommended that a policy be considered that would bar military members from active participation in extremist groups. In his book *Gathering Storm*, author Morris Dees claims there is a clandestine militia group of servicemen at Fort Bragg, North Carolina, who call themselves the "Special Forces Underground." The group's goal is to force the federal government "back into its constitutional prison."[27]

Unfortunately, even though the military tries very hard to discourage its members from joining the militias and other far-right groups, military personnel have a strong role model that pulls in the opposite direction. Former Green Beret colonel and decorated Vietnam veteran Bo Gritz has become a spokesperson for far-right groups such as militias. According to the Militia Task Force of the Southern Poverty Law Center, Gritz delivers "an apocalyptic anti-government message" through his newsletters and syndicated radio program, and claims to be "divinely inspired" and have "prophetic visions."[28] In 1996, however, the police arrested Gritz as he sat in his car on the parking lot of the McAlister Middle School in Suffield, Connecticut. The police believe he meant to kidnap a schoolchild who had become the center of a bitter custody dispute between a husband and wife. The wife's cause had recently been taken up by militia members after she appeared on Gritz's radio show. On the show, she made accusations about corruption in the judicial system, and because of her opposition to the government, she found many friends and supporters in the militia movement.

Because of all the reasons discussed in this chapter, many of the armed civilian militias, even though in existence only four or five years, and once thought by many experts to be just a brief phenomenon that would quickly fade, can today boast a large, diversified, and growing membership. An article in the *Los Angeles Times* a year after the Oklahoma City bombing said: "Most law enforcement officials and private experts thought the public's anger over Oklahoma City would all but shut down the militias and other far-flung extremist groups. But their numbers have increased, by some counts manifold." Gerald A. Carroll, an adjunct professor at the University of Iowa, and a man who has studied society's fringe elements for twenty years, adds, "It's becoming almost monumental. The numbers are quite staggering. Who'd have thought they'd still be increasing like this after Oklahoma City?"[29]

Militia membership, as stated earlier, has increased partly because of economic problems and unwanted social change, but in a large part it is due to the success of heavy recruiting. Some militias recruit by word of mouth; others through advertisements in gun, survivalist, and outdoor magazines; and still others through the militia expos held around the country every year. These militia expos usually go by the name of preparedness/survival expos. Jonathan Mozzochi, executive director of the Coalition for Human Dignity, which tracks right-wing extremist groups, said, "They are the foremost recruiting grounds for militia and patriot activists. The expos also bring militia politics, which has generally existed outside of major cities, into cosmopolitan urban centers."[30]

At a preparedness/survival expo I attended in Atlanta, John Trochmann, one of the founders of the Militia of Montana, told me after his talk, "We don't need just more people involved in the militia. We need everyone involved." At this expo, I got the feeling that the militias represented there were definitely attempting to polish their image, hoping to make themselves look more mainstream in order, as Mr. Trochmann said, to attract a larger segment of the American population to the militia cause.

But as successful a recruiting forum as these expos are, an increasing amount of militia recruiting is done over the Internet. "It is arguably the first U.S. social movement to be organized primarily through nontraditional electronic media, such as the Internet," said Chip Berlet, an analyst with Political Research Associates in Cambridge, Massachusetts.[31]

While doing research for this book, I found that practically every militia of any size in America has an Internet website. There are literally dozens and dozens of them. Militias use the Internet because advertising and recruiting this way has two distinct advantages. First, Internet websites can reach many people quickly and cheaply, and, second, the information provided does not have to be edited or approved by anyone or any organization. The militias do not have to bother with the troublesome and time-consuming task of substantiating anything they say on their web pages.

Some of the militia websites I found during my research simply provide information about the militia and its purpose, with a small portion of the website devoted to how interested parties can inquire about joining. Others have a much more hard-sell approach. "We are a network of doers, not whiners or fakers," says Linda Thompson's Unorganized Militia of the United States of America website. In order to log on to this site, a web surfer must first answer questions such as: "Are you willing to provide a safe house, training area, or equipment and supplies for Patriots defending the Constitution?" The web surfer is also asked about any special talents and skills he or she may possess that might be helpful to the militia, along with other personal information.[32]

Regardless of the recruiting methods used, though, most militia groups will take almost anyone who volunteers, no matter what his or her skills or educational attainments. But this is not universally true. A few of the militias are extremely selective. The 52nd Missouri Militia, for example, wants only individuals with computer, electronics, radio, electronic countermeasures, intelligence, surveying, and mapmaking backgrounds. The 52nd Missouri Militia considers itself the intelligence-gathering unit of American militias. Successfully obtaining membership in the 52nd, even for those with the above skills, can only come on a recommendation from a longtime 52nd member.

Another significant reason for the recruiting success of America's civilian militias is the support and encouragement these organizations receive from powerful members of American society. Several members of the United States Congress, including Representatives Steve Stockman (Texas) and Helen Chenoweth (Idaho), have openly expressed support for civilian militias. Congressman Stockman has sent messages to the Justice Department inquiring about their plans, which he claims he has information on, to attack militias. An editorial in the *Idaho Statesman* said: "Whether she realizes it or not, Chenoweth is quickly becoming the poster child for such groups."[33]

In addition to national politicians, a number of state and local politicians have also openly supported the militias. California State Senator Don Rogers, for example, introduced a measure into the State Legislature calling for safeguards against a global takeover by the United Nations.

This backing from politicians, along with support from media personalities such as J. Gordon Liddy and Rush Limbaugh, gives what should be only small, loosely bound, local groups of angry citizens national legitimacy. They become serious organizations to be reckoned with; thus, to many individuals, joining them looks very attractive. All of this support keeps the membership rolls in these groups swelling.

Yet since many militias keep their membership lists confidential, no one is certain just how successful the militias' recruiting efforts are or how many people across the United States actually belong to civilian militias.

Most experts feel that the number likely runs in the tens of thousands, with the number of sympathizers in the millions. And they also believe the numbers grow larger each year. If this trend does not stop, by the early twenty-first century, the armed civilian militias will become an extremely powerful and dangerous force in our country.

With this large number of people joining the civilian militias every year, training new members so that they can benefit the group becomes increasingly important. But just as there are many different militias across the United States, so there are many different training techniques.

MILITIA TRAINING

In November 1995, a man deer hunting in the Tonto National Forest, about 100 miles north of Phoenix, Arizona, stumbled onto a band of heavily armed men dressed in camouflage. The hunter later complained to the authorities that the group, who hinted they were park security, would not allow him to use a road in the national forest, threatened him when he attempted to, and then forced him to leave the area. The authorities also received a similar complaint from a group of Boy Scouts on a hike through the same area of the national forest. This group of armed men, however, the authorities quickly discovered, were not park security. They were a civilian militia group, and they were holding a training session when stumbled upon by the hunter and troop of Boy Scouts.

Acting on the two complaints, a federal agent went to the location where the confrontations with the hunter and Boy Scouts occurred and found evidence of assault rifle practice. At the site, the agent also discovered a crater six feet wide and three feet deep, apparently made with a bomb. Following up on this evidence, the authorities initiated an official investigation and, after talking with people at gun stores and other hangouts for militia types, they discovered that the group using the forest called itself the Viper Militia.

A clerk at a business in Phoenix called Shooter's World reported to the authorities that he had heard through a customer about the Viper Militia and, after meeting several members, had been invited to join the group. Agents from the Bureau of Alcohol, Tobacco, and Firearms (ATF) recruited the clerk to infiltrate the group for them. In addition, the federal agents deputized an officer with the State Game and Fish Department and also assigned him to infiltrate the Viper Militia, which he did, secretly taping militia meetings and conversations with the members. However, before the two undercover agents could join the group, the Viper Militia members first made them take an oath that included swearing to kill any government agent who tried to infiltrate the Viper Militia, and to take retribution if the police arrested any member of the militia.

On 2 July 1996, after a six-month investigation, federal authorities arrested twelve members of the Viper Militia, ten men and two women, charging them with illegally possessing automatic firearms and explosives. They also charged six of the militia members with conspiracy to furnish instructions in the use of explosive devices as a way of promoting civil disorder. In the criminal complaint, authorities claimed the group had been plotting to blow up a number of buildings in Phoenix, including the offices of the Bureau of Alcohol, Tobacco, and Firearms, offices of the Internal Revenue Service, offices of the Immigration and Naturalization Service, the Phoenix Police Department, and an Arizona National Guard Center.

According to the indictments, the group had been plotting these bombings for two years, and during this time had also been training extensively in the use of automatic weapons and explosives, setting off and testing the capability of several bombs. The government infiltrators claimed the group conducted this training in order to be prepared to fight either the New World Order when it came, or the federal government, if it should decide to declare martial law and begin confiscating weapons from private citizens.

The Viper Militia, the undercover agents also reported, would regularly hold two types of training sessions: A-shoots and B-shoots. During A-shoots, the members would bring only legal weapons and often invite family members and friends to join them. For B-shoots, however, only members of the militia could attend, and during these sessions, they would detonate test bombs and train with illegal automatic weapons. The group trained so extensively and so often that one of the members bragged to the undercover informants that the Viper Militia was so well trained and equipped that it could take on any SWAT team.

Following the arrest of the twelve Viper Militia members, federal authorities seized from their homes almost 100 shotguns, assault rifles, machine guns, and other weapons. They also discovered grenades, grenade launchers, detonation cord, blasting caps, gas masks, and bulletproof vests. Along with this, federal agents found almost a ton of ammonium nitrate, the same chemical used in the April 1995 bombing of the Alfred P. Murrah Federal Building in Oklahoma City, stored at the home of one of the militia members. In addition, the authorities also recovered fifty-five gallons of nitromethane, which bomb makers mix with the ammonium nitrate when constructing a bomb. It took four pickup trucks to carry away all of the evidence.

"The whole house is littered with weapons," said a police officer, when searching the home of one of the Viper Militia members. "You can hardly walk anywhere without stepping on one."[1]

According to the undercover agents who infiltrated the group, the members talked a number of times about "sanitizing" their homes, or removing illegal weapons and explosives. However, one of the members said he had tried to sanitize his home at least six times in the last year, but that he simply "didn't feel secure unless [he had] the ability to take out at least part of [his] neighborhood."[2]

Federal authorities also confiscated a number of training videos the militia members had made, which would later become key evidence against the group concerning their intentions. One of the videos had been filmed by the militia during a B-shoot training session, with segments showing the members firing illegal automatic weapons and detonating bombs. On the tape, following the detonation of a bomb, militia members could be heard shouting, "Yes! Yes! That felt good! Wow! It's a fucking mushroom cloud!"[3]

Another video contained the group's proposed bombing targets in Phoenix. The video, according to the indictment against the militia members, "contains instructions for the placement of explosive devices, illegal entry, control and destruction of the targeted buildings."[4]

On the video, the narrator says, "Today's date is May 30, 1994. This is a reconnaissance tape for American patriots. What you are looking at now is the Phoenix, Arizona, Treasury Building, which houses Alcohol, Tobacco, and Firearms. . . . Notice the structure. These pillars support the entire building. Take out these pillars, simultaneously, with explosives, and the building will collapse." The tape then reveals a plan to place antipersonnel bombs in the mail boxes at the entrance to the building in order to injure and kill the building's workers, and a scheme to blow up a nearby water main so that firefighters would not be able to put out the fire caused by the explosion.[5]

Interestingly, after the authorities announced the arrests and the news media looked into the backgrounds of the militia members, they found that the twelve individuals who had been arrested fit well into the public perception of militia members talked about in the last chapter. All were white, with a high school education or less, and most were stuck in low-paying, dead-end jobs. Because of their life situation, many of the members of the Viper Militia must have felt intense anger and frustration. In 1995, for example, an official of a shooting competition sponsored by *Soldier of Fortune* magazine kicked two members of the Viper Militia out of the competition because of their rowdiness. One of the ejected militia members, who edited a gun-enthusiast bulletin, wrote in the newsletter: "We were too rowdy for *Soldier of Fortune*. Aren't those the guys who frag Serbs for giggles?" Concerning the official who had ejected them from the shooting competition, he also wrote, "Next year, I'm gonna shoot just so I can get a chance to catch you alone and smash your face."[6]

These two men, however, were not the only Viper Militia members who were angry and frustrated. One of the female members reportedly suggested taking retribution against the family members of federal law enforcement officers if any of the Viper Militia members were ever arrested. The female member, who worked for AT&T, claimed she could get the information needed to do this by accessing the telephone records of the targets. The other members, though, felt this was a little too militant and rejected her idea. The group did, however, work out an emergency ambush plan in the event that any of them were ever followed by the police. The tailed militia member would lead the law enforcement officers to a parking lot behind a grocery store, where other militia members would be waiting with guns and other weapons. One of the Viper Militia members had bragged to the undercover agents that he had built a rocket that "could take out a police car."[7]

Despite the elaborate plans, the blustering, and the threats, the twelve members of the Viper Militia surrendered to the authorities without incident. This does not mean, however, that the group was harmless, only that they did not have the courage they thought they would when actually confronted by the authorities. The police frequently see this timid reaction with individuals who exclaim, "The police will never take me alive!" The Viper Militia, however, against unarmed, unprepared targets, such as government workers in one of the buildings targeted for bombing, had the potential to be extremely dangerous.

Ten of the Viper Militia members, despite their initial pleas of innocence, eventually worked out plea bargains with the federal prosecutor. They received sentences ranging from a year and a day to nine years in prison. Two members, though, refused to plea bargain and elected instead to stand trial. A court found one of them guilty and sentenced him to four years and nine months in prison. The other defendant, who had dropped out of the Viper Militia before much of the activity that the others were charged with occurred, was acquitted on one charge and had a hung jury on the other. The government did not say if it would seek a new trial on the hung-jury charge.

As should be obvious from this incident, the Viper Militia showed the potential to be an exceedingly dangerous group, with a mentality similar to that of Timothy McVeigh and Terry Nichols, the two men convicted in the bombing of the Alfred P. Murrah Federal Building in Oklahoma City. Like McVeigh and Nichols, this group held to the belief that bombing government buildings is an acceptable militia tactic. The threat to the public from this type of mentality cannot be overstated. It is one thing to sit around at militia meetings and rant about the government, and even to suggest that violent actions should be taken against the government. This occurs in many, if not almost all, militias. The Viper Militia, however, went much further. They not only talked about taking action against government targets, but they also trained for it. Evidence shows that for two years, the Viper Militia had trained themselves in the use of automatic weapons and explosives. And then, carrying this even further, they actually went out and scouted the locations of possible bombing targets. Only timely intervention by federal agents likely kept a tragedy similar to Oklahoma City from occurring in Phoenix. And for any readers who would argue that the Viper Militia members were not really criminal terrorists, just a group of weekend warriors playing out a fantasy game, I would remind them that the Viper Militia had already purchased a ton of the same explosive material detonated in Oklahoma City, and that they had built and detonated a number of test bombs. The Viper Militia was training for disaster.

As mentioned earlier, and related by the two government infiltrators, the Viper Militia believed that the final goal of their training was to prepare themselves to fight the New World Order. Often, as in this case, training in militia groups can incorporate many of the paranoid beliefs shared by most militia members. According to an article in *Psychology Today*, "When California State University sociologist James William

Gibson, Ph.D., author of *Warrior Dreams: Paramilitary Culture in Post-Vietnam America*, enrolled in combat pistol training as part of his research, he learned 'how the warrior should go to the bathroom.' Urinals leave you vulnerable to rear attack, so the proper technique is to sit on the toilet with the pistol between your legs, ready to fire at any who invade your stall."[8] It does not take too much imagination to see the possible tragedies this type of training and thinking could cause.

Of course, one of the real dangers of militia training is that fringe elements will receive the training, then break away and use the training as terrorists. "The danger of the militia movement comes from the small splinter groups that break off and do things by themselves," said ATF agent George Stoll. "These splinter groups train with the militia, hear the rhetoric, then decide to go out and do something by themselves."

Training in any real military organization (which most militias attempt to imitate), as anyone who has spent any length of time in the military can attest to, is a critical element to the success of the organization. In any military unit, the members must know thoroughly and precisely what their jobs are and what is expected of them. Some of the most elite military units in the world, such as the Army Green Berets or Navy Seals, train continuously in order to keep their fighting edge sharp. This training requirement also holds true for any militia unit that wants to function effectively, and it appears that the Viper Militia conscientiously adhered to this requirement. Unfortunately, the Viper Militia, though unusual, was not a unique case.

Former Green Beret Colonel Bo Gritz hosts a right-wing radio talk show and has also founded a covenant community near Kamiah, Idaho, where he sells home sites. In addition, in 1993, he began a program he calls Specially Prepared Individuals for Key Events (SPIKE) training. Gritz claims that, upon the completion of this ten-phase training program, which takes two years, a group will be as prepared and organized as the Delta Force (the military's elite strike force). Gritz's SPIKE training includes subjects such as stick fighting, counterterrorist driving, and emergency medicine.

For those militia members, though, who do not want to run obstacle courses or train in the woods, but would rather study at home, the South Carolina Militia Corps' Internet website has a list of U.S. Army training manuals that can be downloaded for study. These include manuals on such subjects as sniper training, combat skills, survival, live-fire training, combat in built-up areas, communications jamming, and battle-focused training.

Fortunately, only a few militias in America actually engage in training as intense as the Viper Militia or SPIKE. Also, few militia members would give the U.S. Army training manuals mentioned above the intense study they need in order to be properly utilized. To the contrary, much of the training militias receive turns out to be just a group of men drinking beer and running around in the woods. There is no real organization or content to their training. Jeff Randall, in *Modern Militiaman*, said, "I watched the video of the West Virginia militia training in the woods, and from what I could gather, this 'training' was nothing more than a bunch of guys having fun, rather than real tactics."[9]

The Pennsylvania Minuteman, in an article on militia training, said: "There is also a need for more training and field experience for militiamen. Too many people have no idea what to do after running out their door with rifle and equipment in hand."[10]

An article in *Time* magazine about militia training said: "John Schlosser, coordinator of Colorado's Free Militia, admits that his group's doomsday preparations sometimes amount to no more than 'playing games in the woods.' Militia members, sometimes with their families in tow, play hide-and-seek and capture the flag, all to build conditioning in case of an armed conflict."[11]

Because of the lack of any real, intense, and coordinated training for most militia groups, their chances again trained, disciplined, and equipped military forces are minimal. Most militia groups would be quickly swept aside by units of professional soldiers. However, the danger of the militias does not come from possible confrontations with military units. Their danger comes from confrontations with unarmed citizens and government employees. Heavily armed groups of individuals, holding to the wildest of conspiracy theories and ready to act on the flimsiest of evidence that a takeover conspiracy is unfolding, can and have been extraordinarily dangerous to the American public. The fact that they lack any real training, especially in the use of the weapons they carry, which, as we shall see in the next chapter, are often high-powered and deadly, only adds to their level of danger by guaranteeing that they will not know what to do at the critical moment. Consequently, groups as heavily armed and action oriented as civilian militias pose an imminent danger that cannot be ignored.

❖ ❖ ❖ ❖ ❖ ❖ ❖ ❖ **6**

WEAPONS OF MILITIAS

I had never attended a gun show before, so as I pulled my car into the parking lot, I was not sure what to expect. Even though I have been a police officer for thirty years and have carried a gun all of that time, I have never had much of an interest in firearms other than their use as a last resort backup to a police officer's authority. I only own one gun, which I purchased thirty years ago to carry off-duty, a .38-caliber Colt revolver. The local police, at least in Indiana, do not concern themselves with gun shows. Policing these shows is the responsibility of ATF and the State Police, so consequently, having no interest in guns, I have never needed to attend one.

However, from the research I have done and the people I have interviewed for this book, I discovered that to militia members, guns are revered and worshiped like religious icons. Truly committed militia members, I was to learn, often own dozens of firearms, ranging from small handguns to high-powered assault rifles and machine guns. I also discovered during my research that gun shows, such as the one I was about to attend, have become a major marketplace for militia members looking for firearms. This, I found, has come about because these shows take advantage of a loophole in the gun laws that allow the show's participants to sell firearms without the necessity of paperwork, waiting periods, or background checks. This loophole arose because the McClure–Volkmer Act, passed in 1986, allows "hobbyists" to sell personal weapons without waiting periods or paperwork. This has obviously become a crucial loophole in our nation's gun laws because, reportedly, more than 95 percent of the nation's over 240 million guns are owned by private individuals. Several of the people I interviewed for this book assured me that I could find just about every type of firearm imaginable at a gun show, and that, if I wanted, I could often buy illegal weapons at gun shows. The previous Sunday, I had come across an advertisement for this gun show in the newspaper, and so I decided to see for myself.

At the door, a man asked me if I was carrying any firearms. I was not (I had left my off-duty revolver in the car). I later discovered this was not to stop anyone from carrying firearms in, but only to be certain they were not loaded. I paid the five dollar admission price and then strolled down a hallway into a large auditorium. A few feet inside the door, I stopped, shocked by what I saw. My eyes gaped at what appeared to be thousands of guns of every type and description for sale, rows and rows of tables filled with firearms. I had never seen this many firearms in one place before. Even the police department's property room, which always has a large collection of confiscated firearms, paled against this. After the initial shock had subsided, I walked over to the first table, which had probably a hundred handguns displayed, from blue steel revolvers with black rubber grips to dazzling chrome automatics with polished wood grips, from snub-nosed revolvers to long-barreled target guns, and from guns simply sitting out on the table to guns encased in fancy, velvet-lined boxes. With only two clerks working at the long table, my first thought was how very easy it would be for someone to steal one of these guns. However, when I stepped up to examine a chrome .45-caliber pistol, I found that one of the clerks became very attentive and kept a close eye on me.

A few tables down I found a fully automatic assault rifle with a $1,500 price tag. This weapon is illegal to possess without a federal license. When I apparently made the man behind the table think I had an interest in the weapon, he began expounding on the weapon's reliability, its rate of fire, its magazine capacity, and its unbeatable price. He assured me it was a steal at $1,500 and that I ought to snap it up while I could. He did not inquire whether I had a federal license to own an automatic weapon. Maybe he would have if I had pulled out my wallet, but I am not certain. He seemed awfully anxious to sell it. When I explained that I felt the price was a bit steep, he offered to sell me a semiautomatic version of the same weapon for about one-third of the price. He told me that all I needed to do was walk two tables down, where I could pick up a booklet on how to convert the weapon to fully automatic myself. I thanked him and, sure enough, two tables down, I found I could purchase the booklet he described for five dollars. I bought the booklet and glanced through it. While in several places the booklet mentioned that possessing a fully automatic assault weapon, or even possessing the capability to convert one to fully automatic, could be against the law, it nevertheless provided detailed instructions for doing so. And while a warning printed on the front of the booklet said: "Published for the exclusive use of governmental agencies & Class 2 manufacturers," no one asked me if I was either one of these when I purchased the booklet.

As I strolled through the auditorium, I found that some of the tables sold antique guns and antique gun kits, and a few sold used guns. Most, however, sold new, high-powered weapons. It did not look to me as if many of the tables were those of "hobbyists." It looked like the sellers were mostly professional gun dealers, who made their livelihoods, and apparently good livelihoods considering some of the prices, selling weapons.

Guns, however, were not the only thing for sale at the gun show. Some dealers also sold clips and ammunition for various weapons, from small pistol clips to huge banana clips, and from small caliber ammunition to some that would knock an elephant backwards. As I later discovered, as well as owning many weapons, militia members also believe in amassing a huge stockpile of ammunition. A number of tables there catered to that desire. One table I found to be devoted entirely to knives, many of them strangely shaped and highly ornate. Few of the knives, though, appeared to be designed for whittling or fish fileting. Most seemed to be built more for human disembowelment. Another table sold crossbows and blow pipes, and several tables specialized in Nazi memorabilia. I later learned, after attending several more gun shows, that many gun enthusiasts are also fascinated by items from the Nazi era. One of the items available was a poster of Adolph Hitler that said: "When I come back, no more Mr. Nice Guy."

At a table in the corner of the gun show I found a vendor who sold political, racist, and sexist bumper stickers. The stickers ranged from ones saying "When you come to get my guns, bring lunch and lots of body bags," to "I just got a gun for my wife—it was the best trade I ever made," to "Work—it's the White thing to do."

Interestingly, I found very little hunting paraphernalia for sale. I suppose that the people who attend these shows are not really very interested in hunting, for sport, that is.

As well as browsing the items for sale, I could not help but notice as I moved through the crowded room that even with the hundreds of peo-

ple shopping and browsing there, I did not see a single member of a minority group. Instead, the crowd appeared to be made up entirely of
young to middle-aged white males and a small number of white females.
A surprisingly large number of people wore military-type fatigues, but
most wore jeans and flannel or cotton shirts, with either tennis shoes or
work boots. In addition, many of the attendees had sidearms hung on
their belts or assault rifles and shotguns slung over their shoulders. No
one seemed concerned about this. A number of signs posted throughout
the auditorium, however, proclaimed: NO LOADED WEAPONS IN BUILDING and
NO DRY FIRING. I felt thankful for that.

It occurred to me as I looked at all of the people purchasing firearms
that any measure of gun control in America was at present obviously just
an illusion. I had passed table after table filled with handguns of every
description, tables stacked with shotguns, and tables loaded with assault
rifles. Anyone who wanted a gun of any type, and had the money, could
walk in here and purchase one. By paying the five-dollar entry fee, a person could amass all of the firepower he or she could afford to buy, along
with as many magazines and rounds of ammunition as his or her budget
allowed. While many militia members may worry that the federal government, or agents of the New World Order, want to disarm the American
public, this gun show, only one of thousands held every year across
America, certainly belied that fear.

As I stood at a table that had a tripod-mounted, belt-fed machine gun
on display, I thought of a quote I had seen. Glad Hall, head of the Southern Illinois Patriots League, said, "We advise everyone in our group to be
as well armed as they can afford to be and possess as much ammunition
as they can afford."[1] The people in attendance at this gun show obviously
agreed with that advice. I wondered, though, how militia members, who
are often unemployed or hold low-paying jobs, could afford the items for
sale at this show. I was later to discover that for militia members,
weapons and ammunition come before anything else. They are top prior-
ity. They come before eating out at restaurants. They come before buying
camping equipment or taking vacations. They come before making any
purchases other than the bare necessities. When a militia member was
asked why he owned so many guns, he replied, "Well, I don't play golf."[2]
For militia members, any extra money at all in the family goes for
weapons and ammunition.

When I stopped at one of the tables and asked the man who stepped
up to help me how this gun show fared with others he had attended, he
said that this one was small in comparison to some that have up to a thou-

sand or more tables. He did say, though, that for a small gun show, the sales were brisk.

I lingered at a number of tables not really to look at the wares, but rather to listen in on the conversations of the gun enthusiasts. I was truly surprised by the number of people who bragged about the size of their gun collections, many claiming to own a dozen or more assault rifles, and with plans to buy more. Listening in on the conversations, I also heard at least a dozen comments about the "latest intelligence" concerning the behind-the-scenes workings of the New World Order. It did not take much deduction to realize that was why many of the people there were buying and stockpiling firearms and ammunition. They were preparing to fight the New World Order conspirators when the time came.

To be certain this gun show was not just an aberration, I later attended several others but found them very similar, with many of the same vendors, who apparently travel back and forth across the country from one gun show to another. At one gun show I attended, I stopped at a table full of assault rifles and found a sign that read: THESE GUNS BANNED FOR IMPORT BY FEDERAL LAW. The dealer obviously wanted the people at the show to know that the quantity and availability of these weapons was limited, and that if they wanted to be prepared to fight the New World Order or other conspirators, they had better snatch these weapons up while they could. At another table at this same gun show, I found an interesting item called "Hellstorm 2000." This is a device that fits on the trigger of a semi-automatic assault rifle and allows the shooter to pull the trigger very rapidly, causing the semiautomatic weapon to fire more like a fully automatic one. The vendor assured me that the device was perfectly legal to own and use, which it apparently is.

As I passed the final table at my first gun show and was about to leave, I stopped and looked back at the hundreds of people buying firearms, often several firearms, and the realization struck me of how dangerous these people could be if they suddenly came to believe for some reason that one of their conspiracy theories was actually unfolding. With the amount of firepower available at these shows, and the amount amassed by some of the people attending them, they could commit unbelievable carnage.

There is one creed that every militia group in America believes in, one that most hold as sacred as the Ten Commandments. It is the Second

Amendment right to keep and bear arms. Owning firearms has become as important to most of America's militias as their conspiracy theories. Most believe that only their weapons, or rather the fear of them, has held in check the conspirators who would take over our country. Therefore, militia members believe that any attempt to restrict weapon ownership only plays into the hands of the conspirators. Consequently, militia members truly believe that the only thing that will save our country is their interpretation of what the Second Amendment means, which is unrestricted and unregulated gun ownership.

Although, as we will see in a later chapter, the courts have come to a different conclusion than most militia members about what the wording of the Second Amendment means, militia members believe it gives them the absolute right to buy, own, and carry any firearm they wish, including high-powered, automatic-fire assault rifles. They claim that any attempt to curb this is an unconstitutional and criminal infringement of their rights. An article in *The Pennsylvania Minuteman* said: "It must be understood that every gun 'law' in Pennsylvania and these United States is inherently and unquestionably unconstitutional. The right to keep and bare [sic] arms cannot be infringed or even questioned. Only those bent on tyranny would commit such a treasonable act as the passing of unconstitutional laws abridging the rights of WE THE PEOPLE."[3] An Internet posting from the U.S. Militia said: "We will not disarm and see our freedoms stripped away. . . . A disarmed population will lose—either piecemeal or in one sweeping act—those basic rights for which the citizens of America risked their lives and fortunes for over 200 years ago."[4]

While writing this book, I spoke to a number of militia members, and all agreed with the preceding statements and felt that only by allowing private ownership of large numbers of high-powered weapons would America remain free. However, for any militia member who might have a twinge of hesitation about owning such an arsenal, who might have misgivings that such behavior is not in keeping with Christian principles, there is a religious organization whose message may ease their guilt. Gospel Plow, a Christian ministry in Sedalia, Colorado, has put information on the Internet called "The Christian's Guide to Small Arms." In its Internet posting, the Gospel Plow warns of a United Nations plot to take over the United States. Because of this impending plot, Gospel Plow says good Christians must be prepared to fight back against these anti-Christian forces, and to do this, they must be well armed. The Gospel Plow, insisting that the New Testament instructs Christians to purchase weapons, gives advice to readers on the various types of weapons and ammunition, on firearms safety, and on religious reasons why Christians should be well armed. "The most probable scenario that the Christian American, called to fight for God, family and country, will be presented with is that of guerrilla resistance," says the Internet document in its section on ammunition. "The wisest course in this situation is to choose weapons and tactics that minimize supply, training and maintenance problems."[5]

Given that owning firearms is a central theme to the existence of the various militias across the United States, let us explore how militia members obtain these firearms and weapons, including those banned by law for private ownership. As my experience at the beginning of this chapter shows, many militia members obtain their firearms and weapons through the thousands of gun shows that take place every year in the United States (estimated to be between 2,000 and 5,000 annually). But this certainly is not the only way.

In 1995 and 1996, 6.5 million people in the United States applied to purchase a firearm from a legal gun dealer. Unlike gun shows, purchasing firearms from a gun dealer involves a certain amount of paperwork, often a waiting period, and a background check of the purchaser during this waiting period. Due to the background check, out of the 6.5 million people who attempted to purchase firearms in 1995 and 1996, the government rejected 130,000 applicants because the background check showed they were presently under a felony indictment, had a prior felony conviction, or had a history of drug abuse or mental problems. Still, in 1995 and 1996, this left well over six million guns purchased through legal gun dealers.

However, because of the paper trail, militia members likely made up only a small percentage of the purchases through gun dealers. Many militia members believe that any paperwork required for purchasing or owning firearms is actually a plot contrived by those who want to overthrow the American government. Militia members believe that once this overthrow begins, the plotters will know through this paperwork where to go to confiscate firearms. This is also why militia members refuse to register their firearms. Not surprisingly, militia members prefer buying and owning firearms anonymously.

Because of the ease in obtaining firearms, some militia members travel to states that have lax rules for firearms purchases. "States like Florida and Texas, states with weak gun laws, have become gun bazaars," said Representative Charles Schumer of New York.[6] So many guns come out of Florida and head up to northern states that Interstate 95 has been dubbed "Firearms Freeway." Highlighting this problem, in February 1997, a Palestinian man who had recently arrived in the United States purchased a .38-caliber Beretta while staying in a hotel in Melbourne, Florida. Soon after, he used the gun to fire into a crowd at the Empire State Building in New York City, killing one person and injuring six others before turning the gun on himself.

Some people do not bother to go to gun shows or to travel to other states to purchase firearms and other weapons, but choose to buy them directly through the mail. The Branch Davidians in Waco, Texas, for example, bought much of their weaponry through mail order. This method, however, obviously has a paperwork trail that can be traced. It was the suspicions of a delivery man who had handled several large shipments of firearms, a load of grenade casings, and orders for black powder that alerted the authorities to the possibility that the Branch Davidians possessed and were attempting to manufacture illegal weapons.

Because they fear that clues to their ownership of weapons could be left behind, many militia members do not want to use even relatively anonymous methods of obtaining weapons, such as traveling to states with lax gun laws or visiting gun shows. After all, anyone who believes in far-fetched conspiracies would have to believe that these sources of weapons are monitored by the authorities. Who knows who is watching when they purchase an assault rifle or a hand gun, even at an event that does not require paperwork? Most militia members believe that any clues to their purchase or ownership of weapons must be avoided at all costs, because the one thing many militia members truly fear is a confiscation of their weapons by the government or agents of the New World Order. For this reason, they acquire firearms as clandestinely as possible.

One method some militias use to secretly obtain weapons is to recruit legitimate gun dealers into their groups. This then gives the militia members access to firearms whose paperwork can easily "disappear." Consequently, the weapons will never be traced to them. Reportedly, this occurred during the operation of the Blue Ridge Hunt Club in Virginia, which, despite its name, was actually a militia group. The founder, feeling certain that the federal government would soon begin a confiscation of privately owned firearms, formed the organization to oppose this and eventually recruited a local gun dealer into the group.

"They wanted to grab their guns and head for the hills if the gun control laws got too strict," said Joseph G. Silvey, special agent-in-charge of ATF in Roanoke, Virginia. "They wanted to resist government oppression."[7]

When the authorities arrested the members of the Blue Ridge Hunt Club, they seized illegally converted machine guns, homemade silencers, hand grenades, and other explosives. On a computer disk taken from the home of the organization's founder, the authorities discovered plans to raid a National Guard Armory and blow up bridges, airports, and a radio station. Most of the arrested members, including the gun dealer, eventually entered into plea bargains with the prosecutor.

Military personnel, because of their ready access to weaponry, have become another source of what militia members believe are traceless weapons for the militia movement. In the last few years, this weapons availability has become a very real and large problem for the military. In October 1997, the FBI arrested six Marines and seven civilians for trafficking in illegal military weapons and plastic explosives. During the investigation, called "Operation Longfuse," undercover investigators purchased 150 pounds of plastic explosives, hundreds of hand-held and rocket-propelled grenades, grenade launchers, shoulder-launched rockets, more than fifty machine guns, detonation cord, a handful of antipersonnel land mines, and other military equipment.

According to the investigators, the thirteen arrested individuals would steal the merchandise and then sell it at gun shows or out of private homes. They often sold the plastic explosives out of the back of trucks at gun shows. (This is not unusual. A General Accounting Office report said that its investigators were able to purchase stolen military equipment at thirteen of fifteen gun shows they visited.) Five of the six military personnel arrested were enlisted men, but the operation did include one officer, and all of the arrested individuals had access to the weapons and explosives as a part of their jobs. However, not all military weapons that end up in the hands of civilians are stolen. Often, these weapons are given away or sold by the military.

The Civilian Marksmanship Program began as a government initiative to teach marksmanship and gun safety to civilians, and as a part of this program, the government sells surplus military weapons to its members. Began in the wake of Spanish–American War at the beginning of the twentieth century, this program has sold more than 500,000 surplus firearms to the public, particularly to members of groups that teach firearms proficiency. These weapons can then, through subsequent unregistered sales, end up in the hands of militia members. This program has also sold or given away almost a billion rounds of ammunition.

For those surplus military weapons not sold under this program, regulations require that they be destroyed. However, the government does such a poor job of this that dealers bid vigorously for the weapons scrap. In one instance, a dealer paid $31,800 for 100,000 pounds of "scrap," from which he recovered 250,000 usable parts. This dealer claims he has 500 million weapons parts, enough to build a million assault rifles.

Often though, because they truly believe that a conspiracy to take over the United States is about to unfold, and that, as a result of this takeover, they will be either executed or reduced to slavery, militia members want to own the high power and extremely lethal weapons that are illegal to possess. They want to own the weapons that will strike the most fear in the conspirators.

"They want access to weapons," said Madison County (Idaho) Sheriff Greg Moffat, "and I'm not talking about small arms: tanks, missiles, high explosives."[8]

Routinely, when law enforcement officers raid the residences of militia members, they recover these high-power and illegal weapons, along with thousands of rounds of ammunition. Recently, in Evanston, Illinois, the police recovered eighty firearms and over 50,000 rounds of ammunition from a man's basement. Unfortunately, this is not unusual. In another case, authorities recovered twenty-four firearms, 100,000 rounds of ammunition, and a flamethrower from a private residence in New Jersey. In Denver, the police found not only assault rifles, but also land mines and pipe bombs.

In Los Angeles, in May 1997, the police arrested five members of a militia group, who, the police say, were "filled with hate." According to law enforcement officers, the group was plotting a campaign of domestic terrorism in southern California. The police seized more than 100 weapons, including fully automatic assault rifles and sawed-off shotguns, thousands of rounds of ammunition, including ammunition for a .50-caliber machine gun, a grenade launcher, laser scopes, night vision goggles, and other equipment. The militia group reportedly held bimonthly training sessions, where they practiced firing at dummies made to look like whites, blacks, Latinos, and Asians. In another incident, in January 1998, the leader of the Colorado 1st Light Infantry of the U.S. Militia pled guilty in federal court to possessing four illegal machine guns. Another member of the same group also pled guilty to possessing an illegal weapon.

In addition to possessing high-power, illegal firearms, some militia members want to own even more deadly weapons, such as explosives. Every year, thieves steal an incredibly large amount of explosives from commercial sites that utilize them legally, such as mining companies, quarries, and so on. Like illegal firearms, these items often end up in the hands of militia members. In February 1998, ATF agents arrested three men in Sligo, Pennsylvania, for theft at a Pennsylvania mine. The three men had stolen a ton of high explosives. In Yuba City, California, in 1997, the authorities arrested six men, several of whom were involved in militia activities, during an investigation of stolen explosives believed taken from a Montana mining company. The investigation began when a store of explosives hidden in a tree outside the home of one of the men accidentally detonated and injured him and his two-year-old daughter. The explosion shook homes and broke windows for two blocks around. The police also discovered that one of the men had a quarter ton of petrogel at his home, which authorities said would have leveled three square blocks if detonated. He had stored the high explosive in a motor home parked in his driveway.

Some militia groups, however, do not have access to stolen military explosives, and do not want to become involved in burglarizing private companies for explosives. How then do they obtain explosives? During my research for this book, I came across the claim several times that I could buy bomb-making instructions at bookstores or download them from the Internet. So I tried. With just a bit of searching, I indeed found a book at a local bookstore that provides detailed instructions for making bombs of various types and lethality. It also includes instructions for booby traps, sabotage, and the use of lethal weapons. In addition to this, I also discovered that the claim was true about bomb-making information on the Internet. Again, with just a bit of searching, I came across a computer file that contains instructions for making black powder, ammonium nitrate (the chemical used in the Oklahoma City bombing), napalm, and poison gas. Also included are detailed instructions for making silencers and stun guns. In the Introduction, the author writes: "I wrote this guide a few weeks after the bombing incident in Oklahoma City. I am a member of several militia and right-wing groups, and realized the lack of any real complete guide to a small-time militia member with ideas and information for him to do locally."

Undoubtedly, the most important tenet of the modern militia movement is that American citizens must be permitted to purchase and possess any firearm or amount of firearms they desire. Because of this belief, these same militia groups cry foul at any attempt to control gun sales or ownership, and insist that the government, through gun control laws, is violating their Second Amendment rights. However, from what I have seen while researching this book, this accusation appears baseless. At the gun show I attended, I saw little or no control on the sales of every kind of firearm imaginable. And this is only one of many sources of weapons. This has dire implications for the average citizen. Considering that most militias subscribe to what appear to be fantastic conspiracy beliefs, this free access to firearms for people who also believe it is their mission to fight these conspirators to the death should be an alarming and truly frightening concern. In addition, as I will show in the next chapter, free access to explosives and information on how to use them can also have devastating effects.

❖ ❖ ❖ ❖ ❖ ❖ ❖ ❖ 7

THE MILITIA THREAT

As a part of the research for this book, I went to hear Morris Dees, chief trial attorney for the Southern Poverty Law Center, when he gave a talk at a local university. The Southern Poverty Law Center, located in Montgomery, Alabama, operates the Militia Task Force, a militia watchdog unit. At the end of his talk, I asked Mr. Dees how dangerous he thought the militia movement was.

"I don't think they're going to bring the country down," he answered. "They don't have that power. They do have the power though to hurt individual people."

How very true.

At 9:00 A.M. on 19 April 1995, a twenty-foot, yellow, Ryder rental truck sat parked in front of the Alfred P. Murrah Federal Building in Oklahoma City. Two days earlier, the truck had been rented from Elliot's Body Shop in Junction City, Kansas, by a man using a phony South Dakota driver's license that identified him as Robert Kling. Neither the workers in the federal building nor the people nearby knew that hidden in the back of the rental truck was 4,800 pounds of ANFO—ammonium nitrate/fuel oil.

Ammonium nitrate is most commonly used by farmers as a fertilizer, but it can also become an extremely powerful explosive if fitted with a detonation device that has sufficient power to cause the chemical to decompose violently. Pure ammonium nitrate, however, while explosive, really does not make a very efficient bomb because the chemical tends to absorb moisture, which then makes it extremely difficult to detonate. To prevent this from occurring, a bomb maker must add, in very prescribed amounts, some type of fuel oil to the ammonium nitrate. This then turns the ammonium nitrate into ANFO, a much more stable explosive, powerful enough that businesses such as mines and quarries often use it. Unfortunately, the 4,800 pounds of ANFO packed into the back of the Ryder rental truck had been made with just the correct mixture of fuel oil and had also been fitted with a sufficiently powerful detonation source.

At 9:02 A.M., the detonation source fired and caused the ANFO bomb to explode with a tremendous release of energy, destroying most of the front of the Alfred P. Murrah Federal Building and sending many of the floors of the nine-story structure crashing down onto one another. Several other buildings nearby also suffered severe damage. This explosion would become the most devastating and deadly terrorist attack ever carried out on American soil. And yet, though the force of the explosion disintegrated the front of the building and severely damaged the internal support structure, survivors still remained inside the building's shell after the explosion. For these survivors, escaping before the building completely collapsed became imperative.

"I heard what I thought were the floors falling," said Susan Hunt, a federal worker. "We didn't know what happened except that everything fell on us."[1]

A Marine Corps recruiter, Michael R. Norfleet, escaped from the building down a debris-packed stairwell. "All I remember is following the blood trail from somebody before me. That was like the yarn leading me out of there." Norfleet, a decorated flyer in the Persian Gulf War, lost an eye due to the explosion and consequently was forced to retire from the Marine Corps.[2]

"I started trying to dig myself out," related another survivor, Priscilla Salyers, who said the explosion plunged her down three floors into the building's day care center. "I tried to move rocks from beneath me, and . . . there was a hand."[3]

Florence Rogers, president of a credit union located in the building, tearfully told how the explosion killed all of the co-workers she was meeting with in a conference room. "I had leaned back in my chair to kind of relax while one of them started talking when, literally, the whole building started to blow up. All of the girls who were in the office with me had totally disappeared."[4]

The Oklahoma City bombing stunned not only the people inside the federal building and nearby, but also all of America. No one had expected an act of terrorism of this magnitude to occur in America's heartland. Prior to the Oklahoma City bombing, the most deadly bombing in the United States occurred on 19 May 1927. On that day, a demented farmer, angry over taxes and changes in the school system, used dynamite to blow up a school in Bath, Michigan, killing forty-five people, including thirty-eight children. The 168 people killed in the Oklahoma City bombing dwarfed this event.

"[F]ew say that they foresaw the devastating and brutal incident that occurred in Oklahoma," said an article in *EMS Magazine*. "Most [right-wing experts] said that they may have expected small-scale 'shoot-outs' and other minor violence involving radical members of the paramilitary underground, but few said that they expected a major bombing and mass murder of fellow American citizens."[5]

Regardless of the enormity and unexpectedness of the bombing, rescue workers quickly converged on the scene and began the extraordinarily dangerous task of pulling survivors from a building that could collapse under their feet at any moment. These rescuers also told stories of horror. An Oklahoma City police officer testified that while trying to rescue a woman trapped under a huge pile of rubble, he became concerned that the woman might drown when water began filling the area. To his horror, he discovered it was not water filling the area after all. It was blood. A doctor, James Sullivan, who helped with the rescue, recounted having to amputate a woman's leg with no anesthesia. "Once I started cutting," he said, "she started kicking and screaming." When his surgical scalpel went dull, he pulled out his pocket knife to finish the amputation.[6]

In the end, 168 people died in the Alfred P. Murrah Federal Building and other buildings nearby. Included in this death toll were nineteen children, fifteen of whom were crushed to death in the America's Kids Day Care Center on the second floor, and four who happened to be in the federal building. In addition, three of the 149 adult victims of the bombing were pregnant women whose unborn children also died. Viewers of the evening news on 19 April 1995 gasped in disbelief when they saw the grisly pictures of the young victims being carried out.

"They started bringing our babies out in those sheets, and they laid them by my feet," said Helena Garrett, who discovered that her sixteen-month-old son, Tevin, had died in the blast. "They started making a line of them."[7]

The arrest of the perpetrators of the bombing occurred very quickly, and, as often happens in police work, occurred mostly by luck. An hour and fifteen minutes after the explosion, Oklahoma state trooper Charles Hanger stopped a car on Interstate 35 in Perry, Oklahoma, because it did not have a license plate. While talking with the driver, the trooper noticed a bulge under the man's jacket, and, when asked about it, the driver, twenty-six-year-old Timothy McVeigh, admitted to the trooper that he was carrying a 9 mm Glock semiautomatic pistol in a shoulder holster. The trooper arrested McVeigh for unlawfully transporting a loaded firearm. In McVeigh's pants pocket, authorities recovered a set of ear plugs, which lab analysis would later confirm contained residue from the detonation cord used to set off the ANFO bomb, as did the jeans and T-shirt McVeigh wore. The T-shirt, incidentally, had a picture on it of a tree dripping with blood and a quotation from Thomas Jefferson: "The tree of liberty must be refreshed from time to time with the blood of patriots and tyrants."[8]

Before McVeigh could make bail and get out of the Noble County jail on the firearms charge, federal authorities realized he was their likely bomber and took him into custody. They flew McVeigh on a military helicopter to Tinker Air Force Base in Oklahoma City, where they arraigned him on the bombing charges in a makeshift courtroom.

Thus, began one of the largest criminal investigations in American history. Before its conclusion, the crime scene and other locations would be searched and examined by dozens of law enforcement officers and technicians, and over 30,000 people would be interviewed. However, one of the key pieces of evidence recovered in the bombing case came about because of a new trend in car theft. In the last decade or so, many car thieves, rather than trying to sell the whole car, have begun taking stolen cars apart in "chop shops" and selling the pieces individually. To combat this new trend, automobile manufactures have begun stamping vehicle identification numbers onto major car parts. The police in the Oklahoma City bombing case recovered the twisted axle of the Ryder rental truck that had carried the bomb. Through the vehicle identification number stamped on the axle, police traced the vehicle to Elliot's Body Shop in Junction City, Kansas, and eventually to McVeigh as the man who rented it.

"I saw this humongous object coming straight at us, spinning like a boomerang," said Richard Nichols, telling about the 250-pound axle that crashed into his car and barely missed killing him and his family.[9]

However, despite the hundreds of law enforcement officers working on this case, the thousands of hours put into it, and the early reports saying that the bombing was the result of a large conspiracy, only two people would eventually be charged and tried in the Oklahoma City bombing: McVeigh and his friend and former Army buddy Terry Nichols. When Nichols heard that the police were looking for him, he turned himself in to the authorities at Herington, Kansas, where he lived.

Through their extensive and detailed investigation, the authorities put together what they felt was the likely sequence of events that led up to the Oklahoma City bombing. They learned that McVeigh apparently became enamored with right-wing causes during his time in the Army. He was particularly taken with a 1978 right-wing novel entitled *The Turner Diaries*, which has become almost a bible to antigovernment activists. He reportedly liked the book so much that he read it over and over, and often recommended it to his friends. This book, written by William Pierce, head of the West Virginia-based National Alliance, a neo-Nazi group, recounts the adventures of a group of individuals infuriated by gun control laws and what they see as an oppressive federal government. This group eventually starts a revolution, and as part of this, they blow up the FBI Headquarters in Washington, D.C., using a truck loaded with a ANFO bomb. The Oklahoma City bombing, down to the time of day, patterned itself very closely after the fictional bombing in *The Turner Diaries*. When arrested, McVeigh carried a photocopied page from the novel with the following passage highlighted: "The real value of our attacks today lies in the psychological impact, not the immediate casualties."[10]

During their investigation of the bombing, the authorities also learned that, while McVeigh performed well as a soldier during the Persian Gulf War, he washed out when he applied for Special Forces (Green Berets). Soon after this, apparently disenchanted with the military, McVeigh received a discharge from the Army.

After leaving the military, McVeigh moved around the country for several years, going from job to job. His mental stability soon came under question, though, because he reportedly complained to many people that the Army had implanted a computer chip in his buttocks in order to track his whereabouts. This is a common paranoid belief among militia members. His nomadic lifestyle only seemed to get direction after the 19 April 1993 confrontation between the Branch Davidians and the federal government in Waco, Texas. McVeigh had traveled to Waco during the fifty-one-day standoff, where he sold right-wing literature. After fire destroyed the

Branch Davidian complex and killed all of the occupants, McVeigh became incensed that no one in the federal government was held responsible for what he saw as mass murder. Authorities believe that soon after the Waco incident, McVeigh hatched his plan to retaliate against the federal government for their actions against the Branch Davidians.

McVeigh recruited into his plan of retaliation his old Army buddy Terry Nichols, who also had a long-standing history of sympathy with right-wing causes, as well as a life of failed endeavors. Nichols dropped out of college after one semester. After eleven months in the Army, where he met McVeigh, Nichols received a hardship discharge because of marital difficulties. After his first marriage finally ended in divorce, Nichols reportedly married a mail-order bride from the Philippines. Along with his stormy personal life, Nichols also had a stormy relationship with the authorities. Because of this, he tried to renounce his American citizenship and once mailed an affidavit to the county clerk, claiming he was not subject to federal law. Nichols had also been in and out of court a number of times due to bad debts and run-ins with the police because of his reckless driving.

The actual work on the bombing plot began when McVeigh purchased a book on bomb making. Following this, he and Nichols went on a search for bomb-making materials, including purchasing almost 5,000 pounds of ammonium nitrate from the Mid-Kansas Co-Op in McPherson, Kansas. A sales slip for the ammonium nitrate, which the authorities found in Nichols's home, contained McVeigh's fingerprints. McVeigh also reportedly began calling all over the country, searching for a strong enough detonation device. A former arms dealer said that McVeigh told him he was willing to drive several thousand miles in order to pick up some detonation cord if the arms dealer could obtain it for him.

Continuing their search for explosives, McVeigh and Nichols also reportedly burglarized the Martin Marietta Aggregates Quarry in Marion, Kansas, which used and stored large quantities of explosives. The FBI recovered a drill from Nichols's home that matched marks made on a padlock at the quarry. All of this traveling and purchasing, however, soon began to get expensive for the two unemployed men, and so, in order to finance the bombing plot, McVeigh and Nichols allegedly robbed a gun dealer in Arkansas of almost $60,000 in guns, cash, and precious metals, more than enough to pay for the remaining materials needed. Once the men had purchased or stolen all of the materials necessary, federal agents say they believe McVeigh and Nichols constructed the bomb at Geary State Park in Kansas, the day before the Oklahoma City bombing.

McVeigh reportedly picked Oklahoma City as the site of the bombing for a number of reasons. The federal building there had low security, the truck could be parked right in front of the building, and no one would suspect that such an act could occur in rural, middle America. Probably more important though, McVeigh believed that the federal agents responsible for the Waco incident had come from the Oklahoma City office.

Although the police investigation of the bombing took many months, the trial of McVeigh finally began on 31 March 1997, in Denver, Colorado. The trial had been moved to Denver because the intense publicity made getting a fair trial in Oklahoma City impossible. Despite this move, the government broadcast the proceedings on closed-circuit television to an auditorium in Oklahoma City. There, the victims and their families could witness the trial. The government charged McVeigh with the murder of eight federal agents, conspiracy, and use of a weapon of mass destruction.

While many legal experts believed this would be a lengthy trial, it actually sped along much more rapidly than anyone had imagined. The prosecution called 137 witnesses in only eighteen days, presenting what it felt was a solid case against McVeigh. The defense must have agreed, because it wrapped up its part of the trial in just four days.

During the prosecution, McVeigh's sister testified that, just before the bombing, he told her he was no longer in the propaganda stage but was now instead in the "action stage." Also testifying against McVeigh was a married couple for whom McVeigh had stood up as best man. Michael and Lori Fortier both testified that McVeigh told them about his intentions to bomb the federal building in Oklahoma City months before he actually did it. Michael also testified that he traveled with McVeigh to Oklahoma City to case the federal building, and that he helped transport firearms that McVeigh and Nichols had stolen in order to finance the bombing.

"He was wanting to blow up a building to cause a general uprising in America," Michael Fortier told the court, "hopefully that would knock some people off the fence and urge them into taking action against the federal government."[11] Fortier also testified that "Tim told me that him and Terry had chosen a building in Oklahoma City, a federal building in Oklahoma City. . . . He told me they picked that building because that was where the orders for the attack on Waco came from."[12] Michael Fortier said that McVeigh wanted to spill as much blood as possible. That was why he chose 9:00 A.M., the time when the building's occupancy would be at a peak.

Lori Fortier, as well as testifying about hearing McVeigh talk about the proposed bombing, also told the court that McVeigh once had her wrap up blasting caps as Christmas presents so no one would suspect what they were in the event the police stopped him during a trip from Arizona to Michigan. Both of the Fortiers pled guilty for their part in the Oklahoma City bombing and agreed to testify against McVeigh and Nichols as a part of their plea bargain. On 27 May 1998, a judge sentenced Michael Fortier to twelve years in prison for his part in the bombing. Lori Fortier was allowed to go free.

Also testifying in the trial, a desk clerk at the Dreamland Motel in Junction City, Kansas, told the court that McVeigh, who stayed at the motel, had parked a yellow Ryder rental truck next to their pool. The clerk said he recalled this because he had to ask McVeigh to move the truck when he found it blocked the door of a grouchy guest. The owner of Elliot's Body Shop in Junction City, Kansas, also identified McVeigh as the man who rented the truck used in the bombing. In addition, the jury viewed a tape from a security camera at a McDonald's restaurant in Junction City that showed McVeigh walking to Elliot's Body Shop.

When it became the defense's turn, they attempted to sow doubt in the jurors' minds that McVeigh was the actual bomber. One of the ways they attempted to do this was through pointing out that after the 168 bodies had been pulled from the wreckage of the building, the medical examiner found he had a left leg that did not belong to any of the bodies. The defense suggested it belonged to the real bomber, who had been killed in the explosion. The leg was one of ninety-eight body parts the medical examiner had to match to the mangled remains of the 168 victims. The medical examiner finally determined that the extra leg belonged to a female victim who had been buried with someone else's left leg, though who the wrongly buried left leg belongs to remains a mystery. Although the defense also suggested in their opening statement that they would present evidence of a grand conspiracy behind the bombing, they did not. In addition, McVeigh did not take the stand, nor did the defense offer an alibi for McVeigh during the time of the bombing.

On 2 June 1997, after several days of deliberation, but after taking only one vote, the jury returned with a verdict of guilty on all charges. They said there was no doubt in any of their minds about the guilt of Timothy McVeigh.

The trial then resumed, as did more testimony, to determine the punishment for McVeigh. Since McVeigh's crimes could bring either a life sentence or death by lethal injection, the jury had to decide which punishment was appropriate. Interestingly, during this phase of the trial, McVeigh's lawyers no longer proclaimed his innocence, as they had from the beginning, but instead now admitted he was the bomber and tried to show mitigating circumstances that would preclude sentencing him to death. The defense strove to show the jury that McVeigh had been so distraught over the federal government's actions at Waco that he was driven to commit the bombing.

"We're not using Waco as an excuse," McVeigh's attorney said. "Waco is an event that happened that many people felt impassioned about. One of them was Tim McVeigh."[13]

On 13 June 1997, the same jury then went back into deliberations, and, again after taking only one vote, returned with a unanimous recommendation that McVeigh be put to death for his crimes. As a part of the sentencing formula that discussed mitigating factors, the jurors unanimously agreed that the incidents at Ruby Ridge and Waco were factors that caused McVeigh to commit the bombing. However, the jurors also unanimously agreed that McVeigh was not the patriot he claimed to be, nor did he really believe in the ideals upon which the United States was founded. The judge, bound by the jury's recommendation, sentenced Timothy McVeigh to die by lethal injection. If carried out, that sentence will likely take place in the federal penitentiary at Terre Haute, Indiana, where the federal government constructed a new death chamber after the courts reinstated the federal death penalty in 1988. The chamber has yet to be used.

On 29 September 1997, Terry Nichols went to trial, facing the same charges as McVeigh had six months earlier. His case became a bit more complicated, however, because he had an alibi for the time of the bombing. He was at home on his farm in Herington, Kansas. Also, the prosecution in the Nichols case was more low key than in the McVeigh case, providing less testimony by bombing victims, which had apparently helped to convict McVeigh.

The jurors did hear, however, about FBI agents finding in Nichols's home the drill bit that had been used to burglarize the quarry for explosives. In addition, the gun dealer who had reportedly been robbed to help finance the bombing plot also testified that special armor-piercing ammunition found in Nichols's home had been taken during the robbery.

Michael Fortier, while testifying in Nichols's trial, told the court that McVeigh spoke to him about Nichols's involvement in the planning of the bombing. But in addition, and crucial to the defense, Fortier said that Nichols apparently changed his mind and wanted to back out of the bombing plot. McVeigh, however, would not let him.

As the trial continued, witnesses also testified that they saw a yellow Ryder rental truck parked near Nichols's home the day before the bombing. In addition, FBI agents said that during their initial interview with Nichols, he admitted driving with McVeigh to Oklahoma City three days before the bombing. A neighbor of Nichols told the court that two days after the bombing she saw Nichols, apparently wanting to get rid of the evidence, furiously spreading ammonium nitrate on his lawn so thick it looked like snow.

The jury eventually found Nichols guilty of conspiracy to use a weapon of mass destruction and eight counts of involuntary manslaughter (for the eight federal agents killed in the blast). The manslaughter verdict was a lesser charge than the prosecution had asked for, which was murder. In order to convict him of murder, the jury had to agree that the deaths were premeditated by Nichols, which they could not. The jury then went back into deliberations about Nichols's penalty since the conspiracy conviction could bring a sentence of death. After deliberating $13^{1}/_{2}$ hours, the jury reported back to the judge that they were deadlocked and could not reach a unanimous verdict on the sentence. This then threw the decision of the sentence back to the judge but also assured that the most the judge could sentence Nichols to was life in prison, since in federal cases, only a jury can sentence a defendant to death. On 4 June 1998, the judge sentenced Terry Nichols to life in prison without the possibility of parole.

"I think what it says," said jury forewoman Niki Deutchman, "is that there were a certain number of people who felt very strongly that Terry Nichols was very involved, and there were a certain number of people who felt very strongly that he was only involved in a very small way."[14]

While both McVeigh and Nichols are appealing their federal convictions, the local prosecutor, Bob Macy, said that he intends to try both men in state court for 160 counts of murder. While some might object that this is double jeopardy, it is not, because so far, McVeigh and Nichols have only been tried for eight of the 168 deaths, the murders of eight federal agents. It would only be double jeopardy if they were tried again for those eight deaths. The federal government prosecuted McVeigh and Nichols for only the eight deaths both because it simplified the prosecution and because the murder of a federal agent is a capital crime under federal law.

"It's not over yet," said Macy. "Hopefully we'll have a different verdict to talk about."[15]

"It is a world where loners are never alone, where delusion and fantasy echo back as conspiracy and fact," begins a 1995 *Newsweek* article.[16] This quote applies perfectly to Timothy McVeigh. He certainly could be considered a loner, yet he was not alone, because he felt himself to be a part of a large brotherhood whose members held the same intense hatred of the federal government as he did. The quotation also fits this case perfectly, because when people begin repeating delusion and fantasy over and over, as McVeigh and Nichols did, and as militia members do whenever they meet, the delusions and fantasies eventually become facts in the minds of these people.

And yet the first thing most militia groups will say about McVeigh and Nichols is that, sure, they may have attended a few militia meetings, but they were not official members of any militia. That argument, however, falls apart when one considers the flimsy structure of most militia groups. These groups, which can spring up and then disappear in the same year, are so fluid that membership is a nebulous concept. The fact remains that both McVeigh and Nichols believed in and loudly espoused militia doctrine. An Associated Press article stated: "Evidence surfaced that the two suspects arrested in the terrorist attack traveled in the same circles [as militia members] and showed the same deep rage against the government."[17] A writer for *Soldier of Fortune* magazine analyzed McVeigh's writings and found them full of the usual militia buzzwords. Also, when the authorities searched Terry Nichols' home in Herington, Kansas, they discovered a business card belonging to the leader of the Missouri 51st Militia (named after the fifty-one-day standoff of the Branch Davidians). The leader of the Missouri 51st Militia, however, claims he has never met Terry Nichols.

"McVeigh and Nichols were militia," said ATF agent George Stoll. "There are no rolls of militia members. These groups are too loosely organized to have official membership lists." Agent Stoll helped serve a search warrant on the Nichols farm in Michigan, where McVeigh occasionally stayed. He told me they found a large amount of militia material there.

Actually, whether McVeigh and Nichols were official militia members is not as important as the fact that the militia movement gave the beliefs that McVeigh and Nichols held a strong sense of legitimacy in these two men's eyes. McVeigh and Nichols found that groups of people all over the country held and espoused the same intense hatred of the federal government as they did. This likely made them feel that their actions had at least the moral support of these people.

"While the [militia] movement has not been proven criminally responsible for the bombing," said Steven L. Gardner, research director at the Coalition for Human Dignity, "it has been indicted morally."[18]

One of the greatest threats, therefore, that the militia movement poses to our country is that their dissemination of outlandish conspiracy theories and virulent antigovernment rhetoric gives legitimacy to a radical fringe attracted to their movement. It made McVeigh and Nichols more than just two lone voices calling in the night. Instead, they found themselves echoing what thousands of militia members have been saying about the federal government since Ruby Ridge and Waco: that it is out of control and corrupt.

"You've got a lot of people who are angry as hell, frustrated, afraid, and are simply looking for a forum to vent it," said Joe Roy of Klanwatch.[19] Another Klanwatch report said: "Militias operating in the United States today are breeding grounds for the kind of fanaticism behind the Oklahoma City bombing. . . . The propaganda disseminated by these antigovernment groups is militant, paranoid, and often extremely inflammatory."[20]

But more than simply echoing the rhetoric of the militias, McVeigh and Nichols carried out in reality and gruesome detail what the rhetoric of the militias says they have been amassing their weapons for: a confrontation with the federal government, albeit McVeigh and Nichols's confrontation was probably much more drastic than most militias had envisioned or wished for. And while militias may try to distance themselves from the Oklahoma City bombing, they really cannot. They all share a bit of the blame.

According to Morris Dees, "Even if militia leaders hold to the line of strictly defensive training and throw out the renegades, the damage is likely to be done. The militias will have provided access to weaponry and military training. They will also have brought together like-minded people who may embolden one another and go on to form their own secret cell."[21]

The following is a very clear example of how the militia supports this radical fringe. The Militia of Montana at one time sold a militia training book titled *M.O.D. Training Manual*. This manual advocated guerilla warfare that included such acts as raiding armories, kidnaping prominent individuals, executing government officials, and bombing both government and private installations. The manual goes on to say that these acts must be executed with the "greatest coldbloodedness."[22] When questioned about the manual, officials of the Militia of Montana claimed that they had never read the manual, did not know what was in it, and did not even know what M.O.D. stood for. They no longer sell the manual. But still, the damage is done, because disseminating this kind of material, along with spreading wild conspiracy theories and espousing a philosophy of hatred of the government, only supports and encourages the radical fringe that seeks out the militia.

"The right-wing extremist movement provides a breeding ground for psychotics and psychopaths on the fringe, those who believe and act on the rhetoric," the Senate Judiciary Committee heard in testimony on 27 April 1995, just days following the Oklahoma City bombing.[23]

McVeigh and Nichols, acting on this type of rhetoric, very likely considered themselves to be militia vanguards, the ones who would do what the others only wished they had the nerve to do. McVeigh considered himself very much to be a militia-type thinker. "I was preaching and 'passing-out' [handing out literature] before anyone had ever heard the words 'patriot' and 'militia,'" McVeigh said in a letter to a friend.[24]

In addition, Michael Fortier, in his testimony at McVeigh's trial, told the court that McVeigh had wanted to start a militia group while living in Arizona in 1994. However, he apparently could not find enough people who thought and felt as militant as he did.

While most militias try desperately to distance themselves from McVeigh and the Oklahoma City bombing, some leaders in the militia proudly consider McVeigh a part of their movement. "This means we have won an exceedingly powerful victory, and it has only cost us one soldier," said Norm Olson, the head of the Northern Michigan Regional Militia, referring to the conviction of Timothy McVeigh.[25]

For the victims of the bombing, however, even McVeigh's conviction and death sentence bring no consolation. "There is no such thing as closure for people who lost family in the bombing," said Darlene Welch, whose four-year-old niece died in the explosion. "The only closure is when they close the lid on my casket."[26]

The Oklahoma City bombing demonstrated very clearly the real threat of the militia: "Members . . . see themselves as saviors of society," said William O. Beeman in *The Militia Movement*. "For this reason they are able to justify almost any action, however violent. . . . The unrelenting commitment and conviction of movement members are ultimately what makes them so dangerous for the rest of society."[27]

As might be expected, despite the convictions of McVeigh and Nichols, a number of conspiracy theories have sprung up among militia members concerning the Oklahoma City bombing. The most common one is that McVeigh and Nichols are innocent, and that the federal government actually detonated the bomb for various reasons. Depending on the version of the conspiracy, reasons range from wanting to take public attention away from President Clinton's Whitewater problems, to wanting an incident that would bring strong citizen support for antiterrorist and gun control laws, to wanting an incident that would give the government an excuse to clamp down on the militias. Another version of this conspiracy holds that McVeigh and Nichols were participants, but only as unknowing government patsies who did not realize the truck carried a bomb. Conspiracy spinners insist that the government must have known about the blast ahead of time because several high government officials were not in the building at the time of the blast, and so, in the minds of conspiracy spinners, these officials must have been forewarned.

Another conspiracy theory says that the explosion was a nuclear device set off by the government. "My nuclear experience said it was a nuke," said Galen Windsor, a self-announced expert who claims he has spent forty-five years handling nuclear weapons. "And it was probably under two feet of concrete where they blasted the hole eight feet deep, thirty feet long."[28]

In any set of conspiracies held by militia members, the United Nations and/or the New World Order are likely to appear somewhere. Mark Koernke, a militia leader from Michigan, said the day of the bombing, "As a matter of fact, [my wife] Nancy and the kids, watching initial footage of this, saw what appeared to be United Nations observers badges."[29]

Along with the conspiracy theories, copycat crimes have also followed the Oklahoma City bombing. In Vacaville, California, a bomb seriously injured a federal worker and his wife. A telephone threat that preceded the bombing said, "You guys are all dead. Timothy McVeigh lives on."[30]

In the incident in Vacaville, federal mine inspector Gene Ainslie and his wife Rita were unaware that a pipe bomb had been hidden under the seat of Gene's government truck. After the explosion, in which flying shrapnel sliced through Gene's legs, the vehicle crashed into a concrete median. Gene and his wife both managed to escape from the truck just seconds before it exploded into flames, but Rita, the most seriously injured, suffered burns, a broken ankle, and a dislocated hip from the explosion.

Unfortunately, as we have seen, many militia members on the radical fringe feel that taking violent action, such as in the incident just cited, is an acceptable tactic. As another example, in July 1997, in Spokane, Washington, a jury convicted three members of an antigovernment militia group of eight felony counts involving two bank robberies and bombings. The previous year, the three men had also been convicted of conspiracy, illegal possession of hand grenades, and interstate transportation of stolen vehicles. The three militia members each received mandatory sentences of life imprisonment without parole.

In the Spokane case, four men dressed in camouflage-style military uniforms set off a bomb outside the *Spokane Spokesman-Review* newspaper office, apparently as a diversion for a robbery at a U.S. Bank branch. Several months later, the four men detonated another bomb, this time outside a Planned Parenthood office, again as a diversion before a robbery at the same bank branch. The robbers escaped with $108,000 from the two robberies, which the authorities never recovered.

At their trial, three of the men said they were "ambassadors of Yahweh" (an Old Testament name for God), and as such, they should receive diplomatic immunity. They also said they were part of a militia cell that believed that charging large interest on loans is evil and punishable by death.

In addition to the Spokane bombings, the police also investigated these men as possible suspects in the Centennial Park bombing at the 1996 Olympics. One of the three men convicted, Charles Barbee, was reportedly near the Atlanta area at the time of the bombing, and he fit the description of the likely perpetrator: a domestic terrorist probably involved in a militia-style or hate group. Also, a military surplus dealer reported selling Barbee a backpack similar to the one used by the Olympic bomber.

Another clue pointing to Barbee as a suspect in the Centennial Park bombing was that he worked for AT&T in Georgia, Florida, and Idaho. The Olympic explosion occurred at the AT&T Global Village in Centennial Park. In an interview, Barbee said, "It's not a moral company. Half the people I worked with were women. They were working instead of being helpmates to their husbands, as God requires."[31] Barbee, though investigated, was not charged in the Atlanta case.

A fourth member of the same militia group, who requested and obtained a separate trial, received a fifty-five-year prison sentence after being found guilty. "For our creator, there's no such thing as a bank, so there's no such thing as bank robbery," the militia member told the judge. "Bombing an abortion clinic also is not a crime," he added, "because abortions violate the Ten Commandments."[32]

In another incident demonstrating the threat of fringe militia members, a court convicted two members of the Minnesota Patriots Council on federal conspiracy charges. The men had allegedly manufactured a quantity of ricin—a deadly poison made from castor beans. It is 6,000 times more potent than cyanide, and 15,000 times more potent than rattlesnake venom. Contact with human skin is usually fatal. Authorities say the men had enough ricin to kill 1,400 people and that they had planned to use the poison to kill government employees.

A recent Klanwatch report stated: "The number of groups committed to anti-government extremism . . . is growing, and individuals connected to this movement are involved in a wide range of criminal activity, much of it violent."[33]

Interestingly, not all crimes committed by militia members are the result of a radical fringe striking out at innocent citizens or government employees. Often, financial reasons propel militia crimes. Militia leaders very quickly discover that running even a small militia unit can be expensive; consequently, some militias have turned to crime in order to support themselves. Some, such as the militia members in Spokane, resort to robbery to support their militia activities. Other militias have reportedly found another way to finance their activities: selling drugs.

According to a report from the Southern Poverty Law Center: "The evidence that drugs are funding parts of the extreme right is growing. . . . In Oregon, officials believe three men convicted of operating a major methamphetamine lab pumped a small fortune into the militia movement."[34]

"[He] has all the signs of someone involved in the militia movement," said Lieutenant Michael Tate of the Locust Grove (Georgia) Police Department, who defused explosives found in the home of a suspected militia member and drug dealer. "One of the things these [extremists] do to raise money for their deeds is narcotics trafficking."[35]

In another incident, sheriff's deputies in Gainesville, Florida, while serving a search warrant on a militia member's house, found numerous assault rifles, ingredients for making bombs, potassium cyanide, and a shopping list for the ingredients necessary to make cyanide gas. They also found 811 marijuana plants and equipment for indoor growing.

While the chances are extremely small that a large militia group would openly sponsor a terrorist act such as the Oklahoma City bombing, this does not mean that only fringe members, and not a militia organization as a whole, are dangerous. Anytime a private army that espouses hatred of the government and, as we shall see in the next chapter, often holds racist and/or anti-Semitic views is allowed to exist, innocent Americans are in danger.

❖ ❖ ❖ ❖ ❖ ❖ ❖ ❖ **8**

FRINGE GROUP CROSSOVER

In October 1992, a group of 160 of the nation's leading right-wing activists met at a YMCA Camp in Estes Park, Colorado. They had been summoned there by Pastor Pete Peters of the LaPorte Church of Christ. Pastor Peters is a leader in the Christian Identity movement, which is believed to have between 20,000 and 30,000 adherents, and has its strongest following in the northwest part of the country. While many readers may not have heard of Christian Identity, it is not a new theology, but springs from a nineteenth-century movement called British Israelism. Christian Identity is a theological offshoot of the Christian faith, which holds that the Jews of today are not the Jews of the Bible. Instead, Christian Identity adherents believe that the ten lost tribes of Israel, conquered and taken in captivity from Israel by the Assyrians, rather than returning to their homeland after being freed, instead eventually migrated to and settled in Europe, and that the white, northern European people therefore are the descendants of the actual Jews of the Bible. Christian Identity adherents also hold to the belief that the Jews of today, rather than the Jews of the Bible, are the spawn of a coupling between Eve and the devil, and consequently are children of Satan. In addition, they maintain that all races other than northern European are pre-Adamic, or beasts created by God before he created Adam, who Christian Identity adherents believe was the first white man. Only the white race, Christian Identity adherents insist, descends from Adam and Eve. All other races are subhuman animals, or "mud people." Consequently, harming or killing a mud person or a Jew is not evil since they are animals and do not have souls.

I picked up a pamphlet by Pastor Peters at a preparedness/survival expo I attended in Atlanta. In it, Pastor Peters states: "The Anglo-Saxon, Germanic, Scandinavian, and kindred people are the servant people of the Scriptures, the descendants of Abraham, Isaac, and Jacob, the recipients of the Abrahamic Covenant." Later in the pamphlet, he goes on to say: "Healthy bodies throw off parasites. When there is repentance and obedience to His laws, the porno shop will no longer be on Main Street, the Jewish Hollywood filth will no longer be tolerated. . . . The Jewish bankers will no longer be allowed to charge interest, the drug business will dry up, etc." He then adds this warning: "Today very few Christian ministers speak out against Judaism and Jewish persecution of Christianity for fear of being kicked off the air, having their church foreclosed on, being ostracized from their particular church fellowship, being murdered."[1]

Not surprisingly, most mainstream Christian churches view Christian Identity as simply an attempt at theological justification for bigotry. "As a theology, Christian Identity is nothing more than prejudice in search of divine justification," said Susan DeCamp, coordinator for the Montana Association of Churches in Billings.[2]

Pastor Peters called the meeting of right-wing activists in response to the Randy Weaver incident, which had occurred just a few months earlier at Ruby Ridge in northern Idaho. Peters told the attendees that he had called them together "to confront the injustice and tyranny manifested in the killing of Vicki Weaver and her son Samuel."[3] In attendance at Estes Park were not only people with right-wing sympathies, but also members of the Ku Klux Klan, the Aryan Nations, CAUSE (Canada, Australia, United States, South Africa, and Europe—countries where white people are found), and various offshoot Christian sects similar to Christian Identity. Also attending were tax protestors, pro-gun extremists, members of patriot groups, and publishers and authors of far-right periodicals and racist literature. Pastor Peters also invited United States Attorney General William Barr in order to give him a chance to explain why the government had taken the actions it had at Ruby Ridge. Attorney General Barr, of course, did not attend. Actually, Pastor Peters sent invitations to hundreds of people, including individuals such as David Duke, the former Ku Klux Klansman turned politician. Many, however, either refused the invitation, as David Duke did, or could not attend for other reasons. Still, 160 individuals did attend.

"Men came together who in the past would normally not be caught together under the same roof, who greatly disagree with each other on many theological and philosophical points, whose teachings contradict each other in many ways," said Pastor Peters. "Yet, not only did they come together, they worked together for they all agreed that what was done to the Weaver family was wrong and could not, and should not, be ignored by Christian men."[4] The group set up various committees to work on a solution that would prevent another incident such as Ruby Ridge from occurring again.

The solution that emerged from what became known as the "Rocky Mountain Rendezvous" was armed civilian militias. The group believed militias could prevent another Ruby Ridge, as well as defend homes and families in the event of other incidents such as the then recent Los Angeles riots that had followed the not-guilty verdict in the Rodney King beating case.

"One can only speculate that had there been an effective militia in Naples, Idaho, which could have been mobilized after the U.S. Marshal murdered Sammy Weaver by shooting him in the back . . . [i]t is entirely possible that Vicki Weaver would not have been murdered later on by an FBI-trained assassin while she was holding a baby in her arms," said Larry Pratt, executive director of Gun Owners of America, and the person credited with the idea of forming armed civilian militias.[5]

Those in attendance at the Rocky Mountain Rendezvous agreed, however, that in order for the idea of armed civilian militias to work, the racist and anti-Semitic rhetoric often voiced by some of the groups represented there had to be toned down. The people drawn to these armed civilian militias would be mostly white, middle-class individuals who were not necessarily racist or anti-Semitic, but rather anxious and uncertain about the economy and their future. Any racist or anti-Semitic talk would likely scare these potential members away. The meeting participants readily agreed to this outward elimination of racism and anti-Semitism because they realized the potential of the proposal. Having the large number of armed civilian militias they envisioned could greatly strengthen and invigorate the far right's position of power in this country. These groups could become an army under the invisible control of the far right. And so, rather than targeting Jews, blacks, or illegal Mexican immigrants as the enemy, the enemy became the federal government. Rather than Jewish bankers controlling the economy and the world, it became instead international bankers.

In 1995, many militias received a computer E-mail message from the Texas Militia Correspondence Committee that read, "[I]t is extremely important now to reach out to the general community for their support. Get our story out before our adversaries can get theirs out. Look like respectable businessmen. Emphasize our primary purpose: to enforce the law, especially the Constitution, and that means to expose criminal wrongdoing in government and abuses of power. Forget all the rhetoric about foreign troops, New World Order, and all the rest of the stuff that sounds bizarre to ordinary Americans. Stick to the basics, and hammer it over and over: Corruption and Abuse."[6]

Many of the people at the Rocky Mountain Rendezvous also realized that civilian militias made up of citizens concerned primarily about the economy and the direction of our country would be a perfect hiding place for white supremacists and other right-wing extremists who did not want to advertise their beliefs. These extremists could look like average, middle-class people, yet still have access to weaponry, training, and the support of a group of people who shared their fear and hatred of the government. Most important, though, belonging to a civilian militia would look much more acceptable and respectable than belonging to one of the high-profile white supremacist or hate groups, such as the Ku Klux Klan, the Aryan Nations, and others.

The plan put forth at the Rocky Mountain Rendezvous quickly took seed and, soon after the meeting concluded, armed civilian militias began springing up all over the United States. John and Randy Trochmann, two of the founders of one of the first, and still one of the most influential, militias in the country, the Militia of Montana, reportedly attended the Rocky Mountain Rendezvous.

A 1997 article in *The Christian Science Monitor* warned: "In little more than two years, militias have come to outnumber the membership of the KKK, the neo-Nazis, the racist skinheads, and other hate groups combined."[7]

Despite the groups represented at the Rocky Mountain Rendezvous and the preceding warning, many of the civilian militias that exist in the United States today bristle at the claim that they are racist or anti-Semitic, and some will quickly point to the few blacks, Jews, or Hispanics who belong to the militias as proof of their tolerance. However, the fact that they feel they have to point out these few individuals shows how small a part of the total membership they really are. Many militias also bristle at any claim that they are secretly controlled by racist groups or individuals. However, in the September 1995 issue of the *National Alliance Bulletin*, founder of the neo-Nazi organization the National Alliance, William Pierce, wrote: "Some of the militia groups in the United States are being badly misled in the ideological realm and are in need of some Alliance input. Any member interested in working with a non-Alliance militia group should write to [Dr. Pierce], detailing any past or current contacts he has with a militia group and also mentioning any opportunity of which he is aware for establishing a new contact with a militia group in his area."[8]

Along with the invisible influence of fringe and hate groups demonstrated earlier, some of the present leaders of the modern militia movement, though they try to avoid contact now, have had close association with fringe and hate groups in the past. For example, John Trochmann, one of the founders of the Militia of Montana, reportedly has had considerable contact in the past with the Aryan Nations, a white supremacist organization whose headquarters in Hayden Lake, Idaho, is close to the Militia of Montana headquarters in Noxon, Montana. Trochmann, a popular speaker at many preparedness/survival expos across the country, is one of the most influential militia leaders in the United States. According to Richard Butler, leader of the Aryan Nations, John Trochmann helped set up Bible studies for them and advised the organization on the establishment of a code of conduct.

In a 1995 *Esquire* magazine article about the Militia of Montana, John Trochmann is quoted as saying, "I am following God's law. Blacks, Jews are welcome. But when America is the new Israel, they'll need to go back where they came from. It's just nature's law—kind should go unto kind."[9] That type of rhetoric has now disappeared among militia leaders. It is not that the feelings have disappeared though, they're just well hidden.

"The most recent development in Christian Patriot paramilitarism is the formation of citizen militias," said the Coalition for Human Dignity. "Using convoluted Constitutional and Biblical arguments, Christian Patriots often do not come across as white supremacists. Most hide their bigotry beneath a veneer of pseudo-libertarian ideas and Constitutional literalism. Often a Christian Patriot exterior will conceal a crass racism that emerges only in unguarded moments."[10]

Although most militias as a whole loudly proclaim that they have no contact with fringe hate or white supremacist groups, according to a *Los Angeles Times* article, in 1995, thirty-two militias across the United States and the white supremacist group the Aryan Nations began an identical intelligence-gathering effort using the exact same format called SALUTE, which stands for size/number, activity observed, location, unit, time, and equipment. Militia leaders, however, claim that the simultaneous use of SALUTE by them and the Aryan Nations was simply a coincidence.

"The ties are there despite efforts to play them down," said Thomas Halpern, associate fact-finding director for the Anti-Defamation League.[11]

While doing research for this book, I attended a number of events sponsored by militia groups. Although many of the militia members I spoke with vehemently deny they are racist or anti-Semitic, and well may not be, I have noticed they do not seem to mind occupying booths next to groups that are, and they do not seem to mind that such groups are invited to militia functions.

Also, in their effort to appear nonracist and non-anti-Semitic, most militias proclaim very loudly that they do not discriminate in their membership, that everyone, regardless of race or creed, is welcome. However, very often in the bylaws or statement of purpose of a militia one finds references to white people, to heterosexuality, to Christians, to the Bible, and to an obligation to carry out God's laws. All of this makes a person wonder just how tolerant militias really are of those who are not white and who do not share the Christian faith and other values held by militia members.

The first line of the bylaws of the Missouri 51st Militia, for example, states: "We will not support any specific political party or candidate, nor will we espouse any particular religious ideology or doctrine." Yet a few lines down, when talking about the purpose of the militia, they state: "Educate its members in areas of history, law, and principle from knowledge imparted from this country's historical record *and from the Bible* [emphasis added], which has been the greatest single guiding influence for all nations desiring to be free."[12]

I picked up the Militia of Georgia's Handbook recently while at a function in Atlanta. It says: "We are dedicated to preserving, protecting and advancing *our Christian heritage* [emphasis added] and culture."[13]

The Internet home page for the Louisiana Unorganized Militia states: "As human beings, we are obligated, morally, to provide for the defense of ourselves, our family, and our nation. Under the Declaration of Independence, the Constitution of the United States of America, the laws of Louisiana, and most importantly, the *Holy Bible, King James Version* [emphasis added], we have the unalienable right to self-protection."[14]

A flyer from a militia group in Sepulveda, California, says: "We are a patriotic group that deals mainly with political interest. We are paramilitary, patriotic, and survivalist oriented. . . . Here are just a few items and projects we are currently working on: Prepare for civil war, provide protection for Pro-White candidates . . . educate and inform White people of their culture and heritage."[15]

Under General Policy for the Constitutional Militia of Southern California, it states: "Homosexuality absolutely will not be tolerated. Should any member be found to be homosexual he shall be summarily discharged with prejudice." The document ends with a Militia Prayer.[16]

The Mission Statement of the 7th Missouri Militia says: "As a service organization, we follow the leadership principles *enunciated by Christ* [emphasis added] when he said that the greatest among us would be of the greatest service." Yet despite the benevolence of this religious reference, the same Mission Statement also says: "Strictly following the common-sense concept of 'leaderless resistance' as enunciated by Louis Beam, the 7th Missouri Militia has no chain-of-command or open troop strength."[17]

The Louis Beam referred to above is a former Ku Klux Klan Grand Dragon and Ambassador-at-Large for the Aryan Nations. He has vowed: "We intend to purge this land of every nonwhite person, idea, and influence."[18]

In the September 1997 issue of *Modern Militiaman*, editor Martin Lindstedt wrote: "Well, I have corresponded with Mr. Beam and saw his famous speech 'Enemies of the State' at Estes Park in 1992, and I disapprove of the hatchet job on what seems to be a man of humility. Mr. Beam is recognized by friend and foe alike as being one of the most intelligent and effective of the Resistance leaders."[19] This militia publication's adoration of a man who has belonged to two well-known white supremacist hate groups underlines the racism and anti-Semitism often hidden just below the surface of the militia movement.

This evidence of hidden racism and prejudice in the militia movement becomes even clearer when one begins investigating the various conspiracy theories held by militia groups. Despite the intentions of those at Estes Park in 1992 to downplay anti-Semitism, one of the most popular of the militia conspiracy theories maintains that the United States, and often the world, is secretly run by a cabal of Jewish bankers. A document that has become almost a bible among many militias is a book entitled *Protocols of the Meetings of the Learned Elders of Zion*. Many militia members believe that this text is absolute proof of a Jewish conspiracy to rule the world, even though the book has been proven to be a forgery.

The *Protocols*, researchers believe, was penned in the late 1800s. It is supposed to be a word-for-word record of twenty-four meetings of a secret cabal of Jewish leaders whose intention was to rule the world. Researchers now know that the work is a forgery because parts of it are an exact copy from an earlier work. In 1921, English journalist Philip Graves demonstrated that large sections of the purported minutes of the secret meetings were actually plagiarized from an 1864 book entitled *Dialogues in Hell between Machiavelli and Montesquieu, or the Policies of Machiavelli in the 19th Century*. This latter book, written by a French lawyer, was not about and did not even include any references to Jews, but instead was a satire of French leader Napoleon III, who eventually jailed the author because of it.

Researchers believe the Russian secret police likely compiled the *Protocols* in an attempt to convince Czar Nicolas II that the Jews were a threat to Russia. During this period in history, Russia was going through difficult economic times and the population needed a scapegoat. To the Russian secret police, the Jews seemed a perfect target. Consequently, the first version of the *Protocols* appeared in a St. Petersburg (Russia) periodical.

Czar Nicolas II, however, eventually rejected the *Protocols* after having two high-ranking police officials investigate their authenticity. The police officers discovered through their investigation that the *Protocols* were an obvious forgery, and, following this, the Czar "gave an order that the *Protocols* were no longer to be used, 'since it was impossible to pursue a pure aim by impure means.'"[20]

The *Protocols*, however, refused to die, and the book soon made its way into Germany. It so impressed Adolph Hitler that he had the Nazi Party publish it. Eventually, the book became a basic textbook in German schools. In *Mein Kampf*, Adolph Hitler talks of how the book influenced his thinking about Jews: "To what extent the whole existence of this people [Jews] is based on a continuous lie is shown incomparably by the *Protocols of the Wise Men of Zion*."[21]

The *Protocols* eventually crossed the Atlantic and came to America, where it was widely disseminated by an unexpected source: Henry Ford. In his newspaper, the *Dearborn Independent*, Ford reprinted the *Protocols* in a series of articles entitled "The International Jew." Henry Ford also published this series of articles in book form.

Because of its content, the *Protocols* greatly appeal to individuals who believe in both conspiracies and anti-Semitism. A few quotes from this work should make it very clear how the forgers intended the book to invoke a hatred of Jews.

"On the ruins of the natural and genealogical aristocracy of the Goyim (Gentile)," the book states, "we have set up the aristocracy of our educated class headed by the aristocracy of money. . . . [W]e are compelled to introduce into the constitutions of States to prepare for the transition to an imperceptible abolition of every kind of constitution, and then the time is come to turn every form of government into our despotism. . . . The aristocracy of the Goyim as a political force is dead—we need not take it into account; but as landed proprietors they can still be harmful to us. . . . It is essential therefore for us at whatever cost to deprive them of their land. . . . [I]t is indispensable for us to undermine all faith, to tear out of the minds of the Goyim the very principle of Godhead and the Spirit."[22]

It does not take much of a psychologist to see that the *Protocols* was written with the intent of making the reader view Jews as both evil and a dire threat to all non-Jews. The forgers, however, did a lot of overwriting. When the entire document is read objectively, it becomes clear that any minutes of true secret meetings, which were not meant for publication, would not have the strong propaganda slant that this work has.

Yet still, the *Protocols* has shown an amazing longevity. Today at many preparedness/survival expos and gun shows, copies of it are hawked by people who insist the book is legitimate, that it is a true recording of the twenty-four meetings. And unfortunately, many members of militias hold up this work as positive proof of a Jewish conspiracy against the United States and its citizens.

An offshoot conspiracy of the *Protocols* is ZOG, which stands for Zionist Occupational Government. This is another widely held conspiracy theory among militia members. The gist of this conspiracy theory is that the present government of the United States is really just a puppet government. The country is actually controlled and run by a secret Jewish cabal, or ZOG. Many in the militia movement believe that ZOG has been secretly ruling the United States since the Franklin Roosevelt presidency.

A book I picked up at a preparedness/survival expo in Cincinnati contains a number of conspiracy theories concerning how various organizations other than ZOG secretly control the United States. These other organizations include the Council on Foreign Relations, the Tri-Lateral Commission, the United Nations, and the Bilderbergers. However, in almost any book about national and international conspiracies, anti-Semitism tends to creep in. And it did in this book, which includes a section on how the Rothschild family, which the book clearly identifies as Jewish, now controls the world's money supply and, consequently, the world's leaders. According to this conspiracy theory, the Rothschilds secretly con-

trol every major bank in the world, and it is the Rothschilds who originally set up and still control the Federal Reserve System.

The book states: "To site [*sic*] the Rothschild's remarkable achieve-
ments since 1770, they have established an International Banking Syndi-
cate (IBS) that controls currencies throughout the world; regulates all
banking facilities, including those not owned and operated by the IBS;
today they hold quasi-control of the United States and many other governments, they also control through interlocking directorates, almost all
major corporations, including ABC, CBS, NBC, Hollywood studios, and
all major news sources throughout the world."[23]

This book also contends that the Federal Reserve System is a private
company that, through control of America's money supply, controls
America. This conspiracy theory additionally claims that the only three
American presidents who have opposed the IBS's control of America—
Presidents Garfield, Lincoln, and Kennedy—have been assassinated because of it. It is from believing in and spreading these types of conspiracy
theories that anti-Semitism seeps into the militias.

Often though, racism and anti-Semitism by militia members or their
sympathizers can be symbolic. At 1:15 A.M., on 9 October 1995, the Sunset
Limited, a passenger train carrying 268 people, approached a thirty-foot-
high trestle near the town of Hyder, Arizona, about sixty miles southwest
of Phoenix. Almost everyone on board the train was asleep, but what happened next violently awakened them. As it crossed the trestle at fifty
miles per hour, the train suddenly jumped the tracks, sending the cars
crashing down into the dry creek bed thirty feet below. Passengers and
employees, propelled out of their beds and seats, smashed against walls
and floors, snapping bones and tearing flesh. At 1:16 A.M., at the bottom of
the gorge, the tangled, smashed cars, some with their wheels still turning,
lay in the quiet darkness as many of the mangled but still alive victims,
stunned and confused by the crash and the sudden surreal orientation of
the cars, tried to understand what had happened.

"I heard babies screaming, and their mother was hollering each one
of their names, one after the other," said one of the crash victims.[24]

Unbelievably, only one person died in this crash, though seventy-
eight people suffered injuries, some critical. Compounding the serious-
ness of the crash, though, was the fact that Hyder is so isolated that it took
rescue personnel over thirty minutes to reach the accident site.

Investigators later found that someone had removed a connecting bar
that held the metal rails together and had also removed twenty-nine

spikes, which then freed the rails from the wooden ties beneath them. Ordinarily, this would have set off an alarm that would have activated warning lights. The saboteurs, though, obviously acquainted with railroads,
used a long piece of wire to keep the circuit open and bypass the alarm.
Investigators believe the saboteurs picked the Sunset Limited, not because
of who was on board, but because the train passed through very sparsely
settled areas where the saboteurs would likely not be spotted.

"This type of derailment is a common tactic, taught in Ranger or Special Forces courses, for soldiers of both the United States and many other
countries," said an article by Emergency Net News Service. "You can also
read about it in a number of 'survivalist' and other books that describe
Special Forces or underground types of tactics."[25]

Following the crash, several of the people who stumbled dazed and
injured from the cars found sheets of paper with a typed message on it.
The message made reference to the incidents at Ruby Ridge and Waco,
both hot militia topics. The message also demanded that an agency be created to police government employees, including law enforcement personnel. The letter was signed "Sons of Gestapo."

While some people may find the reference to Nazi Germany puzzling
since most militia groups like to label federal law enforcement officers as
Gestapo or Storm Troopers, anyone who has attended preparedness/sur-
vival expos, guns shows, or other events where militia members gather
would not be surprised. Many gun advocates and militia members seem
to have a fascination with Nazi Germany, and items from this era are
often offered for sale at these events. More importantly, the obviously
anti-Semitic implications in the choice of names for this apparent militia
group is particularly clear.

From this incident, it becomes very clear just how dangerous racism
and prejudice within the militia movement can be. There are many other
examples. For instance, there was a publication previously sold by the
Militia of Montana called the *M.O.D. Training Manual*, which I talked
about in the last chapter. This book includes instructions on destroying
"the firms and properties of people that are not Americans." The manual
advises: "Firms and property in this country that are not owned by Americans must become such frequent targets of sabotage that the volume of
actions directed against them surpasses the total of all other actions
against vital enemy points."[26]

This type of racist, xenophobic thinking, however, can be taken even
beyond the advice given in this manual. In December 1997, the federal

government charged three men with plotting an insurrection against the United States. According to the indictment, once the United States government had been overthrown, the men planned to set up a new country that would be limited to whites only. Since the men worried that, after racial purification, the population of this new country would be small, they decided they would legalize polygamy in order to increase the number of whites in the population. The seven-count indictment charged two of the men with murder, racketeering, and conspiracy. The federal government charged the third man with only racketeering.

Allegedly, two of the men in this case befriended a gun dealer from Tilly, Arkansas, whom they met through gun shows and militia group activities. However, the indictment charges that to help finance the founding of their whites-only nation, the two men robbed and killed the gun dealer, his wife, and their eight-year-old daughter. The third man helped the other two transport stolen materials in support of the plot.

These individuals, incidentally, were not strangers to the police. One of them had been convicted of murdering a man he believed to be a government informant and had also confessed to kidnapping and robbing a couple from the state of Washington. Another of the men had been captured on a police in-car video camera engaging in a gun battle with Ohio police.

Despite all the examples given so far, not all of the fringe groups that cross over to militia organizations are racist, hate groups. Some militia organizations, particularly those in the Pacific Northwest logging areas, have been known to work with the Wise Use movement. This organization, established in 1984, is part of the antienvironmental movement and has allegedly been involved in many incidents of terrorism and harassment. Some of Wise Use's Primary Beliefs include the following: (1) The earth and its life are tough and resilient, not fragile and delicate; (2) humans, like organisms, must use natural resources to survive; and (3) technology can break through natural limits to make earthly goods and carrying capacity virtually infinite.[27] Members of militia groups and Wise Use members, particularly in the West and Northwest, have been known to often join forces in what they see as a common battle against environmentalists: individuals and groups they view as being the ones responsible for making the economy sluggish through their opposition to unrestricted land use for logging, mining, and so on.

Eric Ward of the Seattle-based Northwest Coalition against Malicious Harassment said he has seen an "incredible crossover of people and materials between Wise Use and the militias from Washington to western Montana, eastern Oregon, and northern Idaho."[28]

On 14 November 1994, Ellen Gray, an official from the Pilchuck Audubon Society of Everett, Washington, gave testimony at a county council meeting that favored an environmental issue. When she finished, a man approached her, dangling a noose and threatening that it was for her. "We have a militia of 10,000," another man at the county council meeting told her, "and if we can't beat you at the ballot box, we'll beat you with a bullet."[29]

A 1995 article in *The Nation* stated: "In fact, while nationally the militias have had numerous run-ins with local police, sheriffs, IRS agents and others in the fifteen months since they've gone public, the majority of militia-related incidents have involved people who, one way or another, are associated with the environment."[30]

Notwithstanding everything I have said in this chapter, not all militia groups are filled with racist hatemongers. Actually, many members of militias are not racist at all, nor do they preach hate. Many are simply people frightened and confused by the economy and the direction they see our country taking. These people join militias because they want to do something positive to turn the country around. However, these individuals often mistakenly believe that all members of the militia hold the same beliefs they do, not realizing that many members, despite the nondiscriminatory rhetoric, do not share their tolerance of others who are different.

I found an interesting posting on the Internet from the 52nd Missouri Militia. It said: "We (the 52nd Missouri) would like to apologize for the conduct of the 51st Missouri Militia during the peaceful gathering of 'separatists' at Lone Jack, Missouri. . . . We feel the 51st should NOT have disturbed this picnic in their own intolerant way. We are very surprised that a militia has lowered themselves. . . . Such public actions serve only to harden the souls of those we wish to sway. The 52nd and 51st are NOT associated in any political way."[31]

Yet, as admirable as the 52nd Missouri Militia may sound, far too many militias are still controlled by and contain individuals who do not share this tolerant attitude. While most militias may claim they are fighting to preserve American freedoms and to keep this country the land envisioned by our Forefathers, the racist, intolerant beliefs held by many in the militia movement belie this claim.

❖ ❖ ❖ ❖ ❖ ❖ ❖ ❖ **9**

MILITIA INTERNAL SECURITY

On 26 April 1996, agents of the Bureau of Alcohol, Tobacco, and Firearms (ATF) arrested Robert Starr and William McCranie, charging them with conspiracy to possess unregistered explosive devices. A month later, in the same case, Troy Spain, a former Army Ranger, surrendered to ATF agents. According to investigators, the three men, who lived in Roberta, Georgia, about 85 miles south of Atlanta, had made plans to construct forty shrapnel bombs and distribute them among the members of the 112th Georgia Militia.

As a part of the investigation, ATF agents raided the alleged bomb-making site at Starr's home, where they confiscated bomb-making chemicals and detonation devices. The agents also recovered ten pipe bombs, nine made of one-inch-diameter metal pipe, and a tenth, which was three and a half feet long, made of four-inch-diameter pipe. Investigators learned that the militia members built the bombs for use against the federal government or the New World Order. The three men had become convinced that one of these two organizations would soon come after the members of the 112th Georgia Militia.

How was this plot uncovered? Two government informants had infiltrated the 112th Georgia Militia.

The two infiltrators reported that at a militia meeting, the three men told those gathered that anyone in the militia who wanted one of the bombs, which had nails glued to the outside to make them more lethal, could have one, but that they must bury them in their backyards. The bombs were to be kept hidden until needed in the showdown with the

123

federal government or the New World Order. The informants also reported that the three men claimed they would shoot any law enforcement officers trying to serve a search warrant on them.

"I knew him, Starr, and I can tell you he seemed like a good man," said one of Starr's neighbors. "But he did not like the U.S. government, I can tell you that."[1]

Like many members of militia groups, Starr had a strong hatred of the federal government. The basis of this dislike was primarily financial. Starr's business, the Spectrum Electric Company, had declared bankruptcy in 1995. Among the company debts was a bill for $20,000 owed to the IRS.

The federal government originally became interested in the 112th Georgia Militia after receiving several reports of large amounts of explosives stolen in the Atlanta area. Authorities became concerned that a group might have stolen these explosives in order to sabotage the upcoming Atlanta Olympics. Fifteen hundred pounds of fertilizer capable of being made into a bomb had been stolen from a lawn and garden store in Atlanta, while another large quantity of ammonium nitrate, along with hundreds of blasting caps, had been stolen from an explosives company in Norcross, Georgia, a suburb of Atlanta.

In an attempt to find out where the stolen explosives had gone, the two infiltrators joined the 112th Georgia Militia and began secretly taping conversations and meetings. Although, at first, the conversations centered mostly around the usual militia paranoia about gun confiscation and the New World Order, their paranoia quickly worsened when the FBI began its siege of the Freemen in Montana. This was a group of individuals who claimed that certain parcels of land they owned no longer fell under the jurisdiction of the United States. The siege of this group by the FBI filled the news and lasted for eighty-one days in the Spring of 1996. The three men arrested in the 112th Georgia Militia case inexplicably became convinced that the federal government or New World Order would come after them next. That is when, the infiltrators claim, their efforts turned to bomb making.

At the trial, which began in October 1996, defense attorneys attempted to convince the jurors that the three men were simply country boys who liked to play soldier and talk big, but really were not dangerous. However, tape recordings played in court did not sound that way. During one taped conversation, Starr is heard describing a project to construct bombs big enough to derail trains and destroy bridges. "We ain't got time to be mixing [stuff] up . . . when the ATF's coming down the road," Starr could be heard saying on one of the tapes. "We're going to have these things made up so you can pull it out, hit it and throw it. That's the way we want it."[2]

Defense attorneys also attempted to convince the jurors that the two informants, who were brothers, had been the ones who suggested and instigated the bomb making. They insisted that it had been the two brothers who had encouraged and badgered the three men into breaking the law.

"I got taught how to do it and led into it," claimed McCranie during the trial. "I was messing around with someone I thought was my friend."[3]

The jurors, however, did not buy that argument. They returned guilty verdicts against all three men on charges of conspiracy to use a destructive weapon in a violent crime and possession of illicit explosives. In February 1997, a judge sentenced Starr to eight years in prison. McCranie and Spain both received sentences of six and a quarter years in prison.

This case became a landmark: It was the first time the federal government had ever gone to trial against modern-day militia members. All cases before this had been settled through plea bargains. The way the authorities investigated the case, however, was not unique. It was standard fare for law enforcement. During investigations, police officers regularly use infiltrators and informers to uncover wrongdoing in criminal enterprises. In areas such as narcotics, for example, police officers for years have depended heavily on infiltrators and informants to gain evidence against drug dealers. This has become a necessary part of police work because some drug dealers, knowing the police have targeted them, will not sell to anyone they do not know, making a successful police investigation extremely difficult. However, these type of cases can become much easier to break if the police have someone either on the inside of a drug organization or trusted by it, individuals to whom the drug dealers will consequently sell drugs or in whom they will confide. The same techniques are used with militias. Many of the cases discussed in this book, such as the Viper Militia, the West Virginia Mountaineer Militia, the Blue Ridge Hunt Club, and Ray Lampley and the Tri-State Militia, were all successfully investigated by the police only because of government infiltrators and informers.

"When a group or individuals within a group demonstrates a propensity for criminal acts, an undercover operation is usually the most expedient and valid way of determining their true purpose and direction," said ex-ATF agent Steve C. Wortham. "I think infiltration of any group suspected of posing a threat to the public or which is committing an illegal operation is not only proper and necessary, but obligatory on the part of law enforcement."

Using infiltrators and informants is not foolproof though. Depending on the believability and persuasiveness of an infiltrator's cover story and his or her ability to mix with the group, police investigations of this type can be either complete failures or stunning successes. In the Viper Militia case, discussed in Chapter 5, one of the government infiltrators was so successful in playing his role that there was talk among the Viper Militia members of making him their leader. "We told him 'Absolutely no,'" said an ATF supervisor about the possibility of their informant being elected the militia leader.[4] When he turned down the offer of leadership, the members of the Viper Militia promoted the infiltrator to their chief of security.

In the case against members of the West Virginia Mountaineer Militia, discussed in Chapter 4, the government informant was so persuasive that he became the militia's intelligence chief. Still, the militia members eventually became suspicious of him, and one time confronted him and insisted that he remove his shirt so they could be sure he was not wearing a transmitter. They picked the wrong day, however, the day he was not wearing one.

Yet, although the above cases were successful, using infiltrators and informants can also backfire when an organization suspects that a person is an infiltrator and begins feeding him false information or expels him from the group. However, because of the law enforcement successes in cases such as the ones mentioned here, most militias have begun to strengthen their internal security and are constantly on the lookout for infiltrators and informers.

"It's common knowledge that one out of every five individuals who claims to be a patriot is actually a government informant," said Randy Trochmann, one of the founders of the Militia of Montana. "Everybody in the movement should be thinking about who that fifth guy is."[5]

While law enforcement most likely has not reached this level of penetration, they have been successful in preventing a number of possible tragedies through their infiltration of the militias. Naturally, law enforcement officials have been under tremendous pressure to prevent any more incidents such as Oklahoma City from occurring, and, therefore, if they believe an organization has this sort of potential, they have an obligation to investigate it, which includes using informants and infiltrators if necessary.

However, law enforcement agencies cannot investigate groups simply on a whim. There must be evidence of criminal acts either being committed or about to be committed. All state and local law enforcement agencies have set standards for when they can collect intelligence on private organizations and when they can initiate an investigation.

"We have very strict guidelines we must follow before we can begin an investigation," said First Sergeant Mark Mitchell of the Indiana State Police. "We can only investigate criminal activities. We must see whether the activity is only that of an individual or a group activity, and pursue our investigation on that basis."

The federal government has also established guidelines that its law enforcement agencies must follow when initiating an investigation of an organization believed to have criminal intentions. The United States Justice Department adopted these guidelines in 1975, after it discovered that the FBI was illegally investigating Vietnam War protestors, black activists, and others. The Justice Department found that the FBI had no knowledge or evidence of criminal activities committed by these groups but was acting simply on unsubstantiated suspicion. Therefore, to avoid this type of unwarranted intrusion into private organizations, federal law enforcement agencies must have evidence of actual or imminent criminal activity within an organization before they can conduct an investigation or enlist infiltrators and informants.

However, just infiltrating a militia organization when there is evidence of criminal activity is not enough. Law enforcement agencies must also gather enough evidence to be able to convince jurors or a judge that the accused militia members committed the crimes with which they are charged. This is not always an easy task, because a defense attorney's first tactic, particularly when there is overwhelming evidence of wrongdoing, is to attempt to discredit the infiltrator or informant. He or she will insist that the criminal acts the militia members are charged with were suggested by the infiltrator or informant. The defense attorney will claim that the militia members had no criminal inclinations but were badgered into committing the crimes. The legal defense will contend that the accused militia members are therefore not guilty due to entrapment.

While practically every criminal convicted through the use of an informant or infiltrator claims that he or she was entrapped, this, of course, is very seldom the truth. I have seen drug dealers who have been selling drugs for years suddenly, in court, become law-abiding citizens who were badgered and pressured beyond their will to resist to locate illegal drugs and then sell them to the informant. I have seen prostitutes with a half-dozen prostitution convictions insist in court that they had never in their lives considered the idea of being paid for sex, but rather that the idea came from the undercover police officer or informant who pressured them into saying they would do it. It is equally difficult to believe that individuals with no inclination to do so could be persuaded and entrapped into making bombs. Consequently, this defense of entrapment did not play well to the jury in the preceding case of the 112th Georgia Militia.

However, this is not to say that entrapment by an informant never occurs. Occasionally, it does. The Ruby Ridge case involving Randy Weaver, discussed in Chapter 1, is a classic example of entrapment. For this reason, police officers must use extreme caution when employing infiltrators and informants. They must be certain that these individuals are only recording and reporting criminal activity, not encouraging it. Therefore, to bolster the government's case and refute any claims of entrapment, it is also helpful, along with having an informant inside an organization recording and reporting criminal acts, if one of the members of the organization can be persuaded to testify against the others. This is another common tactic law enforcement agencies utilize, and usually with considerable success. However, this decision by one of an organization's members to assist in the prosecution is seldom the result of a guilty conscience. Usually, the impetus for the decision to testify against former comrades is an offer by the prosecutor of reduced charges in return for cooperating in the prosecution. The next case illustrates this.

In July 1996, law enforcement authorities arrested the founder of the Washington State Militia, John Pitner, and seven others for, among other crimes, conspiracy to make explosives. Some of the individuals arrested, however, were not actually members of the Washington State Militia, but were freemen working in coordination with the militia. Freemen are individuals who hold to a complex legal theory that they believe allows them, as "white sovereigns," to ignore all federal and some state laws. Many militia members also claim to be sovereign citizens, and, as such, exempt from certain laws. I will discuss this legal theory more thoroughly in the chapter on militias and the law.

The authorities arrested five of the individuals in this case while they were attending a bomb-making class in Bellingham, Washington. In the complaint filed in court, the government alleges that the eight individuals arrested wanted "to arm themselves for what they believed would be an eventual confrontation with the United States government or the United Nations." Authorities say that at least seven bombs had already been made by the group.

Earlier that year, John Pitner had publicly proclaimed in several news conferences that his organization was peaceful and sought change only through nonviolent means. He and the Washington State Militia drew high praise from the local news media for not issuing the usual, virulent antigovernment rhetoric. However, it appears that this talk was just a smoke screen, and while the eventual arrests may have surprised many, they did not surprise everyone.

"[It was] good propaganda," said Eric Ward of the Northwest Coalition Against Malicious Harassment. "Their reason for being is an antidemocratic social movement that is seeking to affect mainstream politics either through discourse or through violence."[6]

Following the arrests, a judge ordered Pitner and two others held without bond when a search of several of the arrested individuals' homes turned up evidence that they intended to flee. Also, in an effort to beat the charges, one of the arrested individuals allegedly instructed his family members to gather up all of the bomb-making materials in his house and dump the items far away. The family did so, but the authorities found and recovered the materials.

As in the case of the Georgia 112th Militia, the government had infiltrators and informants inside the Washington State Militia. And, as is customary in most cases involving government infiltrators or informants, the defense attorneys attempted to discredit one of the infiltrators, Ed Maeurer, who, while working for the FBI, had taped many of the meetings and conversations with the arrested individuals. Defense attorneys called Maeurer, a man with a history of writing bad checks, a liar and a scam artist. Also, as is usual in these types of cases, the defense attempted to convince the jury that Maeurer was actually the one who had encouraged the members to commit illegal acts. The defense claimed that Maeurer needed the money the FBI was paying him to be an informant in order to make restitution for the bad checks he had written. However, another person who had also infiltrated the Washington State Militia and had tape recorded meetings and conversations was a bit harder to discredit in court: FBI agent Michael German.

"The feds are coming," Pitner is heard saying at a meeting one of the infiltrators had taped. "We've got to get ready for 'em." At this meeting, in preparation for a confrontation with the federal government or the New World Order, members learned how to make bombs out of Fourth of July sparklers.[7]

Other tapes revealed members talking about how they were the first line of defense against the New World Order, which they believed would attack the United States by coming through Canada. "The more we know how to make, the more dangerous we are," Pitner was recorded saying. "The more dangerous we are, the more heat we can bring on with the U.N. crowd when they decide to do their thing."[8]

However, it was more than just the two infiltrators' recordings that won this case for the prosecution. Initially, following their arrests, all of the individuals charged in this case insisted that the crimes they were accused of were totally false and trumped up, as did many of their family members. However, in January 1997, two of the arrested men entered into a plea agreement. As part of his deal with the prosecutor, one of the men agreed to plead guilty to one count of conspiracy and then to testify against the others. In February 1997, a jury found four of the defendants guilty of possession and transfer of a machine gun, and illegal possession of fire bombs and pipe bombs.

"We have a lot of militia people coming to us," said ATF agent George Stoll. "They joined a militia and then became disenchanted. It's much better for law enforcement to use someone already inside because the violence-prone groups are often closed to outsiders."

The paranoia that every fifth militia member is an informer clearly shows that any militia involved in criminal activity realizes there is a very strong possibility that it either already has been, or soon will be, infiltrated by government informers. For this reason, some militias are splintering into smaller, more compact groups, where all of the members know each other intimately. By doing so, they hope to reduce the danger of government infiltration.

Morris Dees agrees. "I think the movement has become more hard core, operating in smaller units. Their fervor has not lessened at all. They've become more frustrated and more dedicated."[9]

Because of the success law enforcement has had in infiltrating those militias groups engaging in criminal activities, many militias, in addition to forming into smaller cells, have now also instituted more stringent security measures. They are becoming much more vigilant in seeking out and expelling government infiltrators and informants. A recent article in *Modern Militiaman* offers advice on spotting government agents. "Those who have been studying the stories released to the media these days about the arrests of various different people within the militia movement," the article states, "will undoubtedly have noted that government infiltrators are usually involved."[10] The article then describes the three types of government infiltrators to be on the watch for.

The most dangerous and the hardest type of infiltrators to detect, the author advises, are those infiltrators who do not draw any attention to themselves, but rather blend in with the others and simply report back to the government everything they observe about militia activities. The only sign there is such a person inside the militia is that the militia cannot seem to keep any secrets.

A second type of infiltrator, according to the article, is a bit easier to spot. This is the person who tries to create dissension within the militia. This infiltrator attempts to form opposing cliques, and may try to redirect the aims of the militia so that the organization accomplishes nothing.

The third type of infiltrator, the article warns, is extraordinarily dangerous to the existence of the militia but is also the easiest to spot. This is the agent provocateur. This is the person who incites militia members to commit crimes. His or her activities, according to the author of the article, include encouraging bomb making, advocating amassing illegal weapons, and suggesting other clearly criminal acts that members would ordinarily not consider committing.

This article advises militias that if they find any of these individuals within their group, they should throw them out of the organization. If that does not work or cannot be done for some reason, the author says the leaders should completely dissolve the militia and re-form with smaller, more trustworthy cells.

The Oregon Militia did just that. In May 1995, the Oregon Militia disbanded and destroyed all of its records. The leader claimed that the organization had been infiltrated by government informers "to about the highest level." Whether this was true, partly true, or just paranoia, no one knows for sure. The founder, Michael J. Cross, added, "I said to the members if they want to form small cell groups, that would be safer than one big organization."[11]

Because of the high number of government infiltrations of militias, the editor of *Modern Militiaman*, Martin Lindstedt, offers readers some advice about forming infiltrator-resistant militias. Mr. Lindstedt suggests forming two types of militias: open and closed. These two types of militias, he warns, however, must never mix or even have any contact with each other.

The open militia is an educational, politically active group that will take in as new members individuals the long-time members do not know intimately. The open militia never gets involved in anything that even has the appearance of illegality, since all of the members, and particularly the leaders, are known to the authorities. An open militia instead tries to educate people and bring about political reform.

The closed militia is a group of two to five family members or longtime intimate friends. They never take in anyone who is not family or known by the members for years. The closed militia is the action militia. Because of its membership, it is much less likely than the open militia to be infiltrated by government agents. "If you are a member or leader of a closed militia and one of your relatives or close friends in your cell of from 2–5 is an informant," said Mr. Lindstedt, "then you are too stupid to live."[12]

Forming smaller, closed cells is part of an organizational theory called "leaderless resistance," a concept now embraced by some militias, because they have come to realize that if they grow too large and too open, they are more vulnerable, or if their leaders become too important, then they and the movement will be easy to crush. Also, the use of "leaderless resistance" makes infiltration by government agents much, much more difficult.

In his essay on leaderless resistance, Louis Beam, a former Ku Klux Klan Grand Dragon and Ambassador-at-Large for the Aryan Nations, gives credit for the idea to a man named Ulius Louis Amoss, who developed it for use in the event of a communist takeover of the United States. Louis Beam, however, now espouses its use for individuals fighting the federal government.

"The concept of leaderless resistance is nothing less than a fundamental departure in theories of organization," said Louis Beam. "The orthodox scheme of organization is diagrammatically represented by the pyramid, with the mass at the bottom and the leader at the top. . . . This scheme of organization, the pyramid, is not only useless, but extremely dangerous for the participants when it is utilized in a resistance movement against state tyranny."[13]

The essay goes on to say that the orthodox style of organization is especially vulnerable to infiltrators because it is so large and there are so many levels into which an infiltrator can slip. Instead, Louis Beam suggests forming "phantom cells." These are small groups of individuals, from the one-man cell up to four or five individuals, who answer to no central authority but act entirely on their own initiative. No person in the cell is boss or underling, but each member knows what to do and when to do it. There are no orders issued, no commands given. These phantom cells also never know each other or about each other. They therefore do not actively coordinate their activities. The only way they cooperate is that they should all be working toward the same goal. These cells, based on the information they receive from various sources, decide individually when to take or not take action. "These idealists truly committed to the cause of freedom will act when they feel the time is ripe," Beam said, "or will take their cue from others who precede them."[14]

As mentioned earlier, the concept of leaderless resistance has only been adopted by a few of the militias, but the idea is applauded by many. An Internet posting of the U.S. Militia states: "The cell organization is designed to protect the identity of individual members of the organization by circumscribing inter-cell interaction and communication. . . . To see why a cell organization is so effective, consider a line of individuals where each individual knows only the person to his left and to his right. A traitor or an occupation security agent who successfully infiltrates the organization could only identify two other individuals in the organization."[15]

Fortunately for law enforcement agencies conducting investigations, not only has this type of organization not met with wide acceptance, but it also flies in the face of much of what has happened in the modern militia movement so far, where, rather than hiding in anonymous, leaderless cells, there are many people clamoring for status and attention. Few of the people involved in the militia movement, or in the leadership of it, would willingly disappear underground into phantom cells. Most want to stay just where they are, and most want to maintain their status in the organization. For example, when Norm Olson blamed the Oklahoma City bombing on the Japanese government and was consequently voted out as commander of the Michigan Militia, he did not just fade away. Instead, he went to another part of Michigan and formed another militia that he could command.

It must be remembered that many militia members lack strong social ties; consequently, many of these people join militias in order to have some sort of relationship with people they feel are like them. Individuals of this sort are seldom willing to go underground into tiny, unrecognizable cells. That was their life before the militia. These people want fellowship, recognition, and, particularly, status. A number of militia members have complained that at most militia meetings there are almost no soldiers. Practically everyone there is an officer, their rank usually obtained at an Army surplus store. In an article in *Modern Militiaman,* the author observed that, "A man joked to me the other day that the only two things that are in short supply this winter in Michigan are heating oil and general stars."[16]

In addition to the need of its members for social intercourse, if the militia movement actually adopted the concept of underground phantom cells that have little or no contact with each other, a number of the national militia leaders would have to find other jobs. Many of these individuals make their livings by crisscrossing the country every year on speaking tours and by hawking various items that every "real" militia member should have.

Yet regardless of the present lack of acceptance of leaderless resistance by the majority of the militias in our country, readers should still realize just how extraordinarily dangerous this concept is. It is this type of thinking that gives birth to men like Timothy McVeigh and Terry Nichols. McVeigh and Nichols were a two-man phantom cell that acted on their own initiative. As a two-man phantom cell, they had no one to counter their proposed actions with the voice of caution or reason. They had no large membership to discuss and discard their intended bombing plan. If the concept of leaderless resistance were actually implemented by a large number of the militias, the United States could have thousands of McVeighs and Nicholses roaming the country. In an article in *Modern Militiaman,* this very possibility is applauded. The author suggests: "As a result of the lessons which had to be learned, now is the time to build New Model Resistance organizations able to quickly concentrate sufficient force at a point of attack so that the target is always eliminated, but diffuse enough so that the enemy [the federal government] has no idea as to their existence, much less their exact presence."[17] The author recommends the formation of two types of cells.

One type is called the ideological strike cell. "These individuals will usually be men without children to support, men without any ties to bind them except a hatred of the current social order and a need to impose the raw justice of revenge. Such cells are capable of doing anything, such is their alienation from the hated society and the lack of any links which would tend to hold them morally responsible for their conduct."[18] It does not take much of an imagination to realize how well Timothy McVeigh fits this description.

The author also recommends the formation of family cells, made up only of people connected by blood and marriage. The purpose of these cells is primarily survival. Their job is to stockpile food, medicine, and ammunition. However, in addition to this function, they also act as eyes and ears for the ideological strike cells and can give them material support if necessary. Both of these types of tightly formed cells, because of their structure, greatly preclude the chance of infiltration by government agents.

Fortunately, at present, while the concept of leaderless resistance is applauded by many militias, few have actually implemented the strategy. Most militias prefer to stay large and open but, consequently, remain prone to infiltration by government agents.

So, what do militia groups, both large, open organizations and small, closed cells, do when they discover infiltrators and informers in their midst? Most militia leaders recommend expelling them. However, as shown below, some militia members opt for more drastic measures.

In September 1994, during a routine traffic stop in Fowlerville, Michigan, the police pulled over a car they found loaded with weaponry, including a .357 Magnum revolver, three assault rifles, three 9mm semi-automatic pistols, seven hundred rounds of ammunition, and a quantity of military equipment. Following this discovery, the police arrested the two men in the car, Paul Darland and William Gleason, who claimed they were bodyguards for militia leader Mark Koernke, on weapons charges. However, after they were bailed out of jail, rather than returning for trial, the two men went into hiding with the assistance of another militia member, John Stephenson. During the time they were hiding, though, Darland allegedly dragged Gleason into some remote woods, forced him to dig his own grave, and then murdered him. Reportedly, Darland killed Gleason because he thought he was a spy. Gleason died from a gunshot wound to the head. There is some disagreement, however, about who Gleason was spying for: the government or militia leader Mark Koernke. The truth will likely never be known, since both the police and Koernke are not talking about the incident.

"Informants are on the increase in our militias," said Norm Olson, commander of the Northern Michigan Regional Militia. "Gleason was, no doubt, some mole, informer, infiltrator or stooge. This is generally the way justice is meted out to traitors in the militia."[19] While this statement by Mr. Olson may sound extreme, his attitude is not that uncommon. Most militias are extraordinarily paranoid about government infiltrators. The Viper Militia, for example, discussed in Chapter 5, required its members to swear that they would kill any government infiltrators. While in many instances this can be just tough talk, the murder of William Gleason shows it isn't always.

The authorities recovered Gleason's body when a witness to the murder led them to where it was buried. Stephenson eventually worked out a plea bargain with the prosecutor, under which he pled no contest to the charges of being an accessory to murder and possession of a firearm in the commission of a felony. He also agreed to testify against Darland, who is still at large.

Later, the police also arrested Koernke after a process server charged that Koernke threatened him with an assault rifle when he attempted to serve a summons in the Gleason case. A judge set bail at $1,000 cash; Koernke posted the money and was released from jail.

Koernke, however, gives a somewhat different version of the incident. When he spoke at a preparedness/survival expo in Atlanta, Koernke told the audience that his arrest, which led to his being fired from his job as a janitor at the University of Michigan, was actually part of a plot by the federal government to kill him. He said that the plan was for the sheriff to hand him over to the state police, which would hand him over to the federal government, which would then make him disappear. He claimed the government did not go through with its plan, because it realized there would be retribution from the militia.

Ever since members of the militia movement, through the tragedy at Oklahoma City, demonstrated just how dangerous their type of thinking is, the government has taken a serious interest in them as a threat to the public safety. Often, the only way the government can gain information on militia members believed to be involved in criminal activities is through the use of infiltrators and informers. While the many government successes in doing this have forced the militias to beef up their internal security measures, the government cannot let up, but must continue to aggressively penetrate militia groups involved in criminal activities. Only in this way can the government be certain to prevent another incident such as the Oklahoma City bombing.

MILITIA PUBLICATIONS AND PROPAGANDA

At a preparedness/survival expo in Cincinnati, Ohio, while a number of speakers talked about the militia hot topics of preparedness and survival, the gathering also offered many tables filled with militia-related items. These tables contained hundreds of magazines, books, pamphlets, audiotapes, and videotapes about the militia movement and its concerns. Interestingly, a large majority of these publications concerned some plot or conspiracy theory. However, not certain at the time what I should buy that would best suit my research purposes, I spoke with a woman behind one of the tables and told her I was looking for some basic information on the militia movement.

"Oh, then you want our *America in Peril* series," she told me, walking down to the end of the table and pointing to a set of three videotapes she had for sale. "These tapes have all of the important people in the militia movement on them, and they're only $45."

While I was purchasing the videotapes, I noticed she had a sign advertising a videotape about the prison camps for patriots that the government is reportedly building in secret. I told her I would also like that videotape.

"I'm sorry, but I've sold out of that tape," she told me. "But there's a bunch of stuff about the prison camp in Beech Grove, Indiana, on the second tape in the *America in Peril* series."

When I returned home and was watching the second in this series of videotapes, entitled *A Call to Arms*, the speaker, Mark Koernke of the Michigan Militia at Large, spoke very matter-of-factly about a number of things that he apparently felt the audience should accept as true. Although he offered no verification or proof of his claims, which may sound bizarre to ordinary citizens, I have since discovered that many militia members accept them as gospel. He denounced Canada and Mexico as "evil regimes" and explained that the North American Free Trade Agreement (NAFTA) was a plot to keep these evil regimes in power. He told his viewers that the Council on Foreign Relations, which secretly rules the United States, has proposed that, for population control, 75 percent of Americans should be eliminated. He claimed that national health care is actually a secret method of national registry, that we will soon all have microchips implanted in us (which, as well as identifying us, can also track our whereabouts), and that eventually the United States will have an overall tax of 90 percent.

As if these were not enough startling revelations for his audience, Koernke continued by claiming that Fort Polk, Louisiana, is not under American control any longer but is now under the control of the United Nations and that the federal government used foreign troops at Waco. He also told his viewers that Mikhail Gorbachev now works for the United States and is in charge of military base closings, and that street gangs in Chicago recently came to a national conference and signed an agreement to work as shock troops for the New World Order.

While these claims may sound like bad B-grade fiction, from what I have seen and heard at the militia gatherings I have attended, there are tens of thousands of people in the United States who watch militia videos, read militia publications, listen to militia radio programs, and believe every word of it. There are tens of thousands of heavily armed people in the United States who believe and stand by every conspiracy theory militia leaders like Koernke propose.

As we have discussed, one of the most commonly accepted conspiracy theories among militia members is that there will be an eventual takeover of the United States by the New World Order, most believe by the year 2000. After this takeover, the New World Order rulers will immediately suspend all constitutional freedoms and eventually reduce American citizens to slavery status. A large majority of militia members also believe that secret concentration camps are being built all over the United States to hold dissidents, meaning militia members, when this takeover occurs. Militia members, who are both heavily armed and deeply committed to the cause of freedom, fear they will be seen by the rulers of the New World Order as a formidable resistance force if not crushed right away. Consequently, militia members believe they will be rounded up immediately and tossed into these prison camps.

As proof of this part of the conspiracy theory, militia members have reportedly "found and documented" a number of these secret prison camps. The militia members documenting them claim that the facilities found so far, in every part of the country, are presently sitting empty, apparently waiting to be used. Without a doubt, however, the most famous of these secret prison camps is the first one "discovered" and "exposed" by militia members. This is a facility that appears to passersby to be an Amtrak repair facility in Beech Grove, Indiana. At any militia gathering where secret prison camps are discussed, this facility is always talked about and accepted without question as a secret internment facility built by the New World Order. However, in my research, I did not come across any reports of militia members ever trying to get inside this Amtrak facility to confirm that it actually was a prison camp.

However, despite this lack of verification, the claim that this location in Beech Grove is actually a secret concentration camp, rather than a train repair facility, appears on several popular militia videos and in countless militia publications. The first suggestion that this facility is not what it seems to be to passersby appeared on the videotape *America Under Siege* by Indianapolis attorney Linda Thompson, who at one time appointed herself Acting Adjutant General of the Unorganized Militia of the United States of America.[1] Thompson is one of the major figures in the modern militia movement and several years ago attempted to organize a march on Washington, D.C., where militia members would arrest and try government leaders. Thompson's main contribution to the militia movement, however, is the videotapes she has produced about the federal government's actions at Waco, which I will discuss later in this chapter.

On the videotape *A Call to Arms,* narrator Mark Koernke also claims that this facility in Beech Grove, Indiana, is a secret concentration camp. As "proof" that this location is not a train yard but an internment camp awaiting prisoners, the tape, as well as various publications I have read since, point out several "very suspicious" things about the facility. The fence around what is claimed to be a railroad repair yard, for example, has the barbed-wire leaning inward, to keep people in rather than out. The windows of all of the buildings are covered with wood and painted over. There are colored signs throughout the facility that match the colored tags on the back of road signs (as talked about in the chapter on conspiracies, many militia members believe that these road sign tags are meant to guide non-English-speaking invading forces). The facility in Beech Grove also has a windsock and a large radio antenna that militia members believe will be used so that helicopters can ferry the prisoners in without having to pass through city streets, where they might meet opposition from militia members. Finally, military vehicles can often be seen on the property.

When I finished the videotape, I realized it would be extremely difficult for me to investigate whether Gorbachev actually was hiding out somewhere in the United States and working for the government, or whether the street gangs in Chicago really had reached a secret agreement to work as shock troops for the New World Order. But I knew I could investigate the reported secret prison camp in Beech Grove, which is a suburb of Indianapolis.

The chief of police of Beech Grove, Mike Johnson, is an old friend of mine and a former classmate. Back in the late 1960s, we went through the police academy together. A number of years ago, when I was writing articles for a police management magazine, I often used the Beech Grove Police Department as a model small police department. I assumed that because of its proximity (the Amtrak repair yards sit directly behind the police department building), the Beech Grove Police Department would have a good working relationship with the Amtrak police, and so I went to see Mike and explained what I wanted to do.

Mike laughed and told me that he too had seen one of the videotapes that claimed the Amtrak repair facility was actually a secret prison camp. "The radio antenna they show on the video, the one that's supposed to be able to talk to the helicopters," Mike told me, "that's the police department's antenna." I found I was correct in my assumption that the two police departments had a good working relationship. Mike called the head of security at the Amtrak facility, Sergeant John P. Keller of the Amtrak Police Department, and arranged for me to tour the repair yards.

Early the following morning, I pulled my car into the parking lot of the Amtrak repair facility and found that it contained about 450 to 500 cars, which seemed to me a large number for a supposedly empty prison camp. Paradoxically, I noticed that the facility flew a black POW/MIA flag below the American flag.

"You're not the first person who's wanted to do this," Sergeant Keller told me when I arrived at the security office. "Last year, a state senator wanted to come in and look around." Apparently, according to Sergeant Keller, the state senator had received so many calls from constituents wanting to know why he was allowing a secret concentration camp to be built in his district that he called and asked to tour the facility.

After we talked for a few minutes, Sergeant Keller asked me what part of the facility I wanted to see, and I told him all of it. He nodded, and we walked out and climbed into an Amtrak Police Department vehicle and began our tour of the 123-acre repair yards.

According to Sergeant Keller, the facility, which employs around 800 people, repairs and refurbishes Amtrak passenger trains. That is exactly what I saw over the next hour or so as we stopped the vehicle and walked through building after building. I saw workmen stripping down old passenger cars and other workmen refurbishing these stripped-down cars. One building contained a huge, two-story vacuum that, when the workers attached it to one end of a railroad passenger car, would suck out everything loose in the car. In one of the buildings, we came upon several passenger cars that had obviously been involved in an accident. Men with cutting torches were slicing away the damaged parts. In another building, we found huge stacks of large cardboard boxes. Sergeant Keller showed me what they contained: new seats for the passenger cars. In yet another building, I watched workmen converting an old railroad car into a new baggage car. What I saw during this tour was just what a person ought to see at a train repair facility. Sergeant Keller gave me free access to go absolutely anywhere I wanted.

When we returned to the security office, I spoke for a while with the sergeant about some of the items that militia members consider as "proof" that this is really a secret concentration camp. True, the fence along the part of the facility that borders Emerson Avenue, one of the main streets in Beech Grove, does have the barbed-wire on top leaning inward, as if to keep people in. However, before beginning my tour, I drove around the outside of the facility and found that the fence on some parts of the repair yards has the barbed-wire leaning outward, some parts have it straight up and down, and in some places the fence is so old and dilapidated it is falling down. Also, the fence has apparently been there for so long that trees inside the grounds now grow directly up against it, which is hardly a good security measure for a prison, since anyone inside could climb the tree and then over the fence. More importantly, this barbed-wire is not the coiled razor wire found at prison facilities, but simply the basic, straight, three-strand barbed-wire found on many businesses. Several times during my career, I have chased kids who scaled a fence like this one as if it were not there. Sergeant Keller explained to me that parts of the fencing around the facility were built at different times and that is why the barbed-wire leans in different directions.

Two of the other items of proof, the windsock and the colored signs, Sergeant Keller explained, came on orders from the Occupational Safety and Health Administration (OSHA). Several years before, there had been a chemical spill at the facility that injured several dozen workers. The colored signs designate staging areas and instruct employees where to go in the event of another chemical spill. The windsock is there to show employees which direction the wind is blowing, to ensure that none of them get caught in windblown chemicals.

The idea that the New World Order would use helicopters to ferry prisoners into an internment facility always struck me as silly and impractical anyway, something only a person with a delusional belief in his or her own grandiose importance would dream up. According to the conspiracy theory, these secret facilities being built around the country are supposed to hold tens of thousands, or even hundreds of thousands, of prisoners. Bringing all of these prisoners in by helicopter would be tremendously expensive and time consuming. Since railroad tracks lead into most of the buildings at this facility, it seems to me it would be more practical, if I was dreaming up this conspiracy theory, to bring the prisoners into the facility inside closed box cars. I cannot help but believe that the helicopter idea is a subtle way to attach a large measure of importance to militia members and show how very valuable their role is to the cause of freedom.

The claim in militia publications and videos that all of the windows at the Beech Grove facility are boarded shut was only half true. Many windows at the facility were not boarded. However, the large repair buildings, which were built between 1907 and 1910, did at one time have hundreds of windows, which are now covered over. While all of these windows may have been stylish and even effective in the early 1900s when the facility was built, this is no longer the case. Anyone who knows anything about the financial condition of Amtrak realizes how dismal it is, and how far the company must go to cut costs. Amtrak officials found that these hundreds of windows were expensive to replace and clean, and that they allowed the heat to escape too easily from inside the buildings. Since all of the repair buildings are one story and have thirty-five to forty-foot-high ceilings in order to support huge, overhead cranes, heating them becomes very expensive. And so to prevent heat loss and save money, Amtrak officials had workmen cover the outsides of the windows and insulate the insides.

When I was touring the facility, I did notice, as the militia videotapes and publications claim, what appeared to be military vehicles and boxcars at the facility. Sergeant Keller explained to me that because Amtrak is federally subsidized, it can buy surplus military vehicles and boxcars from the General Services Administration at greatly reduced costs.

As I was preparing to leave, I asked Sergeant Keller about the black POW/MIA flag. He told me that about half of the workers at the facility were Vietnam veterans.

A few minutes later, driving out of the parking lot and turning south onto Emerson Avenue, I watched my odometer. I found that the former law office of Linda Thompson, Acting Adjutant General of the Unorganized Militia of the United States of America, sat less than a mile south of the Amtrak facility, also on Emerson Avenue. Since the first report of this facility being a secret prison camp had reportedly been made on one of her videotapes, I could not help but picture in my mind her passing by this facility every day, seeing the barbed-wire leaning inward, seeing the covered up windows, and, with the conspiracy mind-set of most militia members, wondering what was going on inside this place.

The point to the previous anecdote is that the report about the Beech Grove Amtrak repair facility being a secret prison camp is exactly how much of the militia "news" and "intelligence" is gathered and disseminated. One person proposes a theory or a guess, and, without any verification or proof, it becomes accepted as fact by many people. This occurs because militia members will often use one unsupported report to substantiate another unsupported report. It also occurs because militia members do not use the standard methods of obtaining or disseminating information, methods that require fact checking and verification. In fact, militia members often shun the established news and information outlets, such as the morning newspaper or the evening television news. Instead, to obtain or disseminate news and information, they use shortwave radios, the Internet, fax machine networks, homemade or semiprofessional video and audiotapes, privately printed pamphlets and books, and small publishers. The problem with this is that all of these sources of information allow dissemination of news and information without the troublesome and time-consuming task of verification or fact checking. Consequently, many of the wild conspiracy theories talked about in this book get widely disseminated, and, if repeated often enough by different sources, finally become accepted as truth.

"Adding to the geographical distance between militia and government is a striking information gap," said an article in *Psychology Today*. "Militias tend to shun mainstream media, relying instead on their own newsletters, radio broadcasts, pamphlets, and the Internet for news of political or world affairs. So they rarely tap into information or perspectives that might moderate their views. And the Internet's cloak of anonymity further allows extreme views to fester uncensored."[2]

The use of these alternate methods for gathering and disseminating information has emerged because many militia leaders believe that the established news media outlets in America are under the control of the federal government or the New World Order, and that these outlets only do as they are told. In a statement given before the Senate Judiciary Committee on Terrorism, Technology, and Government Information, John Trochmann of the Militia of Montana said, "We the people have had about all we can stand of the twisted, slanted, bias[ed] media in America who take their signals from a few, private, covert interest groups bent on destroying what's left of the American Way."[3]

Many militias also use these alternate methods for communicating news because of their deep-seated suspicion of the federal government, which they believe is constantly monitoring their movements and communication. According to a *USA Today* article, "The surveillance [by law enforcement] has not escaped the attention of the militias, whose message—anti-tax, anti-government, pro-gun—hasn't changed, though the medium often has: Instead of public meetings, many now prefer the anonymity of the Internet, bulletin boards, even encryption codes."[4]

Interestingly, the militias' use of these alternate methods of news and information broadcasting has met with a very high level of acceptance from most of the receivers. This is due to the fact that many people like to receive information they believe has come from underground sources the authorities do not want them to hear from. "People like the notion of the jungle grapevine," said Bernard Beck, Associate Professor of Sociology at Northwestern University. "They take comfort in the idea that there are ways of passing information along that bypasses the establishment. It is very much in keeping with a general distrust of institutions we're seeing more and more in America."[5]

Yet of all these alternative methods for conveying news and information, militias attach particular importance to the use of computer communications, because they are both inexpensive and far-reaching. An Internet site can be set up fairly inexpensively, yet reach tens of thousands of people.

"It's cheap and getting cheaper," said Wallace Wang, author of *Microsoft Office 97 for Dummies*. "Most of these fringe groups used to run cheap flyers, and now they can post them on the Internet with world wide access, for relatively little cost."[6]

In addition, for those militia members seeking information from many different militias, there is the Patriot Network, which is a group of linked computer bulletin boards containing militia information. In an article in *Modern Militiaman*, answers to a questionnaire from a doctoral student at the University of Tennessee touched on militia communications. The responses confirmed that the militias depend heavily on computer E-mail and the Internet for communicating their ideas.

"E-mail can be used for quick, easy communication," the militia member responded. "It is far more common than even WWW pages. While this medium is notorious for its frequent false alerts and flame-wars, still it is unequaled for quick, secure, inexpensive communications."[7]

In an issue of *Minuteman Magazine*, the author states: "Computers provide militia forces with secure, anonymous communications which are essential to the cell structure. The Internet, in particular, is a medium especially well suited to supporting militia command and control. To date, militia use of the Internet has been primarily E-mail, newsgroups, and web. E-mail for point to point, newsgroups for discussion, and web for publication."[8]

The Internet, however, beyond serving as an information source about conspiracies, militia activities, and militia news, can also have a darker side. It can provide information on how to construct devices of mass destruction. An article in *The Police Chief* stated: "Experts say the Internet has been the single most powerful influence on explosive incidents in the past several years. This is especially true for teenagers who take bomb-building information from the Internet—information that at one time was buried in dusty library shelves."[9]

As confirmation of this, a certain address site found on the Internet says in the Introduction: "It's very difficult for a home-experimenter to make a firecracker, but a bomb capable of blowing the walls out of a building is easy. You can find what you need in grocery stores, hardware stores, and farm supplies."[10] In my own research, with a minimal amount of searching, I was able to find on the Internet a document that provides the reader with detailed instructions on bomb making, constructing silencers, creating napalm, and building and designing many other dangerous items.

President Clinton has warned: "Modern technology like the Internet has a 'dark underside' that, combined with America's traditional openness and liberty, leaves the nation very, very vulnerable to the forces of organized destruction and evil."[11]

But the situation is not hopeless. There is help for parents who want to restrict their children's access to this type of information on the Internet. America Online, an Internet service provider, is reportedly working on software that will be able to filter out information on the Internet that customers consider offensive, such as pornography, information from hate groups, and so on.

Along with the Internet as a source of information for militia members, videotapes such as the ones I purchased play a surprisingly large role. A number of them have sold hundreds of thousands of copies. There are literally dozens of tapes covering every aspect of the militia movement, from *Brainwashing for the New World Order* to *The Ruby Creek Massacre* (a video made during the Randy Weaver standoff), from *How to Set Up a Pirate Radio Station* to *30 Ways the IRS Controls Churches*. Some of the most widely viewed videotapes, however, concern Waco and the government's actions there. For example, Linda Thompson has produced two huge selling and widely viewed videotapes entitled *Waco: The Big Lie* and *Waco: The Big Lie Continues*.

In the first videotape, Linda Thompson claims that the Waco incident was really just a subterfuge to cover up the murder of four ATF agents who had been Bill Clinton's bodyguards and knew too much about his misbehavior. In addition, she claims that it was a disgruntled Branch Davidian who made up the stories about David Koresh's reported child abuse and his total domination of everyone in the compound. The federal government, she asserts, used these lies told by the disgruntled Branch Davidian as justification for assaulting the compound and killing innocent people. To support her claim that the government intentionally killed the Branch Davidians, Thompson shows in the video what appears to be a government vehicle using a flame thrower. However, on the unedited version of the tape from which Thompson made her tape, it can clearly be seen that it is not a flame shooting out of the vehicle, but only a reflection of sunlight on some nearby debris. Actually, this is mostly what both of Linda Thompson's videotapes about Waco contain: purposely edited videotape or shots of blurred, unrecognizable images. On the tapes, the narrator explains to the viewer what he or she is seeing, what the blurred, unrecognizable images are, and then moves on, with no concern for verification or proof.

In the *Gun Week* article "*Waco: The Big Lie* Revealed As a Hoax," columnist Ken Carter, after viewing the original, unedited version of the tape that Linda Thompson used to show the alleged flame thrower, said, "Linda Thompson suckered all of us with that one. And she had to have known exactly what she was doing, since the videotape sequence was edited a split second before the vehicle pulls back and executes a hard turn which clearly shows the 'flame' image stabilize and turn out to be a piece of wallboard."[12]

Another videotape about Waco, *Day 51*, figured significantly in the Timothy McVeigh trial. During the penalty phase, jurors watched the videotape, which McVeigh had taken so seriously that he sent copies of it to his friends. In addition to espousing a militia point of view about the incidents at Waco, the videotape also makes various wild claims. For example, it alleges that Iraqi weapons, taken in the Gulf War and smuggled into the United States by the federal government, have been given by local police departments to street gangs, who will use them in their work for the New World Order. This is the type of information that many militia members use when making their decisions. The defense wanted the jurors to see the videotape so they would understand what information Timothy McVeigh had used in making his decisions.

Along with using videotapes as a source of information, there are also numerous books that militia members feel either "prove" the various conspiracy theories they believe in or present a statement about the world as the militia sees it. The book *Report from Iron Mountain*, for example, has recently been pirated on numerous Internet sites maintained or visited by militia members. First published in 1967, this book, while appearing to be an official government document that concludes that war is necessary for society to grow economically, was actually written as a political satire. The author, Leonard C. Lewin, penned the book during the Vietnam War era, when antigovernment and antiwar feelings ran particularly strong. The hardcover copy of this book, rereleased in 1996 (Simon & Schuster), tells the readers that it is simply a political satire. However, the pirated Internet versions do not contain this information about the book's intent, and instead present the book as an actual government report. In 1994, the author settled a copyright infringement lawsuit against the Liberty Lobby, which had published the book after insisting that *Report from Iron Mountain* could not be copyrighted since it was a government document.

"To the majority of the people in the patriots' community, this is not a piece of fiction," said R. J. Tavel, an attorney who had posted *Report from Iron Mountain* on his Internet site, the Sovereign Library. "These patriots are disseminating it to show the evil. Its very premise is to question whether global peace is desirable. Every time I hear from anybody out there about it, they tell me it's factual." However, after receiving a notice from the copyright owner, Tavel removed the book from his Internet site.[13]

Without a doubt, however, the most popular book read by members of the militia movement is *The Turner Diaries*. First published in 1978 and written by Andrew Macdonald, a pseudonym for William Pierce, head of the neo-Nazi organization the National Alliance, this blatantly racist book has sold hundreds of thousands of copies. *The Turner Diaries* is a work of fiction about a man named Earl Turner, who belongs to a group called the Organization. The story, which takes place in the 1990s, starts when the federal government bans the possession of firearms by private citizens and then begins raiding private homes in search of illegal guns (a very real militia fear). Earl Turner and others members of the Organization begin fighting back against the government in what eventually becomes a race war. A few quotes clearly demonstrate the strong racist flavor of this book.

One of the characters in the book, Katherine, a former government employee, is arrested because she owns a gun for protection and does not give it up as the government orders. While under arrest, she meets a member of the Organization and eventually joins up. "She learned the truth about the System's 'equality' hoax," the book says. "She gained an understanding of the unique historical role of the Jews as the ferment of decomposition of races and civilizations."[14]

During the race war, Earl Turner, as part of a salvage crew, inspects a black neighborhood. "We also found gruesome evidence of one way in which the Blacks have solved their food shortage: cannibalism. . . . The unfortunate Whites were dragged from their cars, taken into a nearby Black restaurant, butchered, cooked, and eaten."[15]

The novel ends with the Organization's victory. This victory, however, comes only after a mass slaughter of racial minorities, race traitors, and other "undesirables."

As spoken about in an earlier chapter, *The Turner Diaries* deeply affected Timothy McVeigh. He reportedly read the book many times and gave copies of it to his friends. His bombing of the Oklahoma City federal building eerily mirrors a fictional bombing in *The Turner Diaries* of the FBI Headquarters in Washington, D.C.

Another book that also has a wide readership among militia members is television evangelist Pat Robertson's *The New World Order*. As might be expected from the title, this book talks about (though it offers little proof) the militia's belief in an eventual global takeover by the New World Order.

A final book, one that militia members often hold in near reverence, is entitled *Citizens Rule Book*. This book has been for sale, or in some cases given away, at every militia function I have attended. The intent of *Citizens Rule Book* is to make readers aware that (in the author's opinion) jury members are above the law, that juries can disregard a judge's instructions and find a person not guilty, not because there is no evidence, but because the jurors do not believe the law is just. The book is filled with quotes from the Founding Fathers that the author believes support this idea, along with excerpts from various historical documents. One gets the feeling when reading this book that the author sees a huge government conspiracy to railroad people into prison under unjust laws.

In addition to books, there also exists a number of right-wing newspapers that militia members subscribe to and read religiously in order to get their news and information. The most popular of these is *The Spotlight*. Published weekly by the Liberty Lobby, *The Spotlight* says in its masthead: "You can trust *The Spotlight* to give you 'the other side of the news'—to report on events which are vital to your welfare but which would otherwise be hushed up or distorted by the controlled press. We make no attempt to give you 'both sides.' We'll leave the Establishment side to your daily newspaper, TV and radio."

After reading several issues, I found that *The Spotlight* certainly does offer an "alternate view" of the news. For example, the issues I read contained articles such as "UN Plans World Police Force" (with the subtitle: "If masters of the Global Plantation have their way, there will be a cop on every corner. Problem is, he won't speak English"), "Russia Could Deploy Weather Control System" (an article about a secret satellite system that can cause typhoons, tornadoes, and other weather disturbances), and "Nazi Hunter (Simon Wiesenthal) Named Hitler Collaborator."

While one might suppose that right-wing publications would stick together, at least one popular right-wing publication does not support the ideas in *The Spotlight*. *Soldier of Fortune* magazine said that *The Spotlight* habitually runs "misinformed writings, convoluted reasoning, and out-right fabrications of fact. Any crackpot sighting, no *matter* how insignificant, *Spotlight* will print it, misidentified photo and all."[16]

After reading several issues of *The Spotlight*, one is left with the feeling that its articles have the texture of a supermarket tabloid. Even the advertisements have this questionable quality, with several claiming amazing cures for arthritis, high blood pressure, and clogged arteries, and one advertisement that said for $25 you would be sent proof that the Catholic Church has been infiltrated by Jews, Masons, and homosexuals. However, as do many readers of the supermarket tabloids, many militia members believe everything printed in this newspaper.

In addition to newspapers, dozens of militia newsletters also exist. The larger ones, such as the Militia of Montana's *Taking Aim,* have a wide mail-order distribution. Others, such as the 7th Missouri Militia's *Modern Militiaman,* because they are available on the Internet, also have a wide distribution. Like the information sources already mentioned, though, these newsletters give militia members only the militia view of the news, with no countering views and no verification of facts.

While attending a preparedness/survival expo, I picked up a very interesting newsletter entitled *Flashpoint—A Newsletter Ministry of Texe Marrs.* The copy I purchased was devoted entirely to the belief that the federal government has already implanted biochips in many unsuspecting citizens, and intends to implant biochips in every citizen. According to the newsletter, these biochips, along with identifying who the individual is, can also track his or her movements and location, and, if necessary, turn the person into a mindless zombie who will do the bidding of the New World Order masters. And for readers who think that no one but a few fringe people would take these claims seriously, I would answer that from the contacts I have had with militia members, I have found that thousands of people believe this wholeheartedly. Timothy McVeigh is not the only person convinced that the government has implanted a biochip in him.

Although newsletters, newspapers, and videotapes are fine for information that is not time-critical, for a more immediate dissemination of information, militias also maintain a fairly large and complex fax network. When events occur that the militia leaders believe other militia members, the media, and politicians need to know about, they immediately send this information to dozens of other fax machines. For example, immediately following the Oklahoma City incident, Congressman Steve Stockman of Texas received a fax message about the bombing from a militia member in Michigan. Because of the time-zone differences, it appeared that the fax had been sent before the bombing, and consequently FBI agents became very interested, but soon discovered the time-zone discrepancy.

Computers, videotapes, the printed media, and faxes, however, are not the only media outlets for the militia message or the only sources of information for militia members. Many militia members also listen to call-in and talk programs on shortwave radio. There are literally dozens of these shortwave stations and dozens of programs that feature militia members and right-wing propaganda. The Patriot Network, for example, is a large group of radio stations, many on shortwave, that broadcast militia propaganda. Admittedly, most of these shortwave stations have a small market and serve only small communities, but, then, that is where most militia members live. There are also, of course, larger, and some very large, radio programs that feature material militia members want to hear about and believe in, such as Rush Limbaugh's show, G. Gordon Liddy's program, and the 100,000-watt World Wide Christian Radio in Nashville, Tennessee.

How large an audience does talk radio have? A 1993 *Times-Mirror* poll found that nearly 50 percent of the adults in the United States listen to talk radio.[17] When I went to hear Morris Dees speak, he told the audience, "The danger of the militias is that their message is being mainstreamed." He was referring to the problem he saw in that the militia's antigovernment rhetoric is now being discussed on respectable media outlets, and, through this, given a certain amount of apparent legitimacy, even though most of the claims they make are totally baseless.

In addition to talk radio, however, the introduction of cable television in many parts of America has also brought about the advent of public access television. For a small fee, a number of militias around the country have put together television programs that broadcast their beliefs. Again, as with radio, the audience and market are small, but the message, without the need for fact checking and verification, still gets out.

Actually, there are very few sources that militias have not tapped in order to disseminate their information to interested parties. Militias even use T-shirts to broadcast their message. At the preparedness/survival expos I have attended, there have always been a number of vendors selling T-shirts with militia slogans on them. The Militia of Montana, for example, sells T-shirts with slogans such as "The U.N.—Peace through Terror" and "God, Guts, and Guns Keep Us Free."

Finally, to spread their message, militia leaders crisscross the country every year giving talks at various gatherings where militia members congregate. I attended the preparedness/survival expo in Atlanta specifically because the top two leaders in the militia movement, Mark Koernke, from the Michigan Militia at Large, and John Trochmann of the Militia of Montana, were speaking at this event.

The day I was there, Mark Koernke spoke first. I would guess that the room in which he was scheduled to appear could probably hold 275 to 300 people, and every seat appeared filled. The audience, 100 percent white, could have been expecting a rock star to appear, so great were the anticipation and apprehension as the crowd waited for Koernke to show. As I looked around, I saw no designer clothing, no expensive shoes, no chic sunglasses. Everyone wore jeans, tennis shoes or work boots, and flannel or cotton shirts. The audience was America's white working class, no yuppies allowed.

The audience did not sit idle, though, as it waited for Koernke to appear. Preceding his arrival, people were treated to a warm-up act, a man playing a guitar and singing militia ballads.

When Koernke finally appeared, he received a noisy, boisterous welcome and then launched immediately into standard militia fare. He talked about how the establishment news media ignore the real size and message of the militia, and how militia membership is now in the millions. He then told the audience that Vice President Gore controlled something he called the Directorate of Central Law Enforcement, which controls all law enforcement in the United States (this was news to me), that the Persian Gulf crisis was created for profit, and that secret concentration camps were being built around the United States. He then showed a slide that he claimed was one of these secret concentration camps, discovered by militia members, buried deep in the DeSoto National Forest in southeastern Mississippi. He told the audience that the prison was one mile long and a one-fourth mile wide but sitting empty at present and awaiting prisoners. He also claimed that militia members said they saw white United Nations vehicles parked there. There was, however, a disturbing problem with the slide he showed the audience. This prison was supposed to be hidden deep in the DeSoto National Forest, yet the prison on the slide he showed appeared to be in a desert area. There was not a single tree in the picture anywhere. No one in the audience, however, appeared to notice this discrepancy.

Listening to his presentation, I found Mark Koernke to be an excellent public speaker with considerable skills for holding an audience. He repeatedly got the audience aroused and involved by asking for responses, such as, "Who are they building these prisons for?" The audience would shout in unison, "Us!" A man sitting behind me got so worked up he kept poking me with his finger and saying, "He's right, you know! He's right!" While waiting for Koernke to appear, I had overheard this man talking to the people around him about how the sons-of-bitches (he never did say who these people were) had just taken his house.

Mark Koernke was very well dressed in a nice suit and tie, and stood out among the crowd. He ended the talk with his trademark: "God bless the Republic! Death to the New World Order! We shall prevail!" The audience shouted this in unison with him. Following his talk, a dozen or so people ran up and wanted to speak with him. Any politician would have been delighted to get the type of response he got from the audience.

The next speaker, John Trochmann, was also dressed well, in a gray suit and cowboy boots. In his fifties, with a gray fringe of hair and a beard, Trochmann reminded me of a college professor. The room, as with Koernke, did not appear to have a vacant seat. Trochmann, however, did not possess Koernke's public speaking skills and continually stumbled over words. He gave much the same militia fare, claiming that the United States military no longer belongs to the United States but is now part of a global force, that the government has secret weapons such as energy beam guns that it will eventually use on militia members, and that the government's ultimate aim is to disarm the citizens. He did talk about a few conspiracy theories I had not yet heard. He claimed that the government adds fluoride to the water supply in order to keep people docile, that aircraft daily dump toxic chemicals into the atmosphere in order to kill people and thin out the population, and that lead-based paints were outlawed because spy satellites cannot see through them. He also spoke at length about preparedness and survival, for which he sells products through his Militia of Montana catalog business. As with Koernke, a dozen or so people rushed up after the talk to surround him and ask him questions.

Following these two militia leaders, Larry Pratt, executive director of Gun Owners of America, an organization farther to the right politically than the National Rifle Association, also gave a talk. His audience, though, appeared to be only half to two-thirds the size of those of Koernke and Trochmann. Pratt's talk also turned out to be much more politically oriented, and he openly hawked his organization to the audience. During his talk, he praised a number of politicians who support gun owners and condemned a number who do not. The audience appeared much more subdued during Pratt's presentation, but most seemed interested in what he said, which centered around the belief that private gun ownership in America was at present a very severely threatened right. Pratt is credited in Morris Dees's book *Gathering Storm* as being the person who originated the idea of forming civilian militias.

As readers can surmise from everything we have discussed so far in this chapter, constantly receiving large amounts of news and information almost exclusively from militia sources, with little or no other information sources to balance it, can lead to some serious misconceptions about the state of our country and the world. The following incident demonstrates this problem very clearly.

On 1 May 1996, Defense Secretary William J. Perry traveled to Holloman Air Force Base in New Mexico to attend what he thought would be a standard military ceremony. A training program had been established that would eventually involve 900 German pilots, who would be housed and trained at the base, which the German government had leased from the United States for ten years. This program was supposed to be part of an international agreement to show our appreciation for the many years Germany has allowed the U.S. military to have bases in their country.

News of the German pilots being housed at Holloman Air Force Base zinged over the Internet, flew across militia fax networks, and quickly became a hot subject of discussion on dozens of shortwave radio stations and on many large-audience radio talk shows. From the information they received from these sources, the militias and other far-right groups in America did not see this as a goodwill program. They saw it instead as the beginning of a conspiracy by the New World Order to bring large numbers of foreign soldiers to American bases. They believed the New World Order was doing this because, during the takeover of the United States, foreign soldiers would be much more willing to fire on American citizens than would U.S. servicemen. Militia members saw this program as simply part of a plot by the New World Order to further its scheme of global domination. Consequently, a loud, virulent protest against the training program, one that caught the military completely by surprise, arose almost immediately.

According to an article in the *Washington Post*, "Military officials say the episode demonstrates they have much to learn about how information flows beneath their radar coverage, zapping across media like the Internet, fax networks, and shortwave radio." No one in military public relations had expected this reaction.

"Our phones started ringing off the hook," said Lieutenant Colonel Virginia Pribyla, an Air Force spokeswoman. "It was driven by the talk shows, from California to Ohio, Salt Lake, Arizona, Texas, Arkansas, throughout the West and Midwest. . . . Many questions started off with the assumption something sinister was up, like, 'Is this a precursor to U.N. action in the U.S.?'"[18]

This episode demonstrates the narrowness of the information on which militia members make decisions, and the depth of the paranoia of many militia members. Once a person submerses himself or herself in the various conspiracy theories, all information received is filtered through these beliefs, and receiving only militia-produced information further enhances this. The government needs to realize and take into consideration the immediate and far-reaching grasp of the militia's information network, which they obviously did not in the preceding incident. Information that may have taken weeks or months to reach people a decade ago can now be disseminated to tens of thousands of people in just minutes.

"It's [the militia movement] moving even more swiftly today with our e-mail and World Wide Web hits," said Jack McLamb, a former Phoenix police officer and author of the militia book *Operation Vampire Killer 2000*. "We've got our fax network and our newsletter, the mail and the phone calls."[19]

Yet, as immediate and far-reaching as the militia information network is, it suffers from a significant problem in that the information it disseminates is often only rumor at best and hardly ever substantiated. This brings with it a very real danger, because most militia members believe that the information they receive from militia sources is a true picture of the world, such as Timothy McVeigh's near reverence for *The Turner Diaries,* and it is on this information that they base their decisions. While this danger is large enough with small local militias, the danger could be multiplied many times if, as we shall see in the next chapter, a national militia organization, with national communications capabilities, ever forms.

❖ ❖ ❖ ❖ ❖ ❖ ❖ ❖ **11**

A NATIONAL MILITIA

In October 1996, two of the founders of the Michigan Militia, Norm Olson and Ray Southwell, announced plans to hold a "Third Continental Congress." The three-day event, they hoped, would draw representatives from dozens of militias all over the United States who would meet and examine the problems they see with the present government and draft ideas on what should be done about them. One of the stated goals of this Third Continental Congress was also to form a "Republican Provisional Government," which would be ready to step in and take over the leadership of the United States when the present government collapsed.

"[Our] Congress will meet to discuss the crisis in America being caused by the present government, which patriots generally agree is corrupt and out of control," said Olson, who in 1995, along with Southwell, had been ousted from leadership of the Michigan Militia after the two men blamed the Oklahoma City bombing on the Japanese government.[1]

During the last three days of October 1996, militia representatives from eleven states met in the basement conference room of a Holiday Inn on the south side of Kansas City, Missouri. While the organizers of the Third Continental Congress had hoped to draw representatives from thirty or more states, many militia leaders stayed away because they feared that members of groups such as the Ku Klux Klan or Aryan Nations would show up and bring about a police raid.

Although the Congress did not develop into the huge gathering of militia representatives the organizers had hoped for, it nevertheless did show that there is a feeling of unity and a movement among a number of groups for a national militia organization. This alone should be enough to alarm the American public. The formation of a national militia organization would mean that America would be faced with the possibility of there being in this country a private army of thousands, and possibly tens of thousands, of heavily armed people under the leadership of individuals who subscribe to the wildest of conspiracy theories. This is a recipe for a disaster of unbelievable magnitude.

At the conclusion of their gathering, the attendees at the Third Continental Congress issued a statement of grievances. In this statement, the representatives from the various militias accused the federal courts of becoming an imperial judiciary that has violated the sovereignty of the people. They accused the President of making himself an elected monarch. They accused Congress of being taken over by negligent career politicians who have demonstrated a disregard for the Constitution. And finally, they accused state governments of abandoning their constitutional responsibility to not "make any thing but gold and silver coin a tender in payment of debts."[2] Because of all the problems they saw in the present government, representatives at the Third Continental Congress stated that they believe the present government of the United States will soon fall, and when that occurs, they are ready to step in and take over leadership of the country. As stated earlier, this type of grandiose and delusional thinking, which unfortunately could be backed up by thousands of armed citizens at their command, shows the real danger of a national militia.

This gathering also demonstrated another danger of a national militia. Along with leaders from thirteen states, the congress in Kansas City also brought together a fringe element from across the country, individuals who did not think the leaders of the Congress were aggressive enough or acting quickly enough. Seven people who attended the Third Continental Congress broke away and formed their own cell, which then decided to take action against what they saw as a plot by agents of the New World Order. One of the members of this cell, Bradford Glover, who in a 1995 newspaper interview identified himself as Brigadier General of the 7th Division of the United States Constitutional Militia, had stated several times that he believed the United States government was part of a conspiracy to bring about a New World Order that would be run by the United Nations.

The seven-person cell, five men and two women, became convinced that United Nations troops, who would eventually be used in this takeover of the United States, were training at U.S. military bases, and that Fort Hood, Texas, was one of these United Nations training sites. The break-away cell, upon deciding it had to do something to stop this, concocted a plan to attack Fort Hood during its annual Fourth of July open house cere-monies. They knew Fort Hood would be host to at least 50,000 visitors during its annual "Freedom Fest" celebration. In order to finance this at-tack, a husband and wife, both members of the breakaway cell, reportedly sold the trucking firm they owned.

Fortunately, the police had foreseen the potential threat of a national militia conference attracting and bringing together radical militia mem-bers from across the country. So the authorities sent undercover agents to attend the Third Continental Congress, and, while there, they discovered and infiltrated this breakaway cell.

"They are not to be taken lightly as a bunch of crazies," said Lieu-tenant Richard Coffey of the Missouri Highway Patrol, whose officers in-filtrated the cell. "They feel a responsibility to fight what they believe is a worldwide conspiracy where the United Nations will become a world po-lice force and trample people's rights."[3]

The Third Continental Congress, as well as holding the meeting at Kansas City, Missouri, in October 1996, also held rallies in January 1997 at Independence, Missouri, and in April 1997 at Shelbyville, Kentucky. While attending these rallies, the breakaway cell began compiling intelli-gence about various other military bases believed to be training sites for United Nations troops. They also scrutinized the security at utility loca-tions near the suspected training bases, such as water and power plants. In addition, the breakaway cell began finalizing plans for their attack on Fort Hood. The authorities, however, through their undercover agents, had been tracking the group and knew of its planned assault on Fort Hood.

On 4 July 1997, authorities arrested Bradford Glover and Michael Dorsett while the two men were reportedly en route to carry out the at-tack on Fort Hood. Following the arrest, the police found that the two men were carrying suspected explosives, two rifles, five pistols, a home-made silencer, 1600 rounds of ammunition, night vision equipment, and bulletproof vests. The authorities also knew through their undercover agents that the men's plan had been to attack Fort Hood and then flee to a remote area of Colorado, while other members of the cell would be wait-ing to hide them. The police, therefore, also arrested a man and his wife who were members of the breakaway cell and waiting in Creede, Colorado, where Glover and Dorsett intended to flee. The couple allegedly supplied the undercover officers who had infiltrated the cell with guns and ammunition, and as a consequence, the authorities charged the man and wife with illegal possession of a machine gun.

In addition, the police arrested another husband and wife, also members of the cell, in Wichita, Kansas. Authorities charged this couple with providing undercover officers with a dozen pipe bombs. Finally, the police arrested the last member of the breakaway cell in Wisconsin. They charged him with possession of two pipe bombs and two machine guns.

As many of the incidents in this book very clearly demonstrate, one of the major dangers of the militia movement lies in the fact that it attracts a highly motivated radical fringe. Consequently, a national militia would multiply this problem many times by bringing together members of this radical fringe from all over the United States. As they did in the incident just mentioned, these fringe members, because they are unstable, will often feel that the larger organization is not aggressive enough or moving quickly enough. Consequently, they will decide to break away and form their own action cells, answerable to no one.

Fortunately, however, a national militia remains just a dream of militia leaders such as Norm Olson and Ray Southwell. Yet, although the Third Continental Congress did not forge the national organization it hoped for, it is likely that in the future, more attempts will be made to create an organization such as Olson describes. "As you may know," said Norm Olson, "my intent in forging the idea of a Third Continental Congress was to bring together the militias under a national command authority, subordinate to the Congress of the Provisional Government."[4]

Interestingly, Olson's vision of a national militia runs completely counter to the philosophy of "leaderless resistance," discussed in a previous chapter and endorsed, though not necessarily implemented, by many of the armed civilian militias in the United States. Those who endorse the theory of leaderless resistance maintain that any militia group with an open membership and clearly recognizable leaders becomes easily infiltrated by government informants, and also easily neutralized, since the government knows where to strike and whom to eliminate. A national militia, the argument follows, would therefore be very easy to crush. Supporters of leaderless resistance believe that only small, closed cells can be safe from government infiltration and neutralization.

However, as strong an argument as the proponents of leaderless resistance make for the effectiveness and imperviousness of their organizational structure, the idea that the militia should consist only of small, anonymous cells with no leaders flies in the face of the egos and ambitions of many of America's present militia leaders. These men have often been nobodies before taking over leadership of a militia. Many held small, meaningless jobs and had never received any recognition in their lives. For example, Mark Koernke, a militia leader in Michigan, was previously a janitor, while John Trochmann of the Militia of Montana was reportedly a mechanic. But now, in positions of leadership in the militia, they have become media celebrities, sought after for interviews and opinions. At the preparedness/survival expo in Atlanta, I witnessed the near reverence in which these two men were held by members of the audience. Once a person experiences this type of adoration, it would become nearly impossible just to give it up and disappear into an anonymous cell. Quite the contrary, it is more likely that many militia leaders will want to seek even more authority and more recognition. A drive by such leaders to form a national militia organization naturally follows from this, since heading such an organization would greatly broaden their authority, recognition, and influence. Consequently, as attempted by the Third Continental Congress, even more efforts to form a national militia organization will likely occur in the future.

The Third Continental Congress, however, was not the only time local militias have come together to work as a combined force. In July 1995, a number of local militia leaders attended the first meeting of the National Command Seminar, held in South Dakota. From this gathering, the attendees formed a seven-member National Commanders Council and an umbrella organization called the Tri-State Militia. (This organization eventually fell apart when the government revealed during the trial of Ray Lampley, discussed in Chapter 2, that one of the Tri-State Militia leaders, Colonel John Parsons, had been in the employ of the FBI for some time. Parsons reportedly justified his taking of money from the FBI by arguing that if he had not done so, he would have been forced to close down the Tri-State Militia's Communication Information Center and go back to work as a truck driver.) In October 1995, at the second meeting of the National Command Seminar, one hundred leaders from militias all across the United States gathered at Mountain Spring, Texas, to talk about and analyze the damage done to their image by the Oklahoma City bombing.

On 14 April 1996, representatives of a dozen militias signed a document they called the Knob Creek Declaration, which called for a peaceful resolution to the Montana Freemen standoff. In 1997, an organization called the National Confederation of Citizen Militias worked with the authorities to defuse the standoff with Richard McLaren and his Republic of Texas supporters. Also in 1997, a group called the United States Militia Alliance worked with authorities to bring about an end to a standoff with the police in Roby, Illinois, which we will discuss in a later chapter.

Recently, militias from Alabama, Florida, Georgia, Mississippi, North Carolina, South Carolina, Tennessee, and Virginia formed an organization called the Alliance of the Southeastern States Militia. Their official Articles of Alliance state in part: "Therefore, we the militiamen of the Southeastern United States, do affirm before God that we have entered an alliance against tyranny. . . . We will consider it an act of war to surrender any more of the sovereignty of this nation to the United Nations. Thus, the Southeastern States Alliance will fight the New World Order, and any of its proponents, to the bitter end."[5]

Other multimilitia groups include the American Constitutional Militia Network, which claims to have links with militia groups in fourteen states, and the United States Theatre Command, which claims to have members all over the United States and also has an Articles of Alliance identical to the Southeastern States Alliance. In an attempt to encourage these types of alliances, the 52nd Missouri Militia has designed a medal that it awards to militias that take part in joint militia operations.

Fortunately, none of these organizations or gatherings have ever been able to actually bring together many separate militias under a single command for any lengthy period of time. The leaders of many of the small militias apparently do not want to surrender their authority to a national or even regional organization. However, it is human nature for individuals in positions of power to want to garner more power; consequently, it is likely that attempts to form a national militia will continue.

Therefore, both state and federal authorities should continue to monitor this trend, as they did with the Third Continental Congress in Kansas City. This is imperative for the public safety because the formation of a national militia organization, besides the threat of bringing together likeminded fringe elements from all over the country, also brings with it the very real danger of the sudden emergence of a private army in this country of thousands, and perhaps tens of thousands, of heavily armed people under the leadership of individuals who subscribe to the wildest of conspiracy theories. The likelihood that an organization of this sort could cause a tragedy of immense consequences, particularly, as we shall see in the next chapter, when they have the support of members of Congress and others, is almost unquestionable.

◆ ◆ ◆ ◆ ◆ ◆ ◆ **12**

THE POWER AND INFLUENCE OF MILITIAS

Harry Tootle wanted to be someone important, and his failure to accomplish this did not result from his not trying. Tootle ran and lost in bids to become a United States Senator, Clark County (Nevada) Sheriff, and chief of the Cherokee Nation in Oklahoma. In his attempts at public office, he used the campaign slogan: "Use Your Noodle, Vote for Tootle."[1]

Along with aspiring to high public office, Tootle also operated a UHF television station in Clark County, Nevada, on which, after announcing to the audience his militia membership, Tootle would broadcast his right-wing version of world affairs. He used the television station to warn his audience of excesses and abuses of power by the federal government.

In November 1995, according to later court testimony, Tootle drove to Larry's Villa, a topless bar in Las Vegas, to meet with an informant who reportedly had information about a government cover-up of the Oklahoma City bombing, information that Tootle hoped to use on his television program *Tootle Vision*. However, rather than obtaining this information, Tootle instead found himself incarcerated in the Clark County jail on charges of assault with a deadly weapon, carrying a concealed weapon, and resisting a police officer.

According to his court testimony, a bouncer at the topless bar said he walked over to Tootle's car, which was sitting in the parking lot, reportedly to see if Tootle was being bothered by a nearby panhandler. The bouncer testified that when he approached the car, Tootle made a mumbled claim about being in the FBI and warned the bouncer that he was "in the hot zone" and could get shot. Tootle then allegedly pulled a gun on the bouncer and afterward fled into a nearby apartment complex. Witnesses said Tootle appeared intoxicated.

When the police arrived, Tootle did not try to reason with or talk to the officers. He instead hid behind a large trash bin in the apartment complex. He came out and surrendered only after being surrounded by the officers.

Tootle, however, told the jury a different version of what happened. He said that the man who appeared to be a panhandler was actually the informant he had gone there to meet, and that he ran into the apartment complex in an attempt to catch up with the informant, who had fled from the bouncer. Tootle said he also ran because he feared that the bouncer might be an assassin with orders to kill him in order to keep the Oklahoma City bombing conspiracy a secret.

The jury, though, apparently did not believe Tootle's version of what happened. They convicted him of assault with a deadly weapon and resisting a police officer. A judge later sentenced Tootle to five years of probation. Following the conviction, *Tootle Vision* went off the air and Harry Tootle moved to Idaho.

Harry Tootle certainly is not the only militia member with a desire to run for public office, even though, paradoxically, militia leaders regularly denounce the American political system as corrupt and evil. John Moore, commander of the 1st Missouri Volunteers, ran in the Republican congressional primary for the seat then occupied by Democrat Richard Gephardt. He placed third among eight candidates. Militia member Joseph Keller ran in the Democratic primary, also for Gephardt's seat. He received 20 percent of the vote. Eddie Ebacher, a militia leader in St. Cloud, Minnesota, who claims that his militia has 25,000 members statewide (though law enforcement officers believe the membership numbers are much less), announced in 1997 that he intended to run for mayor of St. Cloud in 1998. He had made a previous run for the mayor's job in 1993 but lost in the primary election.

In November 1997, J. J. Johnson, cofounder of the Ohio Unorganized Militia, and one of the few blacks in a position of leadership in the militia movement, moved to Las Vegas and announced that he might run for Clark County Sheriff in the 1998 election. Johnson was one of the nationally recognized militia leaders who spoke before a United States Senate subcommittee in 1995.

"Clark County has the highest rate of IRS raids in the country," said Johnson. "Perhaps Clark County needs a new sheriff."[2] Although, when making his announcement about a possible run for sheriff, Johnson claimed to have severed his militia ties, the Southern Poverty Law Center reports he still speaks at militia gatherings.

These examples aside, the power and influence of the militia movement does not come from its members holding or attempting to hold public office, but rather from other individuals holding or attempting to hold public office who seek the support of the militia, either through appearing at militia functions or by supporting issues important to the militia. And there are many who do this.

An article in the militia newsletter *Modern Militiaman* stated: "One thing that did impress me about Alabama was the fact that we had a candidate for the U.S. Senate who openly supported the militia movement; he lost his ass in the primary after receiving 10,000 votes. That tells me that even though we lost, we still have 10,000 quiet supporters for what we do. . . . This man was not afraid to come to our militia rally, be photographed, do interviews and say what was on his mind."[3]

However, not just prospective officeholders support the militia. Many of those already holding public office also give the militias their support, or support issues important to the militia movement. State Representative Debra Whyman of Michigan sponsored a resolution calling for state opposition to any "abdication of national sovereignty" to the United Nations, and included references to the New World Order in the proposed resolution. "For whatever reason," said William Ballenger, publisher of *Inside Michigan Politics*, "she has chosen to embrace certain cause celebres of the right."[4]

State Representative Matt Brainaid of Montana sponsored a bill that would make armed civilian militias legal in Montana. He also introduced a resolution in the 1995 Montana Legislature, stating that the right to keep and bear arms is essential for the protection of the people of Montana.

On 12 March 1997, Oklahoma State Representative Charles Key sent out a letter to the general public asking for contributions. This letter was not asking for support for his political campaign, however, but rather for contributions to pay for the expense of impaneling an independent grand jury to investigate the federal government's alleged cover-up in the Oklahoma City bombing investigation. Representative Key pointed out in the letter numerous items that he considers extremely suspicious about the bombing incident, such as the fact that none of the ATF agents assigned to the Alfred P. Murrah Federal Building were inside when the bomb went off, that six different people are certain they saw the bomb squad near the federal building just before the explosion, that the FBI had reportedly allowed the earlier New York City World Trade Center bombing to occur even though they could have stopped it, and that the federal government pressured the ABC network not to air a news story about the government having prior knowledge of the Oklahoma City bombing. "The people couldn't handle the truth," Key claims the United States Justice Department told ABC officials.[5]

"This could be the most important case in our history," Key told a group during a talk he gave at Missouri Southern State College, "and there are too many questions that haven't been answered."[6] This belief in some type of cover-up of the Oklahoma City bombing by the federal government is a conspiracy theory with a large number of adherents in the militia movement. As a result, this attempt at a private investigation by Representative Key has been greeted by applause from many members of the militia.

Representative Key is not the only politician to question the federal government's handling of the Oklahoma City bombing case. Colorado State Senator Charles Duke, according to an article in the *Denver Post*, "drew ire the week of the bombing when he suggested that it might have been the work of the federal government intent on framing members of informally organized right-wing militias." Senator Duke also stated, "If these guys [McVeigh and Nichols] are the ultimate masterminds, which I don't personally believe, then they need to pay the price. If not, it begs the question, 'Who?'"[7] In addition to these statements, the Internet web page of the Stark County (Ohio) Militia contained a letter from Senator Duke. In the letter, Duke harangues about another issue dear to the hearts of militia members: the gun control measures in House Bill 3610. "It is too late to stop this from going into law, because Congress has adjourned for the election season," Senator Duke's letter said. "The lapdog media did their job by stonewalling, again, the information concerning this confiscation of your guns and your rights."[8] House Bill 3610 contained a provision banning gun ownership for anyone convicted of domestic violence.

An article written by Senator Duke also appeared in the January–February 1997 issue of *Modern Militiaman*, a rather radical militia newsletter. In the article, Senator Duke claims that government agents are making illegal searches of citizens' homes and cars, which the citizens unknowingly allow to occur because they do not know they are illegal.

In addition to his letters and articles, Senator Duke also addressed another very popular militia concern when he gave a talk at the national militia gathering in Mountain Spring, Texas, in October 1995. He told those in attendance that they should lobby for a law that would require all bills introduced in Congress to prove there is a constitutional authority for the proposed law.

State Senator Don Rogers of California has had his name included on militia flyers and has appeared at events where the other speakers included former Ku Klux Klan members. Rogers also introduced a resolution in the California State Legislature asking for safeguards against a world takeover by the United Nations, and, in addition, wrote an amendment to the California Constitution that guarantees the right of citizens to bear arms.

Many of Rogers's actions in support of militia causes have made his fellow politicians uncomfortable. "There is no basis in fact of a threat of a takeover by the United Nations," said fellow state senator Richard Polanco. "This measure is just a perpetuation of paranoia in individuals interested in creating a lot of disturbances in this country."[9]

Militia support from elected officials is not confined to legislators alone, however. Graham County (Arizona) Sheriff Richard Mack sued the United States government in order to avoid having to enforce the Brady Bill. Because of his anti-gun-control stance, Sheriff Mack has become a hero and a very popular figure in the militia movement. Actually, there is a surprisingly large number of sheriffs and other law enforcement officers who support the militia movement, or issues popular with militia members, particularly in the West and Northwest. Federal employees working in these areas of the country have occasionally found themselves facing armed militia members who would not allow them to perform their duties. These militia members, the federal employees discovered, were backed by the local sheriff. One federal agency even felt the necessity of giving its employees instructions on what to do if they were arrested for attempting to carry out their job functions.

On a national level, the most vocal supporter of the militia movement is Republican Congresswoman Helen Chenoweth of Idaho. Just days after being sworn in as a member of Congress, Chenoweth began writing a proposed law that would require federal officers to obtain local approval before engaging in any law enforcement function. According to a *New York Times* article, after Chenoweth's election in 1994, a former Ku Klux Klan leader in Georgia hailed her win as a victory for "race-based campaigns." The former Ku Klux Klan member's comments were very likely brought on by Congresswoman Chenoweth's own comments: "White men are an endangered species. I absolutely believe that, what with affirmative action and everything."[10] In addition, also immediately following Congresswoman Chenoweth's election, the Militia of Montana began selling videos of her speeches concerning the danger of a one-world government control of natural resources.

After only two months in office, Chenoweth organized a hearing in Boise, Idaho, that she entitled "In the Matter of Excessive Use of Government Force." In her opening remarks, she told those assembled, "We have a democracy when the government is afraid of the people."[11] During the hearings she questioned government witnesses about their use of "black helicopters," a belief that is at the center of most of the paranoid fantasies of the militia movement: the black helicopters of the New World Order that swoop down on unsuspecting citizens.

Since Chenoweth has been a vocal supporter of the militia movement, the press naturally asked for her opinion of the Oklahoma City bombing. She told the *Coeur d'Alene Press*, "We must begin to look at the public policies that may be pushing people too far."[12] She told another newspaper, "I'm not willing to condemn militias." The newspaper later said in an editorial: "Whether she realizes it or not, Chenoweth is quickly becoming the 'poster child' for the militias."[13]

During her two terms as a congresswoman, Chenoweth has sponsored or cosponsored several bills and resolutions that address core issues in the militia movement. For example, she sponsored a resolution condemning the deployment of U.S. military personnel in the service of the United Nations in the former Yugoslav Republic of Macedonia. The resolution also called on the President to take command of all military personnel participating in United Nations operations, and to ensure that they wear only a U.S. military uniform and carry only U.S. military identity cards. Chenoweth has also cosponsored resolutions that would abolish the Internal Revenue Service; one that would establish English as the official language of the United States; one that would not allow a person born in the United States automatically to become a citizen unless one parent is a citizen, is lawfully in the United States, or has a lawful immigration status at the time of the birth; and a resolution permitting the display of the Ten Commandments in government offices and courthouses.

Congresswoman Chenoweth, however, is not the only politician on a national level who speaks out for the militia movement. Democratic Congresswoman Karen L. Thurman of Florida requested that the United States Justice Department respond to a letter she received claiming that the government had rented an office in Dallas for the purpose of taking out the militias. When questioned about this, a press secretary for Congresswoman Thurman said that the congresswoman was just passing on a constituent's question.[14]

According to an article in *Sierra* magazine, Congressman Don Young of Alaska circulated a letter among his colleagues that said, "Is Boutros Boutros-Ghali zoning land in your district?" In his letter to fellow members of Congress, Young reportedly said, "Our military personnel are giving up their uniforms for the baby blue beret of the United Nations. Now we find out that an area on U.S. soil the size of the state of Colorado [Yellowstone National Park] has been designated as part of the United Nations' Biosphere Reserve program. . . . This, we are told by the Administration, is the New World Order."[15]

In September 1996, the House Resources Committee passed Congressman Young's "American Land Sovereignty Protection Act," which would have required Congressional approval for any future international designations, even though an official from the Interior Department tried to explain to the members of the committee that the World Heritage designation by the United Nations has no force or any effect on sovereignty. Congressman Young's bill was defeated in the House of Representatives by a vote of 246 to 178.

Congressman Steve Stockman of Texas, who reportedly has had militia members working for his election, sent a letter to Attorney General Janet Reno concerning a reported impending raid by federal law enforcement officers against militia groups. In addition, Congressman Stockman also wrote an article for *Guns & Ammo* magazine, in which he suggested that the Clinton Administration planned the deadly 1993 raid on the Branch Davidians in Waco because they hoped to create wide public support for gun control. "These men, women and children were burned to death because they owned guns that the government did not wish them to have," Congressman Stockman wrote. "Waco was supposed to be a way for the Bureau of Alcohol, Tobacco, and Firearms and the Clinton administration to prove a need for a ban on so-called 'assault weapons.'"[16] This belief about Waco is another conspiracy theory widely circulated in the militia movement.

At a preparedness/survival expo I attended in Atlanta, I picked up several press releases from the office of Congressman Ron Paul of Texas.

Congressman Paul is a sponsor of House Resolution 1146, which would end United States participation in the United Nations and diplomatic immunity for United Nations envoys in the United States. In a 2 September 1997 press release concerning payment of back dues owed by the United States to the United Nations, Congressman Paul said, "First and foremost, Congressmen take an oath to uphold the Constitution, and there is nothing in the Constitution which authorizes Congress to tax the hard-earned money of Americans to ship off to power-hungry international bureaucrats. . . . The United Nations is a worthless drain on our scarce national resources." An article by Congressman Paul, again bashing the United Nations, appeared in the March 1998 issue of the Militia of Montana newsletter *Taking Aim*.

While attending the preparedness/survival expo in Atlanta, I also listened to a talk given by Larry Pratt, executive director of Gun Owners of America. After mentioning the names of several politicians in sympathy with gun owners, Pratt introduced a local politician in the audience. The politician, Pat Glanton, a Republican running for Lt. Governor of Georgia, stood up to be recognized and was obviously at the gathering looking for support from militia members.

It is not just law enforcement officers and politicians, however, who give strength and influence to the militia movement. Celebrities can also do their part for the cause. In the newspaper *The Spotlight*, which is read by many militia members and contains many militia-related articles, there is an advertisement with a picture of actor John Wayne. According to the advertisement, John Wayne was a longtime subscriber to *The Spotlight*.

Fortunately, none of the individuals mentioned in this chapter have had enough power or influence to push through resolutions or bills favoring the militia movement, or the power to make the militia a huge force in this country. Yet the support these politicians give to what are basically private armies, and the shared belief of these politicians in many of the wild and baseless conspiracy theories espoused by the militia, should be a frightening wake-up call to the American public, and should certainly make the public want to scrutinize political candidates much more closely.

$$\text{❖ ❖ ❖ ❖ ❖ ❖ ❖ ❖}$$ **13**

MILITIAS AND THE LAW

Emilio Ippolito was at one time Hillsborough County's (Florida) largest property owner. But because of legal squabbles with the government over code violations at the low-income housing he owned, Ippolito eventually lost most of his property. Following this, he and his daughter, Susan Mokdad, decided to set up the Constitutional Common Law Court of We the People. Once they had established this new court, Ippolito then appointed himself as chief justice.

What began as a two-person operation soon gathered followers, and eventually, the new court system had a dozen or so members. The group described themselves at times as vigilantes, at times as freemen, and at times as militia men. Believing that the existing federal and state court systems were a sham, Ippolito's group began holding their own court sessions in public libraries, at a Howard Johnson's, and one time they held a meeting in a warehouse, where, reportedly, forty members of the Brevard County Militia stood guard.

Asserting that all other courts had no authority, Ippolito's group began sending official-looking documents to state and federal court officials and employees, charging them with treason. The group even sent such a document to a grand jury foreman, who is not a court official or employee, but simply an ordinary citizen summonsed to jury duty.

Because the group also threatened several IRS agents, placed phony liens against various pieces of property these agents owned, and because the IRS had received intelligence that a militia group intended to occupy an IRS office in Florida, the government sent IRS agent Robert Quigley undercover to infiltrate Ippolito's group. Playing the role of a tax evader with a strong dislike for the government, Quigley took the name of Robert Chapman and joined Ippolito's newly formed court. At one meeting he attended and secretly recorded, members told Quigley that any government agent they caught trying to infiltrate the group would be hanged for treason.

At one of their meetings, members of the Constitutional Common Law Court of We the People discussed kidnapping a judge, trying him for treason, and then hanging him. They believed this would make the people respect their court. They also discussed sending ten armed militia members into the Orlando federal courthouse to kidnap a judge and hold him for a prisoner exchange, which would involve swapping him for several members of their group who had been arrested.

"If you have 10 or 12 people armed," Quigley taped one of the members of Ippolito's group saying, "I believe you could go in [the courthouse], arrest the judge and take him out in handcuffs."[1]

The Constitutional Common Law Court of We the People also somehow discovered the address of the foreman of the grand jury that had indicted several members of Ippolito's group, and they sent this jury foreman a letter saying that they had charged him with treason, and that he would be put to death if found guilty. During his investigation, Quigley reported to his supervisors that he believed the group also intended to harm other grand jury members if they refused to rescind the indictments lodged against the group's members.

Ippolito's group, however, did not restrict itself only to local matters. The Constitutional Common Law Court of We the People also mailed documents to Washington, D.C., charging the President, Attorney General Janet Reno, and members of the Supreme Court with treason.

In March 1996, the police arrested Ippolito, his daughter, and six members of Ippolito's group, charging them with conspiracy and obstruction of justice. The group went to trial on 3 June 1997. However, just minutes after their trial started, Ippolito leaped up out of his seat and leveled his own charges at U.S. District Judge Steven Merryday.

"I beg to be recognized in an orderly fashion because the Constitution demands that I defend myself," Ippolito told Judge Merryday. "You have been charged with treason. I say this with a heavy heart."[2]

Because of previous warnings given to Ippolito about outbursts he had made during pretrial sessions, Judge Merryday immediately had bailiffs remove Ippolito from the courtroom. "I charge you with compounded acts of treason!" Ippolito shouted at Judge Merryday as bailiffs escorted him from the courtroom. "I say it with humility."[3] Judge Merryday issued an order that Ippolito would watch the remainder of the trial on closed-circuit television.

The following week, however, Judge Merryday brought Ippolito back into the courtroom and asked him if he would behave himself were he allowed to return to the courtroom. "The jury needs to know why the court has not allowed me to present my own defense!" Ippolito shouted. "The jury needs to know they have been charged with treason! The jury needs to know you have been charged with treason, and the prosecutor also!"[4] Bailiffs again removed Ippolito from the courtroom, and he watched the remainder of the trial on closed-circuit television.

In his opening statement, the prosecutor charged that the defendants threatened not just judges, prosecutors, grand jurors, and trial jurors, but also witnesses who might be called to testify against them. "You will find the defendants threatened people for simply doing their jobs," the prosecutor told the jurors.[5]

The defense, on the other hand, claimed the defendants had not committed any crimes, but were simply exercising their First Amendment right of free speech. "Our clients are guilty of nothing more than petitioning the government for the redress of their grievances," said Ippolito's attorney. "And that, of course, is their constitutional right."[6]

As the trial started, prosecutors told the court that members of the Constitutional Common Law Court of We the People considered themselves to be a special class of citizens, and, as such, they believed they were not subject to any state or federal laws. The Constitution was the only law they recognized. They also believed, the prosecutor said, that the Constitution authorizes citizens to form their own courts.

In a tape played during the trial, Ippolito could be heard saying to members of his group during one of their organizational meetings, "You are the highest authority here. This is powerful, what you're doing. This is so powerful that it's almost frightening."[7]

Ippolito's group reportedly believed that, according to the Constitution, the state and federal courts have no authority over citizens unless the citizens give them that authority. Without the citizens' approval of their jurisdiction, the entire court system, the group believed, committed treason if it tried to exert any authority over them. At one meeting, Ippolito told listeners, "If you don't believe in the Constitution, I'll charge you with treason right here and now."[8]

During testimony at the trial, the head of the U.S. Attorney's Office in Orlando told the court that one afternoon he confronted two members of Ippolito's group who had come to the federal courthouse and demanded to talk to the grand jury. After he refused and sent them away, he said he received documents charging him with treason.

The prosecutor also told the jurors that the Constitutional Common Law Court of We the People in both Tampa and Orlando were "counterfeit kangaroo courts presided over by militia men and vigilantes."[9] The defense, in response to this, insisted that members of Ippolito's group were simply talking tough and never really meant to harm anyone.

The victims, however, did not feel the defendants were just talking tough. Hillsborough Circuit Court Judge Dennis Alvarez testified that he began carrying a gun soon after being accused of treason by the group. He also said he received a warrant issued by the Constitutional Common Law Court of We the People that authorized the local militia to arrest him. "This was not something I laughed at or took calmly," Judge Alvarez said. Judge Alvarez told the court that after he received the warrant he knew "we were no longer playing paper games. They were serious."[10] Ippolito's group also sent other judges notices that unless they surrendered themselves to trial before the Constitutional Common Law Court of We the People, they would face physical arrest by militia members at their homes or places of business, which the recipients realized could turn into dangerous confrontations.

On 13 August 1997, after deliberating for four days, the jury found Ippolito, his daughter, and five members of the Constitutional Common Law Court of We the People guilty of most of the charges. The jury acquitted one of the defendants of all charges.

"The common law court has been handed a resounding defeat," said the lead defense attorney after the verdicts were read. "We honestly believed we were covered by the First Amendment and had the right to complain about the way the courts are. The jury didn't see it that way."[11]

While this incident may sound to most readers like just an isolated group of extremists, central Florida is by no means the only location in the United States where such "common law courts" have sprung up. In April 1997, the *San Francisco Examiner* reported that Bay Area judges had been served with phony warrants, orders to appear, and writs from right-wing "common law courts." In August 1997, a common law court in Topeka, Kansas, held a hearing and voted to impeach a United States District Judge.

In Orange County, California, a group calling itself "Our One Supreme Court" notified a local judge that they intended to hold a common law court hearing to determine whether he should remain in office as a judge. He would, they warned, be subject to whatever action the court decided upon. This group also attempted to obtain information on property owned by ten Orange County judges, reportedly for the purpose of filing phony liens against these pieces of property. The Orange County Chief Assistant District Attorney said, "It's definitely an organization we're interested in."[12]

In Arlington, Texas, the Common Law Court of Pleas, meeting at a local motel, issued a judgment of $93,492,827,008,096, in gold, against the United States, the Federal Reserve Board, the International Monetary Fund, and the Holy See of the Roman Catholic Church. The court decreed that this was the amount that had been plundered from Texas since the United States illegally made Texas a state in 1845. The same court also issued an eviction order against the Internal Revenue Service, which they gave just thirty days to leave Texas.

In Yellville, Arkansas, Tom Prahl lives by himself in a small trailer. Although at one time a federal employee, Prahl now lives on disability checks and is judge of a common law court called "We the People." He and a dozen members of We the People have attempted to indict government employees and order them to appear in his common law court. When one of the members of Prahl's group found himself facing a bank foreclosure on his home, the We the People common law court ordered the bank to appear in the common law court to justify their actions.

"Nobody showed up," Prahl said, apparently surprised, since most common law court adherents truly believe they have a legally constituted court system. "So we had to go to their courts, and the guy lost his property."[13]

Actions taken by common law courts, however, have often been over incidents much smaller than a foreclosure. Common law courts have issued indictments and arrest warrants against government officials for infractions as minor as parking tickets. While these courts, of course, have no real legal standing, they believe they do. Their supporters have often researched the law and the Constitution extensively and believe they have found a legal basis for their operation.

An article in *The New York Times* stated: "The supporters of common law courts reject state and federal statutes and all constitutional amendments except the Bill of Rights, and they base their authority on highly selective interpretations of English common law, Bible passages, United States case law and the Constitution."[14] At present, there are believed to be common law courts active in almost every state. And while these courts like to put forth the appearance of being legitimate courts, they are not, and seldom do more than issue nonenforceable findings against government officials and others. Few people other than those associated with common law courts take them seriously enough to believe that they will actually receive any type of legal remedies from them.

The common law professed to be enforced by these common law courts has its roots, as does the American legal system, in the English common law. English common law crimes were actions that all people had accepted as wrong for centuries. For example, everyone knew that robbery was wrong and always had been, as were burglary and murder. In early English history, though, there were no written legal codes that defined all crimes, and much of the population could not read anyway. Instead, there was simply the common law that had come down through the centuries by oral tradition, custom, and court rulings. English common law was a simple legal system that was understandable even to the poorly educated. An act was wrong because everyone knew it was and always had been.

According to *Blackstone's Commentaries*, "[The authority of] all of these doctrines that are not set down in any written statute or ordinance, but depend merely upon immemorial usage, that is, upon the common law for their support . . . rests entirely upon general reception and usage: and the only method of proving, that this or that maxim is a rule of common law, is by showing that it hath been always the custom to observe it."[15]

However, in the case of *U.S. v. Hudson & Goodwin*, the U.S. Supreme Court held that the federal courts could not punish someone merely because he or she committed a common law crime. The court said there had to be a written statute passed by Congress making the action a crime.

Importantly, however, to adherents of the common law movement, the common law did not include such things as income tax filing violations, building or zoning codes, and traffic laws. So, these individuals believe they are not bound by these laws. This, of course, naturally leads to disagreements and confrontations between common law supporters and the authorities.

These disagreements and confrontations turn particularly dangerous when the militia becomes involved in the common law movement. In the incident involving Tom Prahl's We the People common law court, the court did not have an enforcement arm to stop the foreclosure, or the Arlington, Texas, Common Law Court of Pleas an enforcement method for collecting the $93 trillion judgment. However, this is not true for all common law courts. "Since the middle of last year [1995], the trend we have seen the most is common law courts using militias as their enforcement arm," through threats and intimidation, said Robert Crawford of the Coalition for Human Dignity.[16] This development, considering the obviously bizarre and convoluted legal reasoning and decrees of many of these common law courts, and particularly since they have no real legal jurisdiction, can be clearly seen as a recipe for future confrontations that will likely end in bloodshed and violence.

Yet while the legal reasoning of common law courts may sound convoluted and even bizarre to the ordinary person, this type of thinking actually is very common in the militia movement. Many militia members intensely study the Constitution, the Federalist Papers, and other late eighteenth-century legal documents, searching for what they feel is their true meaning. Most believe that the Constitution must be interpreted literally, that every word means only what its precise dictionary definition says it does—nothing more or less. Many militia members also believe there is really only the "Organic Constitution," which consists of the original Constitution and the Bill of Rights. All other amendments and laws are looked upon as part of a plot to undermine the status of a sovereign citizen, which many militia members believe themselves to be.

A sovereign citizen is a person who believes himself or herself to be bound only by the common law. A sovereign citizen believes he or she is master of his or her property and should be completely free from any government interference, taxes, or laws. Sovereign citizens see themselves as free individuals who should enjoy the right of free travel and free commerce, with absolutely no government interference. This means they see no need for driver's licenses, car registrations or plates, traffic laws, gun permits, code enforcement, and so on. A report by the Indiana State Police entitled "Threat Assessment of the Patriot Movement in Indiana" said that a growing trend is for militia members not to carry state-issued driver's licenses, but homemade permits that they believe grant them the authority "to travel the common ways as a Private Christian."[17] Sovereign citizens see not just licensing but most laws and almost all government officials as illegal entities that interfere with a sovereign citizen's rights and freedoms.

In many cases, the only government officials recognized by militia members who have proclaimed themselves to be sovereign citizens are the county sheriff, whom they see as the only legally constituted law enforcement officer, and the county recorder, whom they see as the custodian of public records. Unfortunately, it is the employees of many county recorder's offices who have been bearing the brunt of the actions of militias and common law courts. Militia members have been increasingly bursting into county recorder's offices wanting to file declarations that say they are revoking their U.S. citizenship and declaring themselves to be "sovereign citizens." As sovereign citizens, they believe they will be exempt from federal laws and taxes, even though they still want their right to continue to live in the United States and enjoy all of its benefits. Militia members will also often demand that the county recorder's office file phony liens for them against government officials and others.

Some militia members, however, will come into a county recorder's office with even stranger requests. The members of one group wanted to file documents renouncing their American citizenship and declaring themselves to be "citizens of a nation in exile." This, they felt, would exempt them from state and federal laws, and also from income taxes. Of course, these "citizens of a nation in exile" wanted to remain living and working in the United States, and did not say exactly from what nation they were citizens in exile.

While these claims may sound amusing to readers, they are not amusing to employees of county recorder's offices. When the employees refuse to accept these documents, heated exchanges often occur, and occasionally violence can erupt. A report by the Anti-Defamation League, "Vigilante Justice: Militias and Common Law Courts Wage War against the Government," said that some county clerks are so intimidated by the militias and common law courts that they no longer display their name plates.[18]

"It's become a major problem," said Barbara Bergen, regional director of the Anti-Defamation League. "Recorders are very vulnerable. They usually work in open offices, and these folks are fanatics. They believe they have God and the Magna Carta on their side."[19]

Because of these conflicts and confrontations, in recent years, employees in county recorder's offices have often had to call for security officers when militia members became abusive. Some have even requested constant police protection. In 1994, nine reported militia members physically assaulted Stanislaus County (California) Recorder Karen Matthews with kicks and punches, and then threatened her with an unloaded gun that they dry-fired at her. Why? She had refused to remove a legitimate IRS lien against one of the assailants and also refused to file some phony liens for the militia members. She said the assailants told her she "was a messenger to all recorders, that if we did not begin to do our jobs and record their documents, this would happen to them too."[20] The police arrested the attackers and a court eventually convicted the nine individuals involved in this case.

"These people are, in some sense, like religious zealots—you can't argue with them," said Peter Bartucca, manager of legislative services at the Connecticut Secretary of State's Office, who also says these type of filings are on the rise.[21] He reports receiving a "notice of release" from a man who claims he is a citizen of Connecticut but not a citizen of the United States. Some militia members believe that having a state citizenship, but not a national one, will make them exempt from federal authority and taxes. "They have an enclosed system, which will not recognize anything outside of it," Bartucca said, "so you get these circular arguments that lead to nowhere."[22]

As was shown in the preceding incident involving Mrs. Matthews, common law court advocates and militia members often like to use phony liens as a weapon against government officials and others who they believe have wronged them. This has become a common tactic, because these liens, which are documents that make a claim against a piece of property because of indebtedness, can be filed without having to go to court. In most jurisdictions, a party simply goes to the county recorder's office and files them. They essentially bypass a court system that the militia members believe is corrupt anyway. And while these liens have no legal basis and are not binding, they can still be costly and time consuming to remove, and they must be removed, because they imply serious unsatisfied debts. Left unremoved, they can affect credit ratings and delay the sale of property. It is because of the expense and time involved in removing phony liens that militia members use this technique. They know that filing them against government officials, who must then go through the hassle of removing them, can have the effect of making other government officials reluctant to act against the militias.

Linda Ray, a case coordinator in Pulaski County Circuit Court in Little Rock, Arkansas, has had liens placed against her home, her bank

account, and her automobiles. Consequently, she has had to go to court
numerous times to have them removed. "It's just been an ongoing barrage
of filings and suits that I've had to constantly respond to," Mrs. Ray
said.[23]

While militia members like to use phony liens because they can be
filed without having to go to court, eventually, many militia members end
up in court anyway because of various illegal acts. In these instances,
militia members will often use some very bizarre and convoluted legal
reasoning and arguments that they believe prove the court has no authority over them. One of the legal arguments many militia members and
those from common law courts use to show that the present court system
is illegal and has no authority over them stems from their belief in the
"missing Thirteenth Amendment." This was a proposed amendment to
the Constitution that would have denied American citizenship to anyone
who accepted a "title of nobility" from another country. Apparently,
someone, soon after this amendment had been proposed, printed a copy
of the Constitution with this amendment included, even though it never
attained the needed number of states for ratification. Militia members,
however, because of their belief in conspiracies, insist that the states did
ratify this amendment, but that the government has hidden this fact from
the public, and they have the erroneously printed copy of the Constitution to prove it. Militia members then use this amendment as the basis of
their belief that the present court system is illegal, since lawyers cannot be
American citizens. The reason? Lawyers put "esquire" after their names,
which militia members see as a title of nobility. This, according to their
legal reasoning, denies American citizenship to all lawyers and hence
makes their involvement in the court system illegal. Consequently, since
the American court system is run by individuals without American citizenship, the courts have no real legal standing. Interestingly, no one in the
militia movement has yet figured out what country is bestowing this title
of "esquire," but that does not dissuade militia members from their belief
in this far-fetched legal theory.

This belief in the noncitizen status for lawyers also leads many militia
members to refuse the aid of court-appointed attorneys, which in turn
forces them to handle their own defense. Courts do not, of course, accept
the militia's legal reasoning about their authority but do allow many militia members to discard their court-appointed attorneys and present their
own cases. This explains the extraordinarily high conviction rate of militia members.

Another argument many militia members make for a lack of jurisdiction by the courts revolves around the American flags displayed in courtrooms. If these flags have a gold fringe on them, militia members insist this makes them admiralty (military) flags. Consequently, these are military courts, and, as such, they have no authority over private or sovereign citizens.

A favorite, but far-fetched, legal tactic for some militia members is to claim that the courts have no authority over them because they are not citizens of the United States. They will often supply the court with copies of affidavits they have filed with the county recorder's office in which they have renounced their American citizenship and stated they are foreign sovereigns (though they have no allegiance to any other country). Federal law under Title 8 USC 1481 sets out the provisions for how a person can renounce his or her United States citizenship, and just filing an affidavit with the county recorder is not sufficient. But regardless of this fact, even someone who is not a citizen of a country must still obey the laws of any country he or she is in, or must answer in court for any laws he or she violates. And while all of these legal tactics may sound outlandish and ridiculous, they occur often when militia members come in contact with the law.

As might be expected, the courts have naturally ruled against almost all of the legal theories put forth by militia members. For example, the 5th and 8th Federal Circuit Courts have ruled that a person's claim that he or she is a noncitizen, a nonresident, a freeman, or a sovereign citizen is frivolous. The Texas Court of Appeals ruled that if such a court as the "common law court" ever existed, it ceased to exist in 1846, when the Texas state government was organized. Other court decisions, which I discuss later, have also ruled against militia legal arguments for gun ownership, and even against arguments for their existence as organizations. Despite these adverse rulings against almost all legal arguments put forth by militia members, an article in *U.S. News & World Report* said, "One of the popular services offered at the expos is paralegal training."[24] Indeed, at several of the preparedness/survival expos I attended, I found booths that supplied legal-appearing forms for various purposes, such as declaring oneself to be a sovereign citizen, declaring oneself to be a state, but not federal, citizen, and so on.

Interestingly, despite the claims of many militia members that the American court system is illegal and has no jurisdiction over them, there are many other militia members who believe that the present court system is legal and valid but that jurors in these courts do not know their real rights. Some militia members believe that jurors do not have to listen to a judge's instructions about the law when deciding a case, but can decide for themselves whether a law is just or constitutional, and, in doing so, can find a defendant innocent regardless of the evidence. The argument for this position is included in the *Citizens Rule Book,* discussed in the chapter on militia publications and propaganda.

Militias, however, do more than just preach this legal theory and hand out copies of the book at militia gatherings. They have also been known to mail copies of the *Citizens Rule Book* to jurors in cases important to the militia. During one trial, in which the jurors' identities were supposed to be secret, militia members followed the jurors to their cars, where the license plate numbers were jotted down and traced. The jurors then received copies of the book mailed to their homes.

When I heard militia leader Mark Koernke speak at the preparedness/survival expo in Atlanta, he told the audience that he gives copies of the *Citizens Rule Book* to police officers. He claimed he could judge the officers from their response to it. I found this interesting, since many militia members believe that police officers, particularly high-ranking ones, are part of the New World Order conspiracy to take over the world.

In addition to their various convoluted legal theories, many militia members also believe in a myth about the Fourteenth Amendment. This amendment granted citizenship and equal protection under the law to former slaves following the Civil War. Many militia members believe that the Fourteenth Amendment actually established a new type of citizenship. They believe that individuals made citizens by the Fourteenth Amendment (meaning blacks) are citizens under the authority of the federal government and therefore cannot be sovereign citizens. They also believe that individuals not granted citizenship by the Fourteenth Amendment (meaning whites) can still come under the authority of the federal government, and become "Fourteenth Amendment citizens," but only by unknowingly entering into a "contract" with the federal government. People unknowingly enter into these contracts by paying federal income tax, obtaining a Social Security number, and so on. However, by refusing these contracts with the federal government and declaring themselves to be sovereign citizens, these individuals believe they are not bound by the laws of the federal government. This distinction between the two classes of citizens is, of course, blatantly racist.

Many militia members also believe in a conspiracy theory that says the Sixteenth Amendment, which established the federal income tax, was never legally ratified. Others argue, however, that even if it was legally ratified, it still does not apply to sovereign citizens, only to Fourteenth Amendment citizens.

Interestingly, one finds that many of the convoluted legal theories of militia members often have a financial basis. Many times, militia members are brought into court over matters such as foreclosure on a piece of property, back taxes, unpaid debts, back child support, and so on. A common legal argument used by militia members who want to escape these debts is that federal reserve notes, in which they are expected to pay their debts, are illegal because the U.S. Constitution states that only gold or silver may be used in the payment of debts. The argument then follows that since federal reserve notes are not really money, the Federal Reserve System is also illegal, and, as such, so is the entire banking system of the United States, thereby voiding any debts the person may have. Individuals who believe in this argument have been known to go to real estate auctions, bid a small amount in silver coin, and then file a legal suit claiming that they made the highest bid in "real money." The courts have naturally ruled against this argument. They have also ruled that federal reserve notes are legal tender for the payment of debts. However, this still does not stop many militia members from believing in and attempting to use this argument and other equally spurious legal defenses.

In March 1992, Terry Nichols, who was convicted along with Timothy McVeigh in the Oklahoma City bombing, reportedly sent First Deposit National Bank an affidavit that "revoked" his signature on the application he had filled out for one of their credit cards. He sent this affidavit in the apparent belief that this would void the $14,470.38 he owed them. In the affidavit, he said, "I, Terry L. Nichols, do hereby revoke, cancel, annul, repeal, dismiss, discharge, extract, withdraw, abrogate, recant, negate, obliterate, delete, nullify, efface, erase, expunge, exercise, delete, strike, blot, disclaim, disown, reject, give-up, abandon, surrender, and relinquish all signatures and powers of attorney."[25] Soon afterward, Chase Manhattan Bank sued him for a $17,861.68 credit card bill, which he again argued he should not have to repay.

In April 1992, Nichols attempted to renounce his American citizenship by sending a letter stating such to the State of Michigan. In June 1992, Terry's brother James, because of his rejection of the government, also attempted to renounce his United States citizenship, even though in the previous few years, according to an article in *U.S. News & World Report*, he had taken nearly $90,000 in farm subsidies from the government.[26]

In January 1993, under a court order to pay the credit card companies in the above cases, Terry Nichols attempted to pay them with a "Certified Fractional Reserve Check," which was simply a piece of paper with no value. When facing the judge in his credit card case, Terry said he was a "freedom of common law citizen." He argued that the credit card companies had not loaned him "real money," but simply credit, and that his Certified Fractional Reserve Check was just like their credit. Naturally, his legal arguments were not accepted by the court.

A legal argument that almost all militia members fervently believe in is that the Second Amendment to the Constitution grants them complete and total freedom to own and carry absolutely any weapon they desire. According to an article in *The Pennsylvania Minuteman*, "It must be understood that every gun 'law' in Pennsylvania and these United States is inherently and unquestionably unconstitutional. The right to keep and bare [sic] arms cannot be infringed or even questioned."[27]

When reading the Second Amendment, which says, "A well regulated Militia, being necessary to the security of a free state, the right of the people to keep and bear arms shall not be infringed," members of the militia movement read it with selective vision. All they see is the phrase "the right of the people to keep and bear arms shall not be infringed." There is the qualifier in the Second Amendment before this phrase, however, which legal scholars argue means that the prohibition against restricting the keeping and bearing of arms applies only to state and federal militia operations, and not to individual citizens.

In 1939, the U.S. Supreme Court ruled on the meaning of the Second Amendment in *U.S. v. Miller*. In this unanimous ruling, the court stated that the Second Amendment was written to preserve state militias, and not to give private citizens the right to keep and bear arms.

This landmark case involved a man named Jack Miller, whom the police arrested for transporting an unregistered, sawed-off shotgun between states. In their opinion, the U.S. Supreme Court said that the "obvious purpose" of the Second Amendment was "to assure the continuation and render possible the effectiveness of the militia" (meaning a state or federal regulated militia, not the modern civilian militias that do not answer to anyone). The Supreme Court's opinion then went on to say, "In the absence of any evidence tending to show that possession or use of a [sawed-off shotgun] at this time has some reasonable relationship to the preservation or efficiency of a well-regulated militia, we cannot say that the 2nd Amendment guarantees the right to keep and bear such an instrument."

In 1983, a court cited this case when it held that a city ordinance in Morton Grove, Illinois, which banned residents from possessing handguns, did not violate the Second Amendment. Opponents appealed this decision to the U.S. Supreme Court, who let the decision stand without comment. Regardless, however, of all the cases ruling in favor of the restricted meaning of the Second Amendment, a 1995 *U.S. News & World Report* survey found that 75 percent of Americans believe the Constitution guarantees them the right to own a gun.[28]

Of course, even as important as gun ownership is to militia members, one of the most important legal arguments militia members have with the authorities is the legal basis of their very existence. Many militias claim that the Constitution gives them the authority to form militia groups without government sanction or interference. However, legal experts say that the "well-regulated militia" referred to in the Second Amendment means a militia authorized and controlled by the federal or state governments. Nelson Lund, a professor of law at George Mason University and President Bush's Deputy White House counsel, said that "a well-regulated militia" refers to groups such as the National Guard, and that the armed civilian militia groups that have formed in all fifty states "have no standing as militias under the Constitution."[29]

In a 1950 unanimous decision by the U.S. Supreme Court, which ironically overturned a ruling of U.S. Circuit Judge Alfred P. Murrah, for whom the bombed federal building in Oklahoma City was named, Supreme Court Justice Robert H. Jackson wrote: "No private individual has the power to conscript or mobilize a private army with such authorities over persons as the government rests in echelons of command." In this case, the U.S. Supreme Court stated that the authority and right to raise a militia belonged to the government and not to private individuals.

In addition, Article 1, Section 8, of the United States Constitution states: "The Congress shall have Power . . . To provide for calling forth the Militia to execute the Laws of the Union, suppress insurrections and repel invasions; To provide for organizing, arming, and disciplining the Militia, and governing such Part of them as may be employed in the Service of the United States, reserving to the States respectively, the Appointment of the Officers, and the Authority of training the Militia according to the discipline prescribed by Congress." Nowhere in this article is there any authorization for private individuals to form and operate militias.

In answer to these claims that today's armed civilian militias have no legal basis under the Constitution, Militia leader Norm Olson, in his statement before the Senate Subcommittee on Terrorism, Technology, and Government Information, said, "Citizen militias are historic lawful entities predating constitutions. Such militias are 'grandfathered' (a legal term that means something existing before a law is passed is not affected by the law) into the very system of government they created. The Constitution grants no right to form militias, but merely recognizes the existing natural right of all people to defend themselves."[30] While this sounds impressive, the court decision mentioned above disagrees with Mr. Olson's reasoning.

Regardless of the almost total lack of success in making their legal arguments stand up in various courts, many militia members still believe they are right, just unfortunate victims of a corrupt court system. Most truly believe they have God, the common law, and the Organic Constitution on their side. With this backing, they insist they cannot be wrong, which can be a very dangerous assumption considering their belief in various conspiracy theories, plots, and takeovers that can only be prevented by potentially violent confrontations with an armed militia.

$\diamond$ $\diamond$ $\diamond$ $\diamond$ $\diamond$ $\diamond$ $\diamond$ $\diamond$ **14**

STATE AND LOCAL
RESPONSE TO MILITIAS

On 22 September 1997, deputies from the Christian County (Illinois) Sheriff's Department drove to the residence of fifty-one-year-old Shirley Allen, who lived on a farm in Roby, Illinois, population less than one hundred. Shirley's brother, Byron Dugger, who lived in Arkansas but had traveled to Illinois because of his concern for Shirley, accompanied the deputies. The officers carried with them a court order instructing the sheriff's department to take Shirley to a hospital, where she would undergo a psychiatric evaluation. Shirley's family had become increasingly concerned about her behavior ever since the death of her husband John in 1989, from pancreatic cancer.

"For some reason," her brother Byron said, "she couldn't get over it."[1]

Reportedly, in recent years, Shirley's behavior had become more and more erratic, and, in her family's opinion, dangerous to herself and others. She would claim that items in her house had been mysteriously moved to different locations and that helicopters were spying on her. She wrote and mailed to several relatives a twenty-five-page letter filled with paranoid rambling. However, when her family members, after reading the letter and becoming concerned, came to check on her, she refused to let them in her house, claiming they weren't really her family members at all, but rather were imposters wearing masks and just trying to trick her into believing they were her relatives. But recently, her behavior had taken an even more ominous turn. Allegedly, she had pointed a shotgun at a neighbor and threatened to kill him.

When the deputies and Shirley's brother attempted to persuade her to go with them, she pulled out a 12-gauge shotgun and threatened them, as she had done with her neighbor. The deputies retreated and called for assistance. Thus began the longest siege in Illinois history. Shirley locked herself in her house and held off the authorities for over a month in a standoff that would become known in militia circles, which soon took up Shirley's cause, as Roby Ridge, obviously referring to the disastrous standoff between the FBI and the Weaver family at Ruby Ridge, Idaho, in 1992.

The authorities, not wanting to endanger Shirley or any police officers through a physical confrontation, first tried to force Shirley out of her house by lobbing in tear gas canisters. Shirley, however, a former nurse, had covered her exposed skin with Vaseline and wet towels, rendering the tear gas ineffective. The police then tried firing soft, stun projectiles at Shirley. These projectiles are similar to bean bags, and, fired at high velocity, they usually stun a person with their blunt force but seldom do any serious physical harm. Shirley, however, had prepared herself for this possibility, too. She had dressed in several layers of clothing, which dramatically decreased the projectiles' impact. Following this attempt, however, the atmosphere of the standoff darkened. After the stun projectiles failed, Shirley suddenly grabbed her shotgun and fired at nearby officers but fortunately did not hit anyone.

Once the authorities discovered that all of their nonlethal tactics had failed and that Shirley appeared ready and willing to respond with deadly force, the police found themselves faced with just two options. They could storm the house, and, considering Shirley's responses so far, very likely have to shoot her, or they could just pull back, set up a perimeter, and wait her out.

The Illinois State Police, who had taken charge of the situation since the fifteen-officer Christian County Sheriff's Department did not have the manpower or resources to handle it, decided on the latter tactic. They established a perimeter around the one-story, green house, brought in their forty-foot mobile command post, and set up their operations center just out of sight of Shirley's home. In order to speed up her surrender, the police cut the electricity to Shirley's house and, since she was on a well, shut off her water supply. They also began playing classical music and Barry Manilow CD's on loudspeakers pointed at the house in the hope that this would calm Shirley down and bring about an early surrender.

As with everything else the police had tried, however, none of these tactics worked either. Shirley, apparently an avid canner, had a large supply of canned food on hand. Her well, the police learned, had run dry several times, and so she kept a large supply of bottled water in the house. And so the police sat and waited as the Barry Manilow music played on day after day. From their experiences in similar situations, however, the Illinois State Police felt certain they would eventually pre vail. They had found that in the typical barricaded person situation, if they allowed enough time to pass, the barricaded person's resolve usually began to crumble, and eventually the individual would come out and surrender.

This standoff, however, did not become just another typical police operation. Once it hit the news wires, militia groups began talking about it over the Internet, and the standoff between Shirley Allen and the police became the subject of countless shortwave radio talk shows. Many members of the militia movement saw this as just another example of the government running amok, of a brave woman standing alone in her opposition to "Big Brother" mentality.

One Internet report from a member of the Ohio Militia said: "In this case, a 51-year-old woman has decided to make her stand alone. . . . If Shirley Allen has the resolve to stand, fight, and die for her right of due process, I believe it's irresponsible of her neighbors to stand by idly and witness her execution. . . . There comes a time when good people have to make the sacrifice to stand on principle. If we do nothing, Shirley Allen will certanly die; as we have been informed that she will not surrender."[2]

Another militia Internet message said: "Mrs. Shirley Allen of Roby, Illinois is being held hostage for an unknown reason and for an unknown ransom by the Illinois State Police. The only logical reason she hasn't been killed to this point is because their [sic] are too many eyes (neighbors) watching. She is now surrounded by an all but military police force, who is surrounded by a justifiably angry public at large."[3]

The only part of the above message that bore any truth was the last sentence. At the urging of militia leaders, members of militias from as far away as Texas, New Mexico, and California began converging on Roby, Illinois, certain that this would be Waco and Ruby Ridge all over again. Also joining in the protest, besides a number of local people who supported Shirley, were individuals from around the country who weren't affiliated with, or even sympathetic to, the militia but simply had strong feelings about the situation in Roby, Illinois. Many of these people felt that the government had no right to forcibly take Shirley Allen out of her house and make her undergo a psychiatric examination.

Several weeks into the standoff, the Stark County (Ohio) Militia sent out an Internet alert that said the Shirley Allen situation had deteriorated. "It is possible that this is a clear violation of the 'Articles of Alliance' that we have agreed to uphold," said the Internet alert. "Plainly stated, any unlawful, unconstitutional action that deprives any citizen of life or liberty, will be an act of aggression against all the people, responded to by all of the United States Militia Alliance."[4]

To the militia leadership's credit, however, they advised their members who were coming to Roby, Illinois, to leave their weapons at home, and instead to bring devices such as cameras, binoculars, CB radios, and notepads. Along with the arrival of militia members from all across the country though, a number of nationally recognized militia leaders from across the United States also made their appearance in Roby: J. J. Johnson of the Ohio Militia, John Trochmann of the Militia of Montana, former Green Beret Colonel Bo Gritz, and Jack McLamb, former Phoenix police officer and now a militia recruiter and organizer.

At a rally organized by the militia and held in Taylorville, the Christian County seat, about 200 people showed up to protest the Illinois State Police actions in Roby. Some held protest signs that said: FREE SHIRLEY ALLEN and LAW, LAW, GO AWAY, QUIT HOLDING MRS. ALLEN AT BAY. Several of the local bars sold T-shirts with similar sayings, while protestors circulated petitions demanding that the Illinois State Police call off their siege.

Most of the protestors told the news media that they were very upset by the way the Illinois State Police was trying to take a woman into custody who had not committed a crime. Many believed that the accusations about her mental instability were bogus. But even those who accepted that Shirley Allen had mental problems still felt the police were wrong.

"We believe the danger to self and others should be fairly imminent" before involuntary commitment is justified, said ACLU attorney Benjamin Wolfe. "This is a free society—you have the right to be strange, you even have the right to be ill."[5]

A local bartender said it more bluntly: "It's stupid. They ought to go home and leave her alone."[6]

A neighbor of Shirley Allen agreed with this when he said, "She has the natural right to be crazy."[7]

While many of the people who took part in the demonstrations at Roby, Illinois, protested that the police were trying to take someone into custody who had not committed a crime, apparently they didn't realize, nor did many members of the news media, the reason behind the court order or the task the police were trying to accomplish, which was to prevent a possible tragedy. The first obligation of government is protection of the people. To this end, judges must occasionally order the involuntary commitment for mental evaluation of an individual if it appears there is the clear and very likely possibility that the person in question is a danger to himself or herself or to innocent people. Shirley Allen, by threatening a neighbor with a shotgun, had already demonstrated she could very likely pose such a threat. For the government to do nothing, to simply stand by and allow a tragedy to occur, would have been unconscionable.

Fueling the anger of many of the protestors, however, were the inflammatory messages of the militia conspiracy spinners. Some of the militia Internet messages about the Shirley Allen situation contained hints of the "real" reason behind the attempted mental health commitment. These messages hinted that the whole incident was a conspiracy concocted by Shirley's family to have her committed so they could take her house, forty-seven acres of farm land, and the two oil wells on her property.

"Perhaps stranger still are reports that the earlier estimate of $125,000 for the widow's estate have now grown to current appraisals in excess of a million dollars," said one Internet posting. "It has also been confirmed that there are two oil wells on her large rural property. Yet unresolved is the question of who would control the estate if the court order for mental evaluation succeeds in keeping Mrs. Allen separated from her property. Questions also remain unanswered as to the intentions of Mrs. Allen's out-of-state relatives who initiated proceedings for the court order for involuntary psychiatric commitment."[8]

However, as with most militia conspiracy theories, this one made no attempt to get at the truth. The value of Shirley's total property holdings was less than $200,000, and the two oil wells were dry, their assessed value: zero. Also, contrary to the family conspiracy theory, having a person committed does not mean the other family members automatically gain possession of that person's property, and, in the Shirley Allen incident, her family was not asking for a long-term commitment, only enough time for a mental health evaluation, to be certain she was not a danger to herself or others.

"I don't see how her siblings could gain from having her committed," said Bill Schroeder, law professor at Southern Illinois University, in answer to the militia conspiracy claims. "It seems to me very unlikely that committing her would, in and of itself, deprive her of her land."[9]

In Illinois, if a person such as Shirley Allen is committed to an institution for mental health reasons, a guardian would be appointed to handle her affairs, and if this person were not an attorney, one would be appointed for her. But most important, any actions concerning disposition of her property would have to be approved by a judge.

However, not everyone bought into the family conspiracy theory. In fact, some felt that many of the individuals involved in the protests were misleading the public. "This situation is being spun as if the courts are just handing out (involuntary commitment) orders like they're candy . . . and they're not," said Randy Well, executive director of the Alliance for the Mentally Ill of Illinois.[10]

In the midst of all the clamor, conspiracy spinning, and rallies, the Illinois State Police continued its standoff at the small green house in Roby, Illinois. However, in an attempt to defuse the situation with the militia and other Shirley Allen supporters, the Illinois State Police held a meeting with militia leaders Jack McLamb and J. J. Johnson, and briefed the two men on the situation with Shirley Allen at present, what the police had done so far, and what they planned to do. Later, at a rally set up by the militia, McLamb told the crowd that he felt the Illinois State Police was doing a good job and had handled the situation properly. "I probably would have given the order to shoot Shirley if I'd been in command," McLamb told the crowd, referring to the fact that she had now fired a shotgun several times at the police.

McLamb's words obviously were not what the crowd wanted to hear. They began jeering and booing him. "Go back to Arizona!" the people gathered in front of the Christian County Courthouse yelled. "You're a liar!"[11]

Following this, Ohio Militia leader J. J. Johnson broke with McLamb via an Internet posting. "I believe Jack McLamb felt like a police officer again when we were inside that meeting," Johnson wrote. "For me, maybe it was the uniforms and badges that intimidated me. . . . I told the locals that I would not leave their state knowing that I might have signed Shirley Allen's death warrant. I told them the truth. I told them that I disagreed with McLamb and that the people should not let down their guard for any reason."[12]

This became an interesting development because McLamb has been an extremely popular leader in the militia movement, often sought after to appear at militia expos. I suspect that the militia members gathered in front of the courthouse, so accustomed to hearing from their leaders and trading stories amongst themselves about how corrupt and ruthless the government is, simply could not accept that perhaps in this case the government was right. Believing that would have upset their view of how the world stood. (In another break in the solidarity of the militia leadership, an article in the January 1998 issue of the Militia of Montana newsletter, *Taking Aim,* suggests that the psychological pressure the police used in their attempt to persuade Shirley Allen to surrender had come at the suggestion of militia leader, and former Green Beret colonel, Bo Gritz.)

Amid all of this turmoil, from September 22 through the end of October 1997, the standoff at Roby, Illinois, continued with no resolution. On 27 October 1997, the police, wanting to finally bring the standoff to an end, used a police dog in an attempt to locate exactly where Shirley was in the house. Shirley shot the dog through the nose. On 29 October 1997, in an attempt to win Shirley over, the police dropped off a package of groceries for her. On 31 October 1997, Shirley Allen, for some unknown reason, stepped outside her back door. Waiting police officers shot her with "rubber" bullets, which are soft projectiles meant to stun a person and knock him or her to the ground. Unlike the beanbag projectiles, these projectiles worked, and Shirley fell to the deck at the rear of her house. The officers rushed forward and took her into custody with no serious injury. She talked with state police officers and her relatives for an hour before being taken to St. John's Hospital in Springfield, Illinois. She told them that to avoid being near any windows, she had slept in a narrow hallway throughout the standoff.

On 17 December 1997, Shirley Allen returned to her Roby, Illinois, home. A psychiatrist who examined her told the judge who had ordered the evaluation that she posed no danger to herself or anyone else, even though she had threatened a family member and a neighbor with a shotgun, and had fired the shotgun several times at the police. Ironically, however, considering this evaluation, the state decided not to press any charges against Shirley for her actions during the standoff, because, they said, they believed she was mentally ill when she committed them.

The psychiatrist's evaluation of Shirley Allen is not terribly surprising. Having received my college degree, along with doing graduate work, in psychology, I realize how little we really know and understand about the human mind. And as a police officer, I have seen far too many cases in which two psychiatrists have examined the same person and then come up with completely opposing opinions. I have also seen far too many individuals that psychiatrists or psychologists have deemed either no danger to anyone or completely cured of an earlier mental illness, who, once released, went out and within a few weeks or months committed some horrible crime. Much of psychological evaluation is guesswork, gut feelings, and hunches.

The state's decision not to prosecute Shirley Allen is more surprising and a bit more difficult to understand, particularly since the state-appointed psychiatrist proclaimed her sane, which meant that state officials could proceed with filing charges against her if they wished. The state seems to have overlooked that she fired a deadly weapon at the police several times. Possibly, the decision not to charge her was politically motivated, an effort to offset accusations by the militia that the police had acted like storm troopers when they tried to take an innocent woman out of her house. Perhaps the decision was meant to make the state police look more warm and fuzzy.

Many people may disagree with this decision. Not prosecuting Shirley Allen might not only encourage similar individuals to act violently, but also could give the appearance that the militia is a force that can thwart the law, a force that can make the authorities back down. While the state and local police should not, and cannot, legally target the militias simply because of their beliefs, neither should state and local police, because of the militia threat, soften their standards and let certain individuals get away with criminal activity simply because they enjoy the militia support that Shirley Allen did. If Shirley Allen had been arrested very early in the standoff, before all of the militia members and others had organized their support, or if this had been someone with no support, charges certainly would have been filed. The police would not have backed down.

Actually, there was no reason to back down. The reports show that the Illinois State Police acted properly and did exactly what it was supposed to do, even though it did not sit well with many people. Sometimes a police officer, doing his or her duty, encounters strong resistance from many members of the public and, consequently, with the news media. Police work, however, by its nature, is confrontational and there will always be bad press, even over correct actions. However, regardless of the possibility of protests, bad press, and militia resistance, police departments must continue to fulfill their duties and responsibilities.

Yet the militia presence and the militia-led protests obviously did affect the police, along with other officials. According to an article in the *St. Louis Post Dispatch*, "In the aftermath of the standoff Friday, state police began an internal investigation into how the situation was handled; state legislators were talking about convening hearings on possible changes to the law; and mental illness experts were beginning to worry about a backlash that could make it harder to commit those who need psychiatric help."[13]

The second part of this statement, about lawmakers holding hearings, is not surprising. Whenever any event occurs that elected officials feel might have upset the voters, some kind of response like this is expected. However, the worry is that the legislators will allow themselves to be intimidated and pressured by groups such as militias into making changes in laws that they should not make, as the mental illness experts in the preceding article are clearly worried about.

The incident at Roby, Illinois, though, was more than just a confrontation between the police and the militia protestors. It was actually an event with far-reaching ramifications. Shirley Allen, by her actions, had demonstrated she was a clear danger to herself and others, and that her family members were rightfully concerned. Anyone who has ever had a close family member who they fear is a suicide or homicide risk knows the terrible anxiety this puts on the family members. All they want is to get this person some help before it is too late. From the militia standpoint on this, though, they could not get the troubled family member this help. The militia-led protests in Roby basically said that the police should not be allowed to act until a person such as Shirley Allen actually does kill someone or try to commit suicide.

The anxiety of the mental heath professionals addressed in the *St. Louis Post Dispatch* article is a backlash to the bad press of the Shirley Allen incident, which, it is feared, could cause new laws about involuntary commitment to be passed or old ones changed. Changing these laws in order to make it harder to have someone committed for psychiatric evaluation and help would have important societal consequences. While such changes likely would not last, their results while in effect could be disastrous. The first protest the police usually hear from the public whenever a mentally disturbed individual commits a heinous crime involving innocent victims is "Why wasn't he or she in an institution somewhere? Why was this person allowed to roam free?" If we allow pressure from groups such as militias to make it tougher for family members to have someone with mental health problems evaluated or treated, we will be hearing these questions much more often in the future.

Although concern about the issue of personal freedom, such as militia members demonstrated in the Shirley Allen case, can at times be commendable, the difficulty lies in striking a fine balance between protecting those freedoms and safeguarding the public. The fact is that there are a number of people in this country who are mentally ill and pose a clear danger to themselves and others. Public officials must fend off coercion and pressure from militias to change laws that for the public safety should not be changed.

Unfortunately, the incident involving Shirley Allen is a common one in law enforcement. We are often ordered to perform the unpopular task of serving court orders on individuals who are not criminals, but simply mentally ill and a danger to themselves and others. In addition, no more popular are sheriffs who must evict individuals from homes they have lost in divorces or court cases, or officers who must arrest parents for failing to make court-ordered child-support payments. Both of these last two situations have drawn militia members to a community, as in Roby, Illinois, to protest the actions. The militia members in these cases have insisted that the police should refuse to serve such orders.

However, regardless of the demands of militias, when given such orders by the court, the police cannot decide which orders they will serve and which they will not, which orders they believe are just and which are unjust. Nobody would be very comfortable with giving police officers this much power. The police should be servants in the criminal justice system, not its masters. However, as the most visible arm of the government, the police are often seen as the culprits in any incident such as this, even though they are simply enforcing orders given to them by the courts.

An editorial in the *St. Louis Post Dispatch* said, "As usual, the only thing critics on all sides share is complaints about the police. Despite the fact that the cops had nothing whatsoever to do with creating the situation and somehow managed to bring it to a bloodless conclusion, armchair quarterbacks nationwide are confident that they screwed up. . . . Had this poor woman, because of a diminished mental state, mistaken the neighborhood newspaper boy for a secret agent from Pluto and turned her shotgun on him, a whole new chorus of critics would have demanded to know why nothing was done to prevent the tragedy."[14]

While the police will always encounter individuals who want to second guess and criticize their actions, few of their opponents are as organized as the militia movement. Few have the capability to distribute information, albeit often false, almost instantaneously to thousands of other members across the country, and few have the ability to organize a protest as strong as the one in Roby, Illinois. For this reason, not just the police, but all local and state governments, need to have a plan of how to respond to and deal with the militia use of misinformation.

State and local governments should not wait until an incident such the Shirley Allen situation occurs in their jurisdiction before they decide what to do about countering rumors and half-truths meant to inflame the situation. While the militiao did nothing illegal in Roby, Illinois, their presence and their ability to stir up controversy by spreading rumors and half-truths still caused problems for state and local government. Officials, therefore, must have a plan in place, before such an incident occurs, that outlines how they will disseminate their own information to the public, a plan of how they can be certain the public knows the whole truth about what is happening. Unfortunately, many government agencies, and the police in particular, like to be very secretive about their actions, often when there is really no need for this secrecy. Unless releasing information would endanger someone, the public has the right to know in any incident or confrontation with government officials exactly what the truth is.

Unfortunately, though, not all cases of confrontation between the authorities and militia members are as nonviolent as the one in Roby, Illinois, in which militia leaders advised members to leave their weapons at home. Occasionally, as in the following incident, these confrontations result in tragedy.

On 28 June 1995, a few minutes after 2:00 A.M., Frazeysburg (Ohio) police sergeant Matt May and a civilian passenger, on routine patrol on State Road 16, pulled in behind a car sporting a homemade license plate that read "Militia 3-13 Chaplain." (The 3-13 refers to the part of the Ohio Revised Code that Ohio militia members insist gives them the right of free travel without any interference from the state, interference meaning the requirment of driver's licenses and license plates, the enforcement of traffic laws, etc.). The driver of the vehicle, former Canton (Ohio) police officer Michael Hill, pulled to the side of the road and stopped after Sergeant May activated his emergency lights and siren. Sergeant May later said that Hill climbed out of his car and started walking back toward him, but he immediately ordered Hill to get back into his car.

Hill, a colonel and chaplain in the Ohio Unorganized Militia, did just that, but he also drove away. He was reportedly on his way home from a common law study session. As well as a militia member, he was also chief justice of a common law court the militia had established, which was based on the Bible and the Constitution. Hill had studied the Constitution intensely several years before, when he fought unsuccessfully to stop the demolition of a home he owned in Canton.

Upon seeing the car drive away, Sergeant May chased after Hill and stopped him again. This time, however, according to Sergeant May, Hill jumped out of the car brandishing a .45-caliber semiautomatic pistol, which he held in both hands. Fearing for his life, Sergeant May drew his own weapon and fired four times at Hill, striking him three times and killing him. When the police recovered Hill's weapon, they found it cocked, with a bullet in the chamber and seven in the magazine. Later examination of the weapon showed that one of Sergeant May's bullets had struck Hill's pistol and shattered. Fragments of the shattered bullet entered Hill's hand, elbow, knee, and leg. The passenger riding that night with Sergeant May, a Frazeysburg firefighter, confirmed to investigators that he, too, saw Hill come out of the car with his weapon drawn.

On 27 September 1995, a Muskingun County grand jury found that Sergeant May had acted properly and shot Hill in self defense. Case closed? No.

Three members of Hill's militia group later claimed that they had been caravanning with Hill's car and witnessed the shooting. They said they did not wait around for the police investigation but fled, because they feared for their lives. In signed statements, the three men insisted that Hill had no weapon drawn when he exited his car, but rather that Sergeant May shot him down in cold blood.

"Mike Hill had not given any gestures nor any rapid movements that could be construed as provocation," said Larry Martz, one of the alleged witnesses, in his signed statement.[15] Martz, however, in an incident the following year, would be convicted of assaulting an Ohio state trooper.

The executive director of the National Confederation of Citizen Militias demanded that the State Attorney General investigate the incident. The Attorney General declined, however. Information about the incident was also sent to the FBI, but they too declined to intervene.

Failing this, messages about the shooting blazed across the Internet, fax networks, and shortwave radio talk shows. "Will you be next?" asked one fax message. "This is cold-blooded murder!" said an Internet posting.[16] Another Internet posting claimed that the police planted the gun on Hill and then shot the dying man in the hand to make it appear he had drawn the gun and tried kill the officer.[17]

Soon after the shooting, the local sheriff's office began receiving threatening calls from individuals who identified themselves as members of the Ohio Unorganized Militia. Leaders of the militia, however, stated that they did not condone such behavior. Still, the resulting protests forced Sergeant May to take time off and go into seclusion.

In the end, despite the grand jury finding, Sergeant May's corroborating eyewitness, and the bullet-damaged .45-caliber handgun, Mike Hill became a martyr to the militia movement, seen in militia circles as a patriot shot down in cold blood by a ruthless government. Militia leaders have erected a four-ton granite stone at the Hill's Golden Nugget Ranch in southeastern Ohio as a memorial to him.

This incident clearly demonstrates the constant threat police officers must deal with when confronting militia members. Officers never know when something as minor as a traffic stop or even a summons for a code violation can become a militia member's last stand. With the strong belief in conspiracies that most militia members hold, an officer can never know for certain what a militia member believes is happening. In addition, when stopped, if militia members happen to be carrying illegal explosives or automatic weapons, a deadly confrontation may also result.

Readers should not believe, however, that the danger of such confrontations with militia members does not affect them but is entirely between the police and the militia. Any confrontation that ends in a shooting, such as in the Michael Hill case, very gravely affects everyone. Gun battles are a lot like drive-by shootings. Bullets go everywhere and often strike innocent victims. I have been in several shootouts, and they are notoriously wild affairs, with bullets often flying off in unexpected directions. In any gun battle between the police and militia members, the strong possibility always exists of innocent bystanders being harmed or killed.

Traffic stops of militia members, however, are not the only dangerous confrontations that police officers risk. In another incident, in Atlanta, in October 1997, a police dispatcher sent two officers to an apartment to investigate the report that a man was beating his girlfriend, a very common run for police officers. However, when the police arrived at the apartment, the man reportedly beating his girlfriend, who was a militia member, fired sixteen shots at the officers, killing one and leaving the other in critical condition. Following the shooting, the police confiscated illegal explosives and weapons from the apartment. Again, in this incident, with sixteen shots fired, the police certainly were not the only ones threatened.

Although, as I stated earlier, police departments cannot legally target militia groups simply because of their beliefs, they must still certainly be very cautious of them. Part of this caution should involve the training of all police officers concerning the danger signs when dealing with militia members. But first, police departments need to train their officers on what to look for that might indicate militia membership, such as individuals dressed in camouflage, drivers with no, or homemade, driver's licenses, vehicles with homemade license plates, and so on. Most importantly, police departments need to teach their officers how to deal safely with these types of individuals, not just for their own welfare, but also for the public safety. Unfortunately, though, because the militia movement is so new, few police departments have instituted such training yet.

While admittedly the majority of militia members are law-abiding citizens who present little danger of deadly confrontations, teaching police officers to use caution around militia members is still very important, because there exists a fringe element within the militia movement that is not law-abiding and is definitely a danger. The following incident shows just how dangerous some of these fringe militia members can be.

John Bohlman, County Attorney for Musselshell County, Montana, in his testimony before the Senate Subcommittee on Terrorism, Technology, and Government Information, said, "I want to state that on a personal level I am opposed to such organizations [militias], because I believe they are attempting to impose their political will by force or threat."[18] Backing up this statement, Bohlman told the senators about an incident in his county in which sheriff's deputies arrested on weapons charges two men who they believed had been contemplating the kidnapping of a public official. Later that night, five men driving in two cars appeared at the jail where the two men were being held. Deputies said the men parked their cars in what appeared to be an attempt to control access to the jail. Three of the men, carrying concealed weapons, came into the jail and demanded that the deputies return the weapons and the $86,000 in currency and gold coins they had confiscated from the two arrested individuals. Once the deputies found that the three men were armed, they arrested them also. They then went outside and arrested the other two men, who were waiting in the cars. When taken into custody, one of the men was speaking to someone on a walkie-talkie.

In the days that followed, the Sheriff's Department received hundreds of telephone calls from all over the United States, demanding that they release the seven arrested men. Officials of the Musselshell County Sheriff's Department said that both threats against the deputies and racial slurs were common with these calls.

Because of the possibility of armed confrontations, all police departments need to keep up to date on any militia groups within their jurisdiction. Because they are such a new phenomenon and can often spring up overnight, groups of which police departments often are not aware can exist. While it is illegal for a police department to initiate an investigation of a group unless that group shows evidence of being involved in criminal activity, police departments still need to know what militia groups are in existence in their jurisdiction and how large they are. And, of course, police departments should always be on alert for any information involving possible criminal activity by these groups.

"The militia movement and its individual members should be observed, as any element of the citizenry," said former ATF agent Steve Wortham. "If individual members or the specific group commits a violation of the law, the full force of the law must be used to stop the act and punish the violators."

Lieutenant Michael O'Connor, head of the Indianapolis Police Department's Intelligence Branch, adds, "You can only initiate an investigation if a crime is committed. Police, however, should be aware of the militia groups in the area. You can't have a file on people just because they're in the militia, but you should be aware of them."

Often though, law enforcement officials find that even when they have evidence of criminal wrongdoing by militias, some government officials are reluctant to take action. Many prosecutors, either because of the fear of retaliation by the militia, or the fear of bad publicity, will not press charges against militia members, even when the police have evidence of criminal activity.

A *New York Times* article on 20 June 1997 said: "[S]tate enforcement is largely paralyzed. A long list of state attorneys general refuse to enforce state legislation against militia and paramilitary gangs. The police are out-gunned, or they are afraid politically. In most states, officials supposed to enforce the law get no encouragement from governors."[19]

Presently, seventeen states prohibit the formation of militias, seventeen others prohibit paramilitary training, and seven prohibit both. When Morris Dees of the Southern Poverty Law Center sent a letter to state attorneys general concerning the enforcement of these existing antimilitia laws, he received responses from many who stated a reluctance to enforce the laws because they feared doing so would be unpopular and seen as a violation of the constitutional right of free assembly. This poses a huge problem. The existence of a private army brings with it a very clear and present danger to the public safety. For these officials to allow this to occur, even though in clear violation of some state laws, demonstrates a total lack of commitment to the protection of the public, something these officials are sworn to do.

Incidentally, Mr. Dees has shown that antimilitia laws can be used successfully. He used a Texas statute that outlawed private military organizations to force the Ku Klux Klan to shut down militia-type training camps for members of the "Texas Emergency Reserve," who were allegedly terrorizing Vietnamese fishermen along the Texas coast.

However, in jurisdictions where prosecutors and state attorneys are not afraid to go after lawbreakers, positive results can be obtained. The following incident demonstrates such a case.

In February 1996, a Missouri State Trooper stopped seventeen-year-old Amanda Lenk and issued her three tickets: one for speeding at seventy-eight miles per hour in a fifty-five-mile-per-hour zone, one for not wearing a seatbelt, and another for failure to drive within a single lane. Three weeks later, Amanda filed an affidavit with the county clerk entitled "Declaration of Quiet Claim," in which she declared herself to be a sovereign citizen.

The next month, when Amanda appeared in court, her father, Melvin Lenk, insisted that because Amanda was a sovereign citizen, the court had no jurisdiction over her and warned the judge of severe consequences if he did not drop the charges against Amanda. Judge Patrick S. Flynn, of course, refused to drop the charges. Two weeks later, Judge Flynn received a summons to appear before the common law court "Our One Supreme Court," which, of course, Judge Flynn also refused to do.

On 30 March 1996, a twenty-member "common law grand jury" held a hearing in Bowling Green, Missouri. The grand jury found Judge Flynn guilty of treason, conspiracy, and fraud. The jury ordered that a multimillion dollar lien be placed against property owned by the judge, which Amanda and Melvin Lenk filed on 1 April 1996 in the County Recorder's office. They also filed bogus liens against the prosecutor in Amanda's case and the state trooper who wrote her the tickets.

However, behavior that might in other states have turned out to be an expensive nuisance with no recourse for the victims turned out to be a law violation in Missouri. The State Attorney General, Jay Nixon, ordered the arrest of the members of the common law grand jury for "tampering with a judicial official."

Mr. Nixon even sent special prosecutors down to handle the case, and, eventually, a court convicted eighteen members of the common law grand jury. The two self-appointed leaders of Our One Supreme Court, Dennis Logan and Clifford Hobbs, both received seven-year prison sentences. Three members of the common law grand jury, including Melvin Lenk, received five years of probation, and the remaining thirteen members each received two-year prison sentences. The prosecutor dropped the charges against two of the defendants. Amanda, for some reason, apparently was not charged.

"We told them not to muck up the court system with their liens, not to make threats," said State Attorney General Jay Nixon. "We told them to quit. But unfortunately, a subset of them decided to ignore those signals and take the law into their own hands."[20]

This case clearly demonstrates how aggressive officials can stop the type of harassment many militia members and common law court adherents like to use. But today, there is a limit to what states can do. In the above case, the prosecutors were able to use the law to punish those who would file bogus liens because the defendants had attempted to intimidate a judge. Unfortunately, such protection is seldom available to lesser officials or to ordinary citizens who find themselves saddled with bogus liens. To protect all its citizens, states will have to pass laws that protect everyone from bogus liens, with stiff penalties, both criminal and financial, for those who would attempt to use this method of intimidation.

This suggestion is important, because all of us are potential victims of militia harassment. Bogus liens have often been filed against private citizens who have for some reason angered militia members or common law court adherents. This is not just a minor nuisance, since it can affect the victim's credit rating and prevent him or her from selling property with such a lien against it. Victims are often defenseless against this "paper terrorism" and must spend a considerable amount of time and money to have the liens removed.

In addition to protecting citizens from this paper terrorism, all state legislatures should follow the example of those states that have proposed new laws that would refer any disputes or questions of legality between county recorders and citizens to a local judge. These laws would allow the county recorders to avoid many of the confrontations that occur when they refuse to file questionable liens and affidavits, and would perhaps prevent violence such as occurred in the Stanislaus County (California) Recorder's Office, discussed in the last chapter.

In addition to passing laws preventing paper terrorism and protecting county recorders, certain laws already in existence need aggressive enforcement. As stated earlier, at present, seventeen states prohibit the formation of militias, seventeen others prohibit paramilitary training, and seven more prohibit both. Yet, while these antimilitia laws are on the books, it is obvious, since militias exist in every state, that they are not being enforced.

"Nowhere in the civilized world can you have what amounts to an armed private army," said Morris Dees.[21]

This lack of enforcement is troubling, because when examined closely, militias, since they have no government affiliation, are actually nothing more, as Morris Dees says, than private armies who answer only to their own self-appointed "generals." State officials must take on the responsibility to enforce these laws and vigorously prosecute those who violate them. Also, since common law courts are often affiliated with militias and they, too, are illegal, states should clamp down on and do away with all common law courts.

The Militia Task Force of the Southern Poverty Law Center has drafted a model antimilitia law for states without one. "In an age increasingly populated by militia groups that train to commit violence, states should seriously think about using these anti-militia laws to shut down militias," said Morris Dees and attorney Ellen Bowden, who drafted the model law. "States without these laws should enact them, because they are the best route to prevent the violence that militias can cause before it occurs."

The model law reads as follows:

A. Any two or more persons who associate as a military organization or demonstrate with arms in public without the governor's authority shall be guilty of a misdemeanor.

B. A military organization is any unit with arms, command structure, training, and discipline designed to function as a combat or combat support unit.

C. This section does not apply to any school or college where military training and instruction is given under the provisions of state or federal laws.[22]

However, since most militias form and exist in either rural areas or small communities, where law enforcement is usually thinly spread, enforcing such laws against militias could prove impossible without help. State police agencies, therefore, would need to assist small agencies with enforcing laws against militias.

In addition, because police officers are the most visible representatives of the government, they are held to a higher standard than members of the general public. For this reason, many people believe state and local police officers should not be allowed to join militias. Some might argue that this is a violation of the police officer's right of free association; however, police officers do not have the same right of free association as the general public. A police officer, for example, is not allowed to associate with felons. And since most states have laws against militia organizations, belonging to one is often a law violation anyway.

"Police officers, whether we like it or not, must march to a higher level of values than the rest of the public," said former ATF agent Steve Wortham. "We must follow the law explicitly and we must not conduct business or personal affairs in any way that would lead the public to question our allegiance to the law or our personal values."

Finally, there is another set of laws that needs both tightening up and aggressive enforcement. A serious concern that became very apparent to me while I was doing research for this book is that there are gigantic loopholes in many of our gun laws, particularly where gun shows are concerned. According to an article in the *Indianapolis Star*, there are presently over 22,000 firearms laws and ordinances in the United States, but they are laxly enforced and riddled with loopholes.[23] Because of this, a recent study found that four Southern states where gun laws are lax account for 25 percent of the guns used in Northern city crime.[24] State legislators, therefore, need to tighten up their gun laws and also tighten up restrictions on what can occur at gun shows. Law enforcement agencies must also closely police gun shows to be certain that the gun sales occurring there are proper and legal. From what I have witnessed, any criminal or mental patient can walk into a gun show and walk out with any weapon he or she wants.

No one in America should be prosecuted by the government simply because of his or her beliefs. Most militia members, I have found, truly believe that the government has gotten too large and too obtrusive, and it is their right to feel this way, and even their right to proclaim it from rooftops if they want. However, when a person's beliefs take the form of creating heavily armed private armies, the state or, as we shall see in the next chapter, the federal government must step in. Private armies led by self-appointed generals cannot be allowed to exist in a free society.

◈ ◈ ◈ ◈ ◈ ◈ ◈ ◈ 15

THE FEDERAL GOVERNMENT'S RESPONSE TO MILITIAS

Like many farmers in America during the 1980s, Ralph Clark began falling behind on the payments for a loan he had taken out on his 930-acre wheat farm. His financial crunch began when, like many other farmers, he borrowed heavily to expand and upgrade his farm in anticipation of a huge bounty from the proposed Soviet grain deal. However, when the much-anticipated Soviet deal fell through, Ralph Clark fell onto desperate times. He found he owed the Farm Credit Bank of Spokane $3.1 million that he could not repay.

In response to this personal financial crisis, Clark went a bit further than most distressed farmers. In 1994, he and several dozen other individuals in similar financial circumstances briefly took over and occupied the Garfield County (Montana) Courthouse, establishing a common law court and issuing indictments against government officials. Following this, he and his group set up "Justus Township" on a tract of land near Jordan, Montana, which they claimed was not part of the United States and consequently did not fall under the jurisdiction of its laws. Interestingly, Clark and the others who joined him at Justus Township would proclaim this rejection of the United States government despite the fact they had readily accepted over $675,000 from the federal government in farm subsidies.[1]

The neighbors whose farms adjoined the newly proclaimed Justus Township, but who did not subscribe to Clark's political views, saw the move as nothing more than a desperate act by men who had gambled on the future and lost. According to an article in *Time* magazine: "The common view is that the Clarks and their cohort are sore losers in the perilous game of farming and ranching."[2]

The group who established Justus Township called themselves "freemen." A freeman believes in the doctrine of sovereign citizenry, which says that, as sovereign citizens, freemen reside outside the jurisdiction of the federal government. A freeman, by this group's definition, can only be a white male, since all others are citizens only by virtue of the Fourteenth Amendment. Therefore, all other individuals, including women, the freemen maintain, have only those rights that white males give them. "If these people who are in public office now followed God's Laws and worshiped God truthfully, would we have women in office? No!" said one of the leaders of the freeman in a court document. "Would we have laws to protect gays? No! Would we have laws to compel you to hire colored people to fill a quota? No!"[3]

Freemen believe that the only laws they must obey are the Organic Constitution (the original Constitution and the first ten amendments), the common law, and the Magna Carta (the English "constitution" signed by King John in 1215). The freemen of Montana, besides proclaiming themselves to be sovereign citizens, however, were also ardent believers in the virulently racist Christian Identity sect, discussed in the chapter on fringe group crossover. But mostly, the freemen of Montana became known for their money order scam, which defrauded not just banks and other institutions, but also many small businesses and private citizens.

The money order scam began when Ralph Clark's farm, near Jordan, Montana, became the capital of Justus Township. Soon, other likeminded individuals joined the group, including fugitives from justice LeRoy Schweitzer and Rodney Skurdal. A court had earlier issued warrants against these two men on charges of tax law violations, gun law violations, and running a money scam. Soon after his arrival, Schweitzer become the leader of the freemen group because he offered the debt-ridden farmers what appeared to be a way to escape their problems. According to Schweitzer's political philosophy, the Federal Reserve system was a fraudulent agency that issued currency with no backing. Their debts, therefore, he explained to the farmers, were not valid or real. He then showed his followers how, using liens placed against the federal government as collateral, they could issue their own currency in the form of money orders that he claimed were just as valid as Federal Reserve notes. For the beleaguered farmers, this seemed to be an answer from heaven. The money orders could be used to pay off their huge debts. The only problem with Schweitzer's solution was that the scheme was illegal.

Regardless of the legality of their practices, however, for some time, the freemen on Ralph Clark's farm conducted seminars, which drew hundreds of people from all over the United States. For $300 per head, students could come and learn how to use liens against the federal government as collateral for money orders. The students could then use these money orders not only to pay off debts or to pay for goods and services, but they were advised at the seminars to write the money orders for more than the amount owed and demand a refund of the overpayment. Soon, these types of worthless money orders began showing up all over the country.

In Detroit, in order to pay an $80,000 tax bill, a man sent the IRS a money order, bearing Schweitzer's signature, for $167,427.98, and demanded that the IRS issue him a refund for the overpayment. Also in Detroit, a man used a fraudulent freeman-style money order as down payment on a car lease. In California, federal authorities arrested Elizabeth Broderick, nicknamed the Lien Queen, for selling money orders inspired by LeRoy Schweitzer. Claiming that her "comptroller's warrants" were backed by liens she had against the government, Broderick charged individuals $200 to attend her classes and an additional $100 if they wanted her money orders, which she insisted were just as valid as Federal Reserve notes, and could be used for the same purposes. These fraudulent money orders, however, not only bilked businesses and government agencies, but also many private citizens, who lost money and property when they accepted the money orders as real. By January 1997, the authorities said they were investigating 151 people across the United States for their involvement in the freeman-style money order scam.

Because of the widespread use of these freeman-style money orders and pleas for help from Garfield County officials, who did not have the manpower to confront the large group held up at Justus Township, the FBI sent an undercover agent to one of the seminars at the Clark farm. The agent, gaining the trust of the freemen by promising to build them a tower that could be used for shortwave radio broadcasts, decoyed Schweitzer and several others away from the farmhouse with the suggestion that they inspect the tower site. On 25 March 1996, while Schweitzer and others were looking over the proposed site, federal authorities arrested them. The twenty-one remaining freemen at the Clark farm, upon seeing their leader and several other freemen arrested, barricaded themselves on the farm and began a standoff that would last for eighty-one days and sorely test the FBI's resolve never to have a repeat of Ruby Ridge or Waco.

In late March 1996, a federal indictment charged ten people, most believed to be held up at the Clark farm, with both issuing millions of dollars in phony money orders and threatening a federal judge. Several of the freemen also faced state charges that included criminal syndicalism and advocating violence for political aims. Sending in 100 agents, the FBI surrounded the Clark farm and set up their command post several miles away, beginning the siege of the freemen in earnest. When news of the standoff hit the airways, militia leaders and others around the country held their breath, wondering if the end result of this standoff would be another Ruby Ridge or Waco.

This fear was sparked because it had been the FBI's out-of-control actions at Ruby Ridge and the results of their poorly thought out actions at Waco that had brought the militia movement into being in the first place. For several months, not only militia leaders, but also most of the American public would daily tune into the evening news to see how the FBI was handling the freemen standoff. The FBI, though, obviously having learned lessons from Ruby Ridge and Waco, decided that rather than using those kinds of aggressive tactics, they would instead try to bring the freemen out through negotiation.

"We are engaged in talks, trying to convince them to come out so they can answer to the court," said FBI spokesman Ron VanVranken. "We are trying to approach this in a positive way, with the goal of resolving it peacefully. There have been no shots fired, no injuries, which we are thankful for."[4]

However, as an extra precaution, just to be certain no repeat of Ruby Ridge or Waco occurred, the FBI sent senior officials out from Washington, D.C., to Montana. In addition, the FBI Headquarters in Washington, D.C., activated its Strategic Information and Operations Center in order that the officials there could coordinate and oversee the FBI activities in Montana. FBI Director Louis J. Freeh even flew out to Montana and viewed the area around the Clark farm.

The FBI's apparently peaceful intentions, however, did not stop the conspiracy spinners. Rumors quickly spread that the federal government intended to use military personnel in the freemen standoff. "We had rumors that 200 special forces were up there training at Caspar, Wyoming, and flew up toward the Billings area," said David Trochmann of the Militia of Montana.[5]

The FBI's apparently peaceful intentions also did not convince all militia leaders that their new attitude was in earnest. Norm Olson, a militia leader from Michigan, announced that he and another militia leader would travel to Jordan, Montana. "We're going to use the occasion to meet with other militia leaders and organize a national front," said Olson. "If militia people are killed by federals, roughly 1.5 million armed, uniformed militia are in training and ready. It could reverberate across the country in a firestorm."[6]

Along with Olson, other militia members and leaders from across the country converged on Jordan, Montana. Like the incident in Roby, Illinois, the following year, the militia wanted their presence noticed. However, unlike Roby, Illinois, the freemen did not command the outpouring of support that Shirley Allen would. These were not seemingly innocent citizens set upon by the authorities. These were armed criminals under indictment, individuals who had placed a $1 million bounty on various local government officials, and who were not friendly to outsiders. Anyone approaching the Clark farm was curtly ordered by armed freemen to leave. Twice, news crews shooting film in the area had their camera equipment forcibly taken away by armed members of the freemen group. The freemen also did not have the support of other community members. Actually, most residents of Garfield County did not like the freemen, because many of them had been threatened by members of this group.

Because of this lack of community support for the freemen, during the FBI siege, local residents who were fed up with the freemen held a meeting and about 100 of them volunteered to be deputized by the local sheriff. They wanted to help him arrest the freemen. "These jerks have to be stopped," said a man whose property bordered Justus Township.[7] Petitions began circulating in Jordan, Montana, urging the FBI to use "reasonable force" to arrest the freemen. The FBI, however, maintained its siege, and would not allow itself to be drawn into a Randy Weaver-type confrontation. Many members of the news media covering the standoff at Justus Township said they believed the FBI was suffering from "Weaver Fever."

Relatives of some of the people held up at Justus Township, seeing this lack of support for the freemen and hoping to end the standoff without bloodshed, asked Gerry Spence, one of the attorneys who had defended Randy Weaver after his surrender at Ruby Ridge, to mediate between the authorities and the freemen. Spence said he would only mediate at the request of the FBI. Norm Olson, a militia leader from Michigan, offered his services as mediator, but the FBI declined his offer. Former Green Beret Colonel Bo Gritz, who successfully convinced Randy Weaver to surrender, did attempt, with FBI approval, to act as negotiator, but after several days at Justus Township, he gave up in disgust, complaining about the freemen "legal mumbo-jumbo."[8] He claimed that, several times, he had worked out a plan to which most of the people inside the Clark farmhouse agreed. "But any time that happens," Gritz said, "they are immediately put down verbally by these vitamin salesmen who would have to get a job if this whole thing collapses."[9]

Colorado State Senator Charles Duke also attempted to act as a mediator but, like Gritz, gave up in disgust. "They're just scam artists," Senator Duke said of the freemen.[10] During the first two months of the standoff, the FBI used forty-two different people as intermediaries, but without any success. Unlike at Waco, however, where the FBI ignored advice from experts, in this standoff, the FBI actively used experts who advised them about the freemen's style of thinking.

After several months passed and no resolution to the standoff appeared near, those watching it closely feared that the FBI's patience had finally begun to wear thin, and that a Waco-type assault was imminent after all. They feared this because, in late May 1996, the FBI began moving several armored vehicles and a helicopter to the site.

On 11 June 1996, however, an apparent break in the standoff occurred. The FBI gave Edwin Clark, a relative of Ralph Clark, "free passage" to leave the farm so he could consult about a possible surrender with freemen leader LeRoy Schweitzer, who was being held by the authorities in Billings, Montana. The FBI flew Edwin Clark there and back in an FBI airplane. The FBI did this because they knew that the freemen, after two and a half months, were now seriously considering surrendering. A week before, a man, his wife, and their two daughters had left the freemen compound. They told the FBI that food supplies were running low and that water was becoming scarce. They also said the freemen were running out of fuel for their generators, which were needed because, earlier in the siege, the FBI had cut off electricity to the farm. Also, due to the siege, the freemen had recently run out of toothpaste and toilet paper.

On 13 June 1996, woefully lacking in necessities, and realizing they had no widespread public support, the remaining sixteen freemen at the Clark farm finally surrendered to the authorities. However, they made one of the conditions of their surrender a promise from the authorities that a Montana state legislator would agree to safeguard a Ryder rental truck full of documents that the freemen insisted proved their claims of government misconduct. Thus, the eighty-one-day siege of the Montana freemen ended with no shots fired and no one injured. Although this siege cost the FBI millions of dollars and involved 633 federal agents, it demonstrated that the FBI had learned valuable lessons at Ruby Ridge and Waco.

"The message that comes out of it is very clear," said FBI Director Louis Freeh. "If you break the law, the United States government will enforce the law. It will do it fairly, but firmly."[11]

Attorney General Janet Reno, who had approved the assault on the Branch Davidian compound in Waco, added her thoughts. "From the first day of the standoff in Montana, the Justice Department and the FBI have worked with steadfast determination to reach (Thursday's) result—arrest of the Freemen without loss of life or injury and without compromising our mission to fully and firmly enforce federal laws."[12]

But the most pertinent comment was made by Deputy Attorney General Jamie S. Gorelick, who said, "The most significant point here is that it shows that the FBI and the Justice Department learned from the tragedies at Ruby Ridge and Waco."[13]

Even though jailed, however, it seemed the freemen just could not quit. An Internet posting, dated 25 September 1996, from the "Freedom Center," offered electronic copies of all legal briefs filed in the freemen case and periodic news releases involving the trial. Subscribers could get all of this for a nominal fee, the ad said. How much? Only $100 per year. However, the ad warned, only federal reserve notes or postal money orders would be accepted.[14]

On 2 July 1998, a federal jury returned thirty-five guilty findings against the freemen. The jury told the judge they were deadlocked on the remaining counts. U.S. District Judge John Coughenour ordered the jurors to resume deliberations. On 8 July 1998, the jury returned with twenty-two more convictions.

The ending of the Montana freemen standoff turned out almost storybook perfect for the FBI. No shots fired, no injuries incurred, no major deals struck about reduced criminal charges. The freemen simply gave up to the authorities.

The peaceful resolution to this standoff, however, did more than just put a little shine back on the FBI's reputation, a reputation that had been seriously tarnished by Ruby Ridge and Waco. It likely saved the United States from a militia backlash. Militia members and sympathizers had watched the incident closely during the eighty-one days that the FBI maintained its siege. A violent end to this standoff would have only confirmed the militia's belief in a brutal, corrupt government, and would have dashed forever any hopes of ever convincing the more moderate militia sympathizers that the federal government could be an entity that has the best interests of the people at heart. It would also possibly have resulted in retaliation by the more violence-prone militia members, not to mention alienating a large segment of the general population.

"These people [militia members] are very sensitive to their constitutional rights," said Clark R. McCauley, professor of psychology at Bryn Mawr College. "The downside is that there are people who sympathize in general with their concerns who can be motivated and stirred into action by mistakes by the government."[15]

Chip Berlet of Political Research Associates adds this thought: "There is at least an unwritten policy among the people in the federal government not to create martyrs. I feel treading cautiously is better. It spends money, but it will save money because you won't create people who join these movements."[16]

Just this one incident, though, no matter how well handled and resolved, will not be enough to stop the militia accusations of government brutality and corruption. And it will certainly not be enough to stymie militia recruiting. To do this, the federal government must make a number of positive changes. First, there must be no more Ruby Ridges or Wacos. This means that the federal government must continue to show restraint when facing situations where there is no imminent danger. Federal law enforcement officers must use the resolution of the Montana freemen incident as a model for any future standoffs of this type.

In addition to this change in law enforcement policy, however, more must also be done to change the public's view of the federal government. In the past, when the government has made a mistake, it has covered it up rather than admitting it. The federal government has already been caught in so many lies during cover-up attempts, such as Agent Orange and Gulf War Syndrome, that anything but complete honesty and openness will be seen as only more of the same deceptiveness. And regardless of any new guidelines and models for behavior, if more future incidents like Ruby Ridge and Waco occur, they must be thoroughly and openly investigated, and, most important, wrongdoers, no matter who or how highly placed, must be punished. To do otherwise simply perpetuates the militia movement's feelings and beliefs that the federal government is basically corrupt and unchangeable in its present form.

While much of the militia's distrust and dislike of the federal government centers around the actions of law enforcement agencies such as the FBI and ATF, many members of the public believe that other federal agencies must also be cleaned up. A considerable amount of the friction between militia members and the federal government involves the IRS. A surprisingly large number of militia members have had serious problems with being unable to pay their taxes. These tax problems are often what has driven them to join the militia movement. And because of serious problems at the IRS, militias attract more and more individuals every year. During Congressional hearings in 1997 and 1998, members of Congress heard horror story after horror story about IRS abuse of citizens. They heard stories about hordes of overly aggressive agents storming into private businesses without warning, and of IRS supervisors measuring employees by how much tax money they could squeeze out of citizens. They heard stories of IRS agents breaking the law to pad their statistics and of agents seizing homes, bank accounts, and businesses.

Along with the seizure of their property and bank accounts, though, I found that an unusually large number of militia members have been hit with huge penalties from the IRS. The chairman of the Senate Committee that oversees the IRS said he believes that the IRS penalty system is "out of control." Senator William V. Roth said that problems with the IRS are the "reason the income tax is losing the confidence of the American people. Make no mistake about that."[17] Part of the problem with the penalty system, Senator Roth's committee found, is that the IRS often unfairly allows a long time to pass before notifying taxpayers of mistakes in their tax return, sometimes years, but the penalties for these mistakes start from the day the tax is due. Consequently, the interest on the penalties can often be enormous. Also, the committee found that, until 1997, the IRS used the amount of penalties and interest generated as a measure of employee performance. This type of unfair treatment only solidifies the militia belief that the federal government is evil, corrupt, and completely uncaring about citizens. This type of unfair treatment also drives many citizens to join the militias, or at least become sympathetic to their cause.

A point many people in government service tend to forget is that the government's job is to serve the people, not the other way around. I am not saying that agencies such as the IRS should not go after tax cheats or call in people for audits who have made mistakes in their tax returns. They should. There are a number of people in this country who do not want to pay their fair share as the rest of us do, and the IRS should go after these individuals. But they should do it fairly, honestly, and respectfully. However, Congressional hearings in 1997 and 1998 found that the IRS pursued audits very aggressively, so aggressively in fact that the public was outraged. Citizens want to be treated fairly, honestly, and respectfully by government employees, and they felt the IRS was not doing this. Until the IRS and every federal agency changes, the militia rhetoric will continue to find sympathetic ears among the public.

However, even if all government employees followed strict regulations that prohibited unnecessarily aggressive tactics with the general public, it still would not be enough for some people. There is a small percentage of fringe individuals involved in the militia movement who cannot change their feelings about the government and cannot rein in their intense hatred. They like to blame the government for everything, even though the government is really not the source of their problems. There are a number of people in the militia movement who, like the freemen of Montana, have suffered severe economic losses due to gambles they ventured on that did not work out. And there are a number of people in the militia movement who, due to their lack of education or training, cannot meet the demands of the modern workplace; consequently, they hold menial, low-paying jobs, with little or no room for advancement. Yet because these individuals, due to their psychological makeup, cannot accept that perhaps they are the cause of their own problems, they instead look for a scapegoat on which to vent their bitterness and frustration. The militia movement's virulent antigovernment rhetoric fills this need perfectly. Due to this intense hatred and bitterness toward the government, these fringe individuals are the ones most likely to be involved in crime and violence. They are the Timothy McVeighs, the dangerous people the police need to go after.

In an attempt to supply law enforcement with the tools necessary to stop the bloodshed and violence that people like Timothy McVeigh wreak on society, the Clinton Administration, soon after the Oklahoma City bombing, suggested giving law enforcement additional power to fight domestic terrorism. The administration suggested increasing covert surveillance and relaxing the ban on military involvement with civilian law enforcement. The administration also offered proposals that would give police the authority to investigate groups that have not yet shown any criminal activity, the power to tap phones and computer lines without court authorization, and free access to hotel registers, credit records, and the files of common carriers.

FBI Director Louis Freeh has also proposed to federal legislators that any encryption codes (the keys used in decoding messages) used for any type of communication, on the Internet or otherwise, be supplied to law enforcement upon court order. "The looming specter of the widespread use of robust, virtually uncrackable encryption is one of the most difficult problems confronting law enforcement as the next century approaches," the FBI Director told a Senate Judiciary Committee. "At stake are some of our most valuable and reliable investigative techniques and the public safety of our citizens."[18]

Freeh has also talked about "reinterpreting" the FBI's rules concerning when it can initiate an investigation of a group. As it stands presently, a group must show the intention to become involved in criminal activity before law enforcement can begin investigating it. Freeh said the FBI's new interpretation would mean there will be no need to find "an imminent violation" of the law, as the guidelines have in the past been interpreted to mean, but simply any conduct which "might violate federal law."[19] The chasm-size difference between these two guidelines would give the FBI the power to investigate many, many more groups and individuals than it could in the past.

While most people applaud Director Freeh's intentions of wanting to protect American citizens from more Oklahoma City–type bombings, many do not agree with most of the proposals to expand law enforcement's authority to combat domestic terrorism. The power to circumvent constitutional rights should never be given simply to make law enforcement's job easier. Opponents of expanding the FBI's power believe that while protecting the public safety is important, so is protecting constitutional rights. History has shown far too many times that giving law enforcement too much power almost always ends in an abuse of this power. One has only to remember the COINTEPRO scandal of J. Edgar Hoover's FBI, in which federal agents investigated individuals who were not necessarily criminals but simply held unpopular beliefs. During COINTEPRO, federal agents investigated civil rights leaders, members of the antiwar movement, and other people whose beliefs conflicted with Mr. Hoover's. In addition, the FBI, along with investigating these individuals, also planted false information in an attempt to discredit them. In order to prevent a repeat of this, there must be a careful balance between aggressive law enforcement, which includes surveillance, wiretaps, informants, and so on, and the respect of every citizen's constitutional rights. Regulations that state that those groups or individuals investigated by law enforcement *must* have shown intent to commit a crime exist to protect citizens' rights.

"Any time you abandon the idea of a criminal predicate for an investigation, you have to find something else," said the Executive Director of the ACLU. "What would that be? Maybe national origin, maybe race, maybe political beliefs, maybe militia rhetoric. . . . When you don't use a criminal predicate, you must find some other proxy that inevitably tramples on constitutional rights."[20]

During thirty years in law enforcement, I've seen firsthand the dangers of unsupervised or uncontrolled power. All of the proposals that would allow the police to conduct investigations on a whim, to initiate wiretaps without court approval, or to have free access to personal records, run the risk of ending in the abuse of citizens' constitutional rights. Not only would this be a disservice to all citizens, but it would also further polarize militia members from the government. Law enforcement officials must aggressively pursue criminals—which include militia members who violate the law—but they must do it within the parameters of the Constitution.

"There must always be a balance between guaranteeing the public safety and individual rights," said ATF agent George Stoll.

In the last few years, as shown by many of the incidents reported in this book, federal law enforcement officers have been very successful with moving in and arresting militia members who have built bombs and planned terrorism—before the event occurred. They have been able to do this legally and successfully without the expanded powers suggested by some, and without violating the public's constitutional rights.

Two opinion polls reflect the public's point of view on this subject. A poll published by the *San Francisco Chronicle* found that two-thirds of the respondents were against the formation of armed civilian militias; half of the respondents felt that the militia groups posed a possible threat to society; and one-third felt the militia to be a *severe* threat to society.[21] However, a poll by the *San Francisco Examiner* found that while over sixty-seven percent of the respondents felt the government should crack down on unregulated militias, almost 90 percent believed it should not be done at the expense of civil liberties.[22]

Along with keeping within the bounds of the Constitution while aggressively pursuing militia members who violate the law, federal law enforcement agencies also need to assist small communities that experience militia problems. These communities are often too small to have officers who are trained or experienced in dealing with militia problems, and many times the community's police department is dwarfed by the much larger militia. For example, in Garfield County, Montana, where the freemen standoff occurred, law enforcement consisted of the sheriff and one deputy. It would have been extremely hazardous and foolhardy for these two men to have attempted to enter the heavily fortified Clark farm. Federal authorities must come to the aid of such small communities.

As I discussed in the last chapter, many state attorneys general today are reluctant to prosecute militias, even though they are illegal. While the existence of militias and/or paramilitary training is against the law in forty-one of the states, these state laws are useless if they are not enforced. Morris Dees, of the Southern Poverty Law Center, and Kenneth Stern, of the American Jewish Committee, have recommended that a federal law be passed that would prohibit the existence of militias not authorized by state laws. "Militias are private armies," Mr. Stern said. "Many contain small cells designed to conduct guerilla warfare against American government and American society. America is not Somalia. Why do we tolerate private armies? Why are they not illegal under federal law?"[23] This proposed federal law could be used in jurisdictions where local officials are reluctant to enforce state laws against militias.

In addition to passing a law prohibiting militias, however, the federal government also needs to promulgate rules that would prohibit government employees, including military personnel, from belonging to militias. Most taxpayers would likely question the appropriateness of government employees belonging to organizations that espouse antigovernment rhetoric.

Another important area that needs federal intervention involves explosives manufacturers. For a number of years, an idea has been proposed by law enforcement lobbyists that would greatly assist law enforcement in tracking down bombers. That idea is that the manufacturers of chemical explosives should be required to add identifiers to their explosives. These identifiers are microscopic chemical tracing elements called "taggants." These taggants survive the explosion and can identify the explosive used. This idea is not just theory but has already been successfully implemented in other countries. In Switzerland, for example, according to an article in the *New York Times*, chemical explosive markers have been used to track suspects in more than 500 bombings in five years.[24] Regardless of this success in other countries, though, the use of taggants in the United States, while proposed in Congress a number of times, has always been defeated through aggressive lobbying by gun rights advocates. As with lobbying against the restriction against assault rifle ownership, gun rights advocates feel this taggant requirement would be just one step in a total government crackdown. The federal government, however, must not allow these special interest groups to derail efforts to ensure the public safety.

While enacting the new federal laws and rules suggested here would be extremely helpful, it is not enough. Existing federal laws also need to be more strictly enforced. The assault rifle ban, for example, needs to be enlarged and enforced without exception. What logical reason exists for a private citizen to own an assault rifle? Such a weapon is far more powerful and deadly than anyone needs for personal protection or for hunting. Assault rifles are meant for only one thing: to kill many human beings.

While the federal government, through its actions at Ruby Ridge and Waco, may have unwittingly initiated the birth of the modern militia movement, it can also play an integral part in bringing the militia movement to an end. The reason militias are tolerated in many states, even though in violation of the law, is because of the sympathy they receive from many citizens who agree that the federal government appears to be out of control. The federal government can pull the rug of support out from under the militia movement but only by becoming a government that serves the people, not the other way around.

❖ ❖ ❖ ❖ ❖ ❖ ❖ ❖ **16**

CITIZEN'S RESPONSE TO MILITIAS

B eginning in 1995, in several small communities in Michigan, normally quiet township meetings suddenly began to heat up. Militia members, many of whom didn't even live in the township, began to attend the meetings and essentially tried to take them over. The reason behind this move was the militia's belief that the township government is superior to the state or federal government. Consequently, amid shouts and threats, the militia members have attempted to bully their way into control in several small communities. At one point during a Norman Township meeting in Wellston, Michigan, a militia member stood up and threatened to have a township official forcibly removed from the room. The militia members have also attempted through their intimidation to demand that every matter brought before the township board be voted on, not by the township board, but by those attending the meeting, usually with a show of hands. This then allows the decisions made at the township meetings to be controlled by the militia, which packs the meetings with their members and supporters.

The militia's intrusion in the Michigan township meetings usually results in a division into factions of those attending. Some support the militia's ideas, some don't. One of the ideas the militia members in Michigan espouse is that their interpretation of the law is that all a group of voters has to do is post a notice for a township meeting, then they can get together, with or without the township board, and pass any measure they want. This right, the militia members insist, has been kept secret from the public in order to make it easier for the New World Order to take over control of the country.

"They want to take away your God-given rights," said a militia leader in Wellston, Michigan. "They're saying you have no say-so. Are you going to let someone else run your life?"[1]

Of course, in reality what the militia members want is control—to be able to impose their view of the world on the community—and they use these threatening and disruptive tactics in an attempt to do so. Because of the commotion, intimidation, and threats at some township meetings, many people no longer attend. Those that do attend are often angry at those who don't take their side.

"I'm not pro-this side or pro-that side," said a resident of Wellston. "I am pro-Norman Township. And look at us here. We are screaming and arguing. We are calling each other names."[2]

All of this, naturally, is what the militia wants. Less attendance at the township meetings and a divided community allow them to have control. Interestingly, through their actions, these militia members are opposing what they preach, which is a return to the ideals and values of our Founding Fathers. To make this return, however, many militia members believe they must intimidate into silence all voices but their own, something with which the Founding Fathers certainly would not have agreed.

These types of disruptive events do not occur, however, just in Michigan. According to an article in *USA Today*, in Montana, the threat of violence by militia members at public meetings has discouraged attendance. "Some residents, fearing for their safety, have stopped attending [land use and other community] meetings altogether, allowing a vocal minority to dictate public policy."[3] Militias in California have also advised their members to pack local meetings.

A letter to the *Indianapolis Star* from a member of the Wabash River Heritage Corridor Commission tells of a county commission meeting called to consider the idea of applying for an American Heritage River designation for the Wabash River. This is an honorary designation that makes receiving federal funding easier but gives away no local control to anyone. The local militia group, however, took the view that this was actually an international plot by the United Nations to take over land in the United States. "The land-rights extremists repeated their nonsense to anyone who listened and bullied those who did not," the letter said. "They told the corridor commission people that we were 'satanic' and 'unconstitutional.' Individuals asked me how I could sleep at night since I was handing private property over to the United Nations."[4]

While the militia movement may be for many readers only an interesting item in the news, a short report about a distant event, for others, it has become much more personal. For many communities, the reality is that the militia has suddenly appeared and found a home there. And while many militia members are good people who simply believe that our government has problems that need to be addressed, other members are not. Some militia members are blatantly racist, given to the wildest of paranoid fantasies, and prone to violence or intimidation. What can private citizens do to stop the racist rhetoric, stop the threats and intimidation? How can private citizens successfully expose the fallacies of the conspiracy theories proposed by militia members, or successfully reject the racist teachings of Christian Identity? There are a number of ways, regardless of how threatening and intimidating these groups of angry, armed individuals appear to be, that ordinary citizens can stop them from taking over the community and spreading their doctrine of paranoia, racism, and hatred.

To begin with, citizens must keep themselves aware and up to date on national and worldwide events so they can counter with facts any conspiracy spin that militia members may give to these events. Informed citizens likely will not change the militia member's mind, who will possibly instead accuse them of being part of the conspiracy, but with knowledge and facts, citizens can debunk the conspiracy theories for anyone with an open mind who has not yet been fully indoctrinated into the militia.

In some communities, though, a much stronger opposition is needed. In areas of the country where the militia movement is particularly influential, such as the Pacific Northwest, private citizens have formed their own antimilitia groups. These citizen groups teach racial tolerance and mutual respect. For example, in Bonner County, Idaho, citizens have formed the Bonner County Human Rights Task Force, which, through education, attempts to counter the influence of extremist groups that inhabit the area.

A group called Nine Mothers against Hate, in Bellingham, Washington, has begun spreading its message of love and racial tolerance. "What we are trying to say is there are moments in time when you have to draw a line in the sand and say, 'What's across this line is wrong,'" said Emily Weiner, the group's leader.[5] The group began its campaign by disseminating racial tolerance messages using the symbol of multiracial hands grasping each other. This symbol has appeared on homes, bumper stickers, and buttons.

In Everett, Washington, the Human Rights Coalition for Snohomish County gives its antimilitia message at schools, churches, and public gatherings. "The more of us who speak up and say this is not acceptable, then the louder our voice is going to be," said a Coalition member.[6]

However, militia problems are not confined just to the Pacific Northwest. In Chicago, the Center for New Community, a religious group, sponsored a conference and workshop in December 1997 that showed the attendees how to oppose the rhetoric and intimidation of the militia movement. "The white supremacist movement is alive and well in the Midwest," said Reverend David Ostendorf, director of the Center. "Its cutting edge includes a resurgent Klan and the so-called Christian Patriot organizations [which includes the militia movement] with their vicious antigovernment agenda."[7]

Along with these small, local groups, there are also several much larger and more well-organized groups of private citizens who oppose the intimidation and racial intolerance preached by some militias. The Simon Wiesenthal Center in Los Angeles monitors television and radio broadcasts all over the world, looking for racist and anti-Semitic messages. It also maintains an extensive record of groups espousing hate and racial intolerance. When the U.S. Army became concerned that some of its soldiers were involved with racist groups, Army representatives met and conferred with officials from the Wiesenthal Center, asking for input concerning their knowledge of this possibility.

In 1987, the Northwest Coalition Against Malicious Harassment was founded. Formed in response to the rhetoric and violence of extremist groups in the Northwest, this group has been a vocal opponent of racist and hate groups, including militias that espouse racist and hate doctrines. The Coalition often works in coordination with other human rights groups, sharing information and expertise.

Without a doubt, though, the largest and most successful private organization opposing the militia movement is the Southern Poverty Law Center (SPLC) in Montgomery, Alabama. Beginning as a small civil rights law firm in 1971, the SPLC has grown into a national organization that opposes any group who would deny minorities equal rights. The SPLC has won some impressive legal victories against hate groups, and through these, they have essentially bankrupted the groups and/or put them out of business.

In 1987, the SPLC won a $7 million verdict against the United Klans of America for its involvement in the lynching of a young black man. To settle this judgment, the Klan was forced to sell its headquarters and end its operation in the United States. In 1990, the SPLC won a $12.5 million judgment against the White Aryan Resistance movement for its involvement in the murder of an Ethiopian student. Soon afterward, the SPLC began the seizure of the White Aryan Resistance movement's assets. In 1994, a lawsuit won by the SPLC forced the Ku Klux Klan's Invisible Empire to disband and sell its assets.

In 1994, the SPLC, finding links between armed civilian militias and white supremacist groups, established the Militia Task Force. Sensing a growing threat of violence from some of these militia groups, the SPLC sent a letter to Attorney General Janet Reno warning her of this threat. The bombing in Oklahoma City soon afterward underscored the danger the SPLC had foreseen. The Militia Task Force continues today, tracking militia activity and issuing reports on developments in the movement.

In addition, the SPLC also involves itself in education through distributing a number of books and videotapes teaching racial tolerance. Supported by private donations, the SPLC presently has over 300,000 sponsors. And while the SPLC is not officially supported by the government, a large number of police officers and other government employees applaud their work. During the writing of this book, I spoke to a number of police officers who told me that Morris Dees of the SPLC was one of their heroes.

In 1995, in response to the intrusion of militia groups in many small-town government meetings, the American Jewish Committee published a thirty-page booklet entitled *What to Do When the Militia Comes to Town*. The Foreword of the booklet states: "The main impact of the militia movement has been its thuggish intimidation of grass-roots democracy in small communities across America. In some counties the fear created by the militia is akin to that produced in the South by the Ku Klux Klan in the 1960s. Public officials and private citizens actually have to weigh whether speaking their minds will result in an armed response from the local private armies."[8]

This booklet warns readers that by not opposing militia activity in a community, the residents are giving the field of public opinion over to the militia organizers, who will attempt to insinuate that they have a broad base of support, whether they do or not. The author of the booklet, Ken Toole, director for the Montana Human Rights Network, advises concerned community members to begin organizing to oppose militia influence as soon as a militia group makes its first appearance and to seek allies from groups such as minority organizations, churches, labor unions, schools, the business community, the news media, and others who can help. In addition, in the booklet, Mr. Toole offers valuable information about how to get a community organization off the ground that can counter the militia, how to sustain the organization, how to involve the news media in the group's efforts, and how to develop campaigns that can oppose the militia message. I heartily recommend this booklet for any community facing the invasion of a militia group. It can be obtained from

The American Jewish Committee
165 East 56 Street
New York, NY 10022-2746

However, before any readers might begin to think that the militia threat in America really does not affect them because they live in a large city and most militias exist in small communities and rural areas, let me advise them to think again. As I have said several times in this book, although serious danger certainly exists whenever a private army, such as a militia group, is allowed to form, a significant threat also comes from the radical fringe that the militia message attracts. These fringe members often feel that in order to right things they see as wrong, they have to strike at what they view as the evil force in our society: the federal government or the feared New World Order. Unfortunately, as in Oklahoma City, this radical fringe also feels that its strike must be large and dramatic in order to be effective. By necessity, this means the strike has to take place in an urban area.

As a consequence, all citizens need to be involved and aware of militia activities in our country. But just as important, all citizens also need to be aware of which politicians are supporting the militia movement. By giving their support to the militia movement, politicians are in effect condoning the formation of private armies that do not answer to the government the politicians represent and often vehemently oppose it. By supporting the militias, politicians are also giving legitimacy to the radical fringe attracted to the militia message. Every citizen needs to make his or her elected officials aware that private armies cannot, under any circumstances, be allowed to exist in America. Only then can we be certain to avert another Oklahoma City disaster.

❖ ❖ ❖ ❖ ❖ ❖ ❖ ❖

FINAL THOUGHTS ABOUT MILITIAS

Morris Dees of the Southern Poverty Law Center, in gauging the danger of the militia movement, said, "Assessing the magnitude of the threat posed by militia groups operating today is a bit like gauging the risk to shipping posed by icebergs. The number that can be seen is important, but the real danger lies beneath the surface."[1]

Before I began writing this book I thought of the militia movement in America as simply a bunch of ultra-right-wing conservatives. They were, I believed, just a group of gun lovers who fantasized about being soldiers, and consequently spent their weekends running around the woods playing military games. I have since learned they are something much more dangerous than that.

Like Mr. Dees, and as many of the incidents reported in this book have shown, I have found that while the average militia member the public sees may be just an ordinary citizen frustrated with the direction our government is taking, there is a hidden militia, inspired by the militia message and made up of fringe individuals intent on bringing about their own agenda by violence. There is a hidden militia that puts every citizen in this country at risk of injury or death, a hidden militia that will willingly use firearms, bombs, and violence to achieve their ends.

But even as dangerous as this hidden militia is, the visible and public militias that exist in this country also present a very clear and present danger to innocent citizens. Even though militias consist mostly of ordinary citizens who individually may mean no harm, they are essentially heavily armed private armies under the command of individuals of questionable stability and unknown leadership qualities. The possibility that one of these leaders, seeing an event through the veil of paranoia, could exhort his followers into committing violence under the cloak of patriotism is unquestionable. When a militia leader states in a militia publication that our present system of government must be replaced by violence of arms if necessary, when a militia leader tells an audience that the present government leaders should be arrested by militia members and hung, I think it is time for the authorities to move in, enforce the law, and put the militias out of business.

"No modern country in the world allows private armies," said Danny Welch of the Southern Poverty Law Center. "If we let fanatics run around the countryside plotting armed resistance against any law or government action they don't like, we are flirting with anarchy."[2]

The only thing I could add to this statement is to say, "Amen."

NOTES

1. The Birth of the Modern Militia Movement

1. "Aryan Nations" (25 November 1997). Internet posting at http://www.storm-front.org/aryan_nations/.
2. Gerry Spence, *From Freedom to Slavery* (25 November 1997). Internet edition at http://www.ruby-ridge.com/gspence.htm, p. 3.
3. *Department of Justice Report Regarding Internal Investigation of Shootings at Ruby Ridge, Idaho During Arrest of Randy Weaver* (25 November 1997). Lexis Counsel Connect Internet edition at http://www.cs.cmu.edu/afs/cs.cmu.edu/user/wbardwel/public/nfalist/ruby.ridge1, p. 32.
4. Ibid., p. 2.
5. Ibid., p. 13.
6. Ibid., p. 132.
7. Ibid., p. 163.
8. "SWAT Team Members: FBI Shooter Rules 'Crazy' at Ruby Ridge" (14 October 1995). CNN Internet posting at http://cnn.com/US/9510/ruby_ridge/index.html.
9. *Department of Justice Report Regarding Internal Investigation of Shootings at Ruby Ridge, Idaho During Arrest of Randy Weaver*, p. 35.
10. David Johnston, "F.B.I. Leader at 1992 Standoff in Idaho Says Review Shielded Top Officials," *The New York Times* (10 May 1995), p. D-21.
11. Mark Warbisa, "Federal Judge Dismisses Charges against Agent in Ruby Ridge Shooting," *Indianapolis Star* (15 May 1998), p. A-4.
12. Tim Weiner, "U.S. Won't Bring More Charges against F.B.I. Officials in Ruby Ridge Siege," *The New York Times* (16 August 1997), p. A-1.
13. Morris Dees, *Gathering Storm* (New York: HarperCollins, 1996), pp. 49–67.
14. Richard Abshire, "Terrorism in America," *Law Enforcement Technology* (July 1996), p. 42.

15. Dave Delany, "The Great Militia," *Modern Militiaman* (July–August 1996). Internet edition at http://www.mo-net.com/~mlindste/mmmisu2.html.
16. Gary E. McCuen, *The Militia Movement and Hate Groups in America* (GEM Productions, 1996), p. 67.
17. Martin Lindstedt, "Interview: The Militia Movement and the Media," *Modern Militiaman* (September 1997). Internet edition at http://www.mo-net.com/~mlindste/mmmisu7.html.
18. Lesley Pearl, "Militias' Numbers Drop While Violence Rises, ADL Finds," *Jewish Bulletin of Northern California* (25 November 1997). Internet edition at http://shamash.org/jb/bk970425/sfamili.htm.
19. Keith W. Strandberg, "The Extreme Right and Militia Groups," *Law Enforcement Technology* (March 1997), p. 47.
20. Militia Task Force, "Active Patriot Groups in 1997" (1 June 1998). Internet posting at http://www.splcenter.org/klanwatch/patriotst.html.
21. Strandberg, p. 47.
22. Chip Berlet and Matthew N. Lyons, "Militia Nation," *Progressive Magazine* (14 December 1997). Internet edition at http://www.publiceye.org/pra/rightist/milnatbl.html.
23. Ibid.
24. Larry McMurtry, "Return to Waco," *The New Republic* (7 June 1993), p. 170.
25. Strandberg, p. 45.
26. Dees, p. 200.

2. The Beliefs and Philosophies of Militias

1. "Four Accused of Plotting Series of Bombings in U.S.," *The Detroit News* (14 November 1995), p. 1.
2. Richard Abanes, *American Militias* (Downers Grove, Illinois: InterVarsity Press, 1996), p. 2.
3. "Mission Statement of the 7th Missouri Militia" (27 November 1997). Internet posting at http://www.mo-net.com/~mlindste/misn7mom.html.
4. Harold Sheil, *MacNeil/Lehrer News Hour* (26 April 1995).
5. Abanes, p. 10.
6. "Thanks For Checking Us Out" (26 November 1997). Internet posting at http://militia.gen.mi.us/thanks.html.
7. "Who We Are" (26 November 1997). Internet posting at http://members.aol.com/starkmil/who.htm.
8. "What Is the 52nd Missouri Militia?" (26 November 1997). Internet posting at http://www.wws.net/52ndmo/whatis.html.
9. "South Carolina Militia Corps Organization" (26 November 1997). Internet posting at http://pw1.netcom.com/~dan3/scmcorg.htm.
10. Donald A. Manson and Darrell K. Gilliard, *Presale Handgun Checks, 1996* (Washington, D.C.: U.S. Government Printing Office, 1997), p. 1.
11. Michael Winerip, "Ohio Case Typifies the Tensions between Militia Groups and Law," *The New York Times* (23 June 1996), p. A-1.

12. "Tennessee Volunteer Militia," *Tennessee Volunteer Militia Newsletter* (February 1996), p. 5.
13. Chris Williams, "Militia Leaders Dispute Reports," *San Antonio Express-News* (1 October 1997), p. 1.
14. Abanes, p. 13.
15. Ralph R. Reiland, "New American Revolutionaries March to a Very Different Beat," *Insight on the News* (19 August 1996), p. 29.
16. Abanes, p. 18.
17. Todd Kepple, "Ken Medenbach's Half-Finished Home Flaunts His Distaste for Regulation," *Klamath Falls Herald and News* (25 April 1997), p. 1.
18. "Thanks For Checking Us Out," p. 1.
19. "Militia—History and Law FAQ" (27 November 1997). Internet posting at http://www.militia-watchdog.org/faq6.htm.
20. "Our Mission" (27 November 1997). Internet posting at http://www.ipser.com/usmilitia/mission.htm.
21. "Our Vision" (27 November 1997). Internet posting at http://www.ipser.com/usmilitia/vision.htm.
22. Serge F. Kovaleski, "Women in Militias Say Ranks Are Not Just for Angry White Males," *The Washington Post* (9 September 1995), p. A-3.
23. Martin Lindstedt, "Always Use a Tool Which Works or the Myth of Non-Violence," *Modern Militiaman* (July–August 1996). Internet edition at http://www.mo-net.com/~mlindste/mmmisu2.html.
24. Martin Lindstedt, "Second Interview with Editor of *Modern Militiaman*," *Modern Militiaman* (September 1997). Internet edition at http://www.mo-net.com/~mlindste/mmmisu7.html.
25. "Virtue, Liberty, and Independence," *The Pennsylvania Minuteman*, Vol. 10, p. 3.
26. "Developing a Mental Trigger" (27 November 1997). Internet posting at http://www.ipser.com/usmilitia/minuteman/1997spring/mentaltrigger.htm.
27. "Missouri 51st Militia By-Laws" (27 November 1997). Internet posting at http://www.tfs.net/personal/sbarnett/5100001.htm.
28. "A Well Regulated Militia? Today?" (27 November 1997). Internet posting at http://mmc.net/text/today.txt.

3. National and Worldwide Conspiracies

1. "Report on Military Internment Camps" (28 November 1997). Internet posting at http://members.aol.com/starkmil/gard_3.htm.
2. "What We Believe," *Militia of Georgia Handbook*, p. 9.
3. David Neiwert, "An Interview with John Trochmann/Randy Trochmann" (14 February 1996). Internet posting at http://www.militia-watchdog.org/dn-troch.htm.
4. Michael Kelly, "The Road to Paranoia," *The New Yorker* (19 June 1995), p. 60.
5. Paul Feldman, "Militia Promoters Draw a Crowd," *Los Angeles Times* (8 May 1995), p. A-3.

6. Richard Abanes, *American Militias* (Downers Grove, Illinois: InterVarsity Press, 1996), p. 76.
7. Jason Vest, "Leader of the Fringe," *The Progressive* (June 1995), p. 28.
8. Chip Berlet and Matthew N. Lyons, "Worried about the Secret Conspiracies Running the World?" (3 May 1998). Internet posting at http://www.public-eye.org/pra/tooclose/conspi.html.
9. Abanes, p. 109.
10. Mike McIntire and Rick Hartford, "The Government as Enemy," *The Hartford Courant* (23 November 1997), p. 1.
11. Glenn Frankel, "Blast's Shock Was Its Source," *The Seattle Times* (3 June 1997), p. 1.
12. Richard Hofstadter, *The Paranoid Style in American Politics* as quoted in Paul Feldman, "Conspiracy Theories in America," *Los Angeles Times* (31 May 1995), p. 4A.
13. Chip Berlet and Matthew N. Lyons, "Militia Nation," *The Progressive* (June 1995), p. 22.
14. Jill Smolowe, "Enemies of the State," *Time* (8 May 1995), p. 58.
15. *The Alien Files*, offered by the Patriot Report Online Catalog at http://www.logoplex.com/resources/patriot_report/alien.html.
16. Michael Janofsky, "'Militia Man' Tells of Plot To Attack Military Base," *The New York Times* (25 June 1995), p. 14.

4. Who Belongs to Militias?

1. Ruth Mullen, "IPD Officer Apologizes for Remarks About Mayor," *Indianapolis Star* (5 May 1995), p. A-1.
2. Ibid., p. A-2.
3. Ruth Mullen, "IPD Chief Demotes Officer for Slur Against Mayor," *Indianapolis Star* (6 May 1995), p. A-2.
4. Ibid., p. A-1.
5. "IPD Officer Apologizes for Remarks About Mayor," p. A-2.
6. Ibid.
7. R. Joseph Gelarden, "City Undecided about Appealing Order and Restoring an Officer's Rank," *Indianapolis Star* (24 August 1996), p. B-2.
8. Ibid.
9. Gregory Weaver, "Court Upholds Officer's Demotion," *Indianapolis Star* (20 November 1997), p. B-1.
10. Richard A. Serrano, "Militias' Ties to Public Safety Officials Feared," *Los Angeles Times* (13 October 1996), p. A-1.
11. Serge F. Kovaleski, "A Show of Strength for Militia Movement," *Washington Post* (24 September 1995), p. A-6.
12. Serrano, p. A-18.
13. Brad Knickerbocker, "Militia Leader Decries Racism, Violence," *The Christian Science Monitor* (9 April 1997), p. 4.
14. Marc Cooper, "Montana's Mother of All Militias," *The Nation* (22 May 1995), p. 714.

15. Paul Feldman, "Militia Promoters Draw a Crowd," *Los Angeles Times* (8 May 1995), p. A-24.
16. "FBI Claims Men Planned Attacks against Government," *Las Vegas Review-Journal* (2 August 1997), p. 1.
17. "Flip Burgers or Die!" (2 February 1998). Internet posting at http://www.publiceye.org/pra/rightlist/flip_die.html.
18. Richard Abanes, *American Militias* (Downers Grove, Illinois: InterVarsity Press, 1996), p. 100.
19. Ibid., p. 10.
20. Mella McEwen, "Militias Looking to Replace Soviet Bogeyman," *Midland Reporter-Telegram* (22 August 1997), p. 1.
21. Chris Bouneff, "The Extremist Movement Still Exists," *Idaho Press-Tribune* (25 April 1997), p. 1.
22. Jo Thomas, "Militias Hold a Congress and Not a Gun Is Seen," *The New York Times* (1 November 1996), p. A-20.
23. David McHugh, "Black Members Find a Place in Militias," *Indianapolis Star* (28 January 1997), p. A-15.
24. "Women in Militias Say Ranks Are Not Just for Angry White Males," p. A-3.
25. Peter Applebome, "Increasingly, Extremism Is Heavily Armed," *The New York Times* (30 April 1997), p. A-27.
26. Jonathan S. Landay, "Army Brass Rattled by Ties of Soldiers to White Supremacists," *The Christian Science Monitor* (19 December 1995), p. 3.
27. Morris Dees, *Gathering Storm* (New York: HarperCollins, 1996), p. 212.
28. Jonathan Rabinovitz, "Militia Leader Sought Arrest In Custody Case, He Asserts," *The New York Times* (3 October 1996), p. B-8.
29. Richard A. Serrano, "Militias: Ranks Are Swelling," *Los Angeles Times* (18 April 1996), p. A-1.
30. Kovaleski, p. A-6.
31. Brad Knickerbocker, "New Armed Militias Recruit Growing Membership in US," *The Christian Science Monitor* (3 April 1995), p. 14.
32. Jason Vest, "Leader of the Fringe," *The Progressive* (June 1995), p. 28.
33. Janet Hook, "Militias Have Forged Ties to Some Members of Congress," *Los Angeles Times* (28 April 1995), p. A-1.

5. Militia Training

1. "Agents Seize Arsenal of Weapons in Militia Home," *The Detroit News* (3 July 1996), p. 1.
2. Angie Cannon and Jodi Enda, "Arizona Group Nondescript on the Surface But Allegedly Well-Prepared for Bloodshed," *Indianapolis Star* (7 July 1996), p. D-5.
3. Patricia King, "'Vipers' in the 'Burbs," *Newsweek* (15 July 1996), p. 20.
4. James Brooke, "Agents Seize Arsenal of Rifles and Bomb-Making Material in Arizona Militia Inquiry," *The New York Times* (3 July 1996), p. A-18.
5. Tony Ortega, "Sticking By His Guns," *Phoenix New Times* (2 January 1997), p. 1.

6. James Brooke, "Volatile Mix in Viper Militia: Hatred Plus a Love for Guns," *The New York Times* (5 July 1996), p. A-16.
7. Christopher John Farley, "A Nest of Vipers," *Time* (15 July 1996), p. 24.
8. Peter Doskoch, "The Mind of the Militias," *Psychology Today* (July–August 1995), p. 12.
9. Jeff Randall, "West Virginia Wannabe Syndrome?" *Modern Militiaman* (October 1996). Internet edition at http://www.mo-net.com/~mlindste/mmm isu3.html.
10. "When Will the Standoffs End?" *The Pennsylvania Minuteman*, Vol. 10, p. 4.
11. Christopher John Farley, "Patriot Games," *Time* (19 December 1994), p. 48.

6. Weapons of Militias

1. Kathy Marks, *Faces of Right Wing Extremism* (Boston: Branden Publishing, 1996), p. 100.
2. Peter Baker, "Va. Hunt Club Was Aiming to Battle Government, U.S. Says," *Washington Post* (27 April 1995), p. C-6.
3. "Virtue, Liberty, and Independence," *The Pennsylvania Minuteman*, Vol. 10, p. 3.
4. "We Will Not Disarm" (12 December 1997). Internet posting at http://www.ipser.com/usmilitia/minuteman/1997fall/disarm.htm.
5. Charles H. Featherstone, "Ministry Groups Call Christians to Arms," *Logan Herald Journal* (25 April 1997), p. 1.
6. Carol Rosenberg, "Gun Laws Blasted by Lawmakers," *Indianapolis Star* (10 April 1997), p. A-6.
7. Baker, p. C-1.
8. Peter Doskoch, "The Mind of the Militias," *Psychology Today* (July–August, 1995), p. 12.

7. The Militia Threat

1. Michael Fleeman, "Bombing Survivors Recall Horror of Blast," *Indianapolis Star* (26 April 1997), p. A-3.
2. Ibid.
3. Michael Fleeman, "McVeigh Evidence Lacks Fingerprints," *Indianapolis Star* (16 May 1997), p. A-16.
4. Tom Kenworthy, "Prosecution Ends McVeigh Case," *Indianapolis Star* (22 May 1997), p. A-2.
5. Clark Staten, "Domestic Terrorism: The Enemy from Within?" *EMS Magazine* (July 1995). Internet edition at http://www.emergency.com/domsterr.htm.
6. Michael Fleeman, "McVeigh Jury Suffers Through More Gruesome Testimony," *Indianapolis Star* (6 June 1997), p. A-8.
7. Fleeman, "Bombing Survivors Recall Horror of Blast," p. A-3.

8. Michael Fleeman, "FBI Chemist Testifies Explosives Residue Found on McVeigh's Clothing," *Indianapolis Star* (20 May 1997), p. A-7.

9. Michael Fleeman, "Camera Tracked Truck's Movement," *Indianapolis Star* (15 May 1997), p. A-3.

10. "The Turner Diaries," ABC News Internet edition at http://www.abcnews. com/sections/us/oklahoma/turner_diaries.html.

11. Richard A. Serrano, "Ex-Friend Tells of McVeigh's Bomb Plans," *Indianapolis Star* (13 May 1997), p. A-2.

12. "Testimonial" (1 December 1997). Militia Task Force Internet posting at http://www.splcenter.org/klanwatch/kw-10d.html.

13. Michael Fleeman, "Writings, Videotapes Used to Trace McVeigh's Rage over Waco," *Austin American-Statesman* (9 June 1998). Internet edition at http://www.austin360.com/news/features/mcveigh/waco.htm.

14. Howard Pankratz and Michael Booth, "Nichols Escapes Death Penalty," *Denver Post* (8 January 1998), p. 1.

15. Peggy Lowe, "More Trials Could Come," *Denver Post* (8 January 1998), p. 1.

16. Evan Thomas, "The Plot," *Newsweek* (8 May 1995), p. 28.

17. Sharon Cohen, "Militias Have Moved Out of the Spotlight," *Indianapolis Star* (31 March 1997), p. A-2.

18. Serge F. Kovaleski and Susan Schmidt, "Bombing's Repercussions Rattle Militias," *Washington Post* (6 May 1995), p. A-12.

19. Cohen, p. A-2.

20. Gary E. McCuen, *The Militia Movement and Hate Groups in America* (GEM Productions, 1996), p. 49.

21. Morris Dees, *Gathering Storm* (New York: HarperCollins, 1996), p. 200.

22. Keith Schneider, "Manual for Terrorists Extols 'Greatest Coldbloodedness,'" *The New York Times* (29 April 1995), p. 10.

23. McCuen, p. 101.

24. "Text of Alleged McVeigh Letter," *The New York Times* (9 May 1997), p. 1.

25. Phil Linsalata, "Militias See Verdict as Confirmation of Conspiracy," *The Detroit News* (3 June 1997), p. 1.

26. Libby Quaid, "Death for McVeigh," *Indianapolis Star* (14 June 1997), p. A-1.

27. McCuen, p. 43.

28. George Lane, "Militias: Murrah Blast Set Off by Nuclear Device," *Denver Post* (24 February 1997), p. 1.

29. Jill Smolowe, "Enemies of the State," *Time* (8 May 1995), p. 58.

30. Julian Guthrie, "FBI Probes Vacaville Car Bomb Connection," *San Francisco Examiner* (15 April 1996), p. A-1.

31. "Spokane Link to Olympic Bombing," *The Seattle Times* (27 January 1997), p. 1.

32. "Last Spokane Bomber Gets 55 Years," *Washington Post* (3 December 1997), p. 1.

33. David McHugh, "Militias Now Are Smaller, But Angrier," *Detroit Free Press* (26 March 1997), p. 1.

34. "Drug War" (2 December 1997). Internet posting at http://www.splcenter. org/klanwatch/kw-12.html.

35. Ibid.

8. Fringe Group Crossover

1. Pastor Pete Peters, *The Real Hate Group* (LaPorte, Colorado: Scriptures For America), pp. 25–26.
2. Michael Dorgan, "A Radical Religion Motivates Montana 'Freemen,'" *The Seattle Times* (3 April 1996), p. 3.
3. Lou Kilzer and Kevin Flynn, "Militia Movement Had Roots in Estes," *Inside Denver* (14 May 1997). Internet edition at http://www.insidedenver.com/extra/bomb/0514okc2.htm.
4. Morris Dees, *Gathering Storm* (New York: HarperCollins, 1996), p. 50.
5. Larry Pratt, *Safeguarding Liberty, the Constitution and Citizen Militias*, as quoted by Dees, p. 55.
6. John Roland, "Rumored March 25 Arrests," newsgroup message #180430 (24 March 1995), posted on Internet to talk.politics.guns.
7. Brad Knickerbocker, "Militia Movement Ideas Seep into the Mainstream," *The Christian Science Monitor* (7 February 1997), p. 4.
8. Dees, p. 202.
9. Daniel Voll, "At Home With M.O.M.," *Esquire* (July 1995), p. 46.
10. Gary E. McCuen, *The Militia Movement and Hate Groups in America* (GEM Productions, 1996), p. 25.
11. Eric Harrison, "Data-Gathering by Militias, Neo-Nazis Set Off Violence Alarms," *Los Angeles Times* (11 September 1995), p. A-5.
12. *Missouri 51st Militia Bylaws*, p. 2
13. *Militia of Georgia Handbook*, p. 9.
14. "The Louisiana Unorganized Militia Home Page" (12 December 1997). Internet posting at http://www.orion-cs.com/freedomforum/.
15. Neil A. Hamilton, *Militias in America* (Santa Barbara, California: ABC-CLIO, Inc., 1996), p. 107.
16. "Charter of the Constitutional Militia of Southern California" (12 December 1997). Internet posting at http://pw1.netcom.com/~stevep/charter.htm.
17. "Mission Statement of the 7th Missouri Militia" (12 December 1997). Internet posting at http://www.mo-net.com/~mlindste/misn7mom.html.
18. Dees, p. 35.
19. "Interview: The Militia Movement and the Media," *Modern Militiaman* (September 1997). Internet edition at http://www.mo-net.com/~mlindste/mm-misu7.html.
20. Richard Abanes, *American Militias* (Downers Grove, Illinois: InterVarsity Press, 1996), p. 141.
21. Adolph Hitler, *Mein Kampf* (Boston: Houghton Mifflin, 1971), p. 307.
22. Hamilton, pp. 125–127.
23. John Rakus, *IBS* (Sacramento, California: The National Justice Foundation of America), p. 2.
24. Luna I. Shyr, "Terrorists Suspected in Derailment," *Boulder Daily Camera* (10 October 1995), p. 1A.
25. Paul Anderson, "Domestic Terrorism Strikes AMTRAK" (9 October 1995). Internet posting at http://www.emergency.com/azdrail.htm.

26. Keith Schneider, "Manual for Terrorists Extols 'Greatest Coldbloodedness,'" *The New York Times* (29 April 1995), p. 10.
27. Sarah Horn, "Wise Use Movement" (25 April 1997). Internet posting at http://www.newswest.com/crossingline/group14.html.
28. David Helvarg, "The Anti-Enviro Connection," *The Nation* (22 May 1995), p. 722.
29. Ibid.
30. Ibid.
31. "Public Apology" (18 November 1997). Internet posting at http://www.wws.net/52ndmo/index.html.

9. Militia Internal Security

1. William Booth, "Neighbors Wondering if Members of Georgia Militia Crossed the Line," *Washington Post* (28 April 1996), p. A-4.
2. Alan Sverdlik, "Georgia Militia Members Who Conspired against ATF Found Guilty," *Washington Post* (7 November 1996), p. A-9.
3. Alan Sverdlik, "Prosecutors Finish Case against Georgia Militiamen," *Washington Post* (3 November 1996), p. A-9.
4. Louis Sahagun, "Pursuit of Viper Militia May Backfire on U.S.," *Los Angeles Times* (14 July 1996), p. A-1.
5. David Foster, "Feds Balancing Free Speech, Security," *Daily Ardmoreite* (1 June 1997), p. 1.
6. Carol M. Ostrom and Danny Westneat, "Militia Leader Sought 'Peaceful' Image for Group," *The Seattle Times* (30 July 1996), p. 1.
7. Lily Eng, "Court Hears Audio of Militia Meeting," *The Seattle Times* (26 January 1997), p. 1.
8. Ibid.
9. "Militias Move Out of Spotlight, Feds Move In," *USA Today* (31 March 1997), p. 1A.
10. Mike Johnson, "How to Spot a Government Infiltrator," *Modern Militiaman* (July–August 1996). Internet edition at http://www.mo-net.com/~mlindste/mmmisu2.html.
11. Serge F. Kovaleski and Susan Schmidt, "Bombing's Repercussions Rattle Militias," *Washington Post* (6 May 1995), p. A-12.
12. Martin Lindstedt, "Forming In-Fill-Traitor Resistant Patriot Organizations," *Modern Militiaman* (June 1996). Internet edition at http://www.mo-net.com/~mlindste/mmmisu1.html.
13. Louis Beam, "Leaderless Resistance," *Modern Militiaman* (October 1996). Internet edition at http://www.mo-net.com/~mlindste/mmmisu3.html.
14. Ibid.
15. "Organizing the Militia: The Militia Cell" (3 March 1998). Internet posting at http://www.ipser.com/usmilitia/minuteman/1997/winter/organizing.html.
16. Randall, "West Virginia Wannabe Syndrome?" p. 19.

242 **Terrorists Among Us**

17. Martin Lindstedt, "Principles of Resistance Organization," *Modern Militiaman* (September 1997). Internet edition at http://www.mo-net.com/~mlindste/mmmisu7.html.
18. Ibid.
19. Jeremy Pearce, "2 Militia Members Charged in Shooting Death of 3rd Man," *The Detroit News* (17 December 1996), p. 1.

10. Militia Publications and Propaganda

1. Jason Vest, "Leader of the Fringe," *The Progressive* (June 1995), p. 28.
2. Peter Doskoch, "The Mind of the Militias," *Psychology Today* (July–August 1995), p. 12.
3. Gary E. McCuen, *The Militia Movement and Hate Groups in America* (GEM Productions, 1996), p. 69.
4. "Militias Move Out of Spotlight, Feds Move In," *USA Today* (31 March 1997), p. 1A.
5. James Coates, "Internet Is Thick with False Webs of Conspiracy," *Chicago Tribune* (10 November 1996), p. 1.
6. Keith W. Strandberg, "The Fringe on the Net," *Law Enforcement Technology* (April 1998), p. 51.
7. "Interview: The Militia Movement and the Media," *Modern Militiaman* (September 1997). Internet edition at http://www.mo-net.com/~mlindste/mmmisu7.html.
8. "Militia Force XXI: Command and Control," *Minuteman Magazine* (Summer 1997). Internet edition at http://www. ipser.com/usmilitia/minuteman/1997summer/forcexxi.htm.
9. Lois Pilant, "Building a Better Bomb Squad," *The Police Chief* (September 1997), p. 38.
10. Timothy Egan, "Terrorism Now Going Homespun as Bombings in the U.S. Spread," *The New York Times* (25 August 1997), p. A-1.
11. John F. Harris, "Clinton Rejects 'Patriot' Claim of Armed Groups," *Washington Post* (6 May 1995), p. A-1.
12. Dean Speir, "*Waco: The Big Lie* Revealed as a Hoax," *Gunweek* (21 January 1994), p. 15.
13. Doreen Carvajal, "Left-Wing Satire Pirated on Internet as Right-Wing Fact," *The New York Times* (1 July 1996), p. A-1.
14. Andrew Macdonald, *The Turner Diaries* (Hillsboro, West Virginia: National Vanguard Books, 1978), p. 29.
15. Ibid., pp. 150–151.
16. Richard Abanes, *American Militias* (Downers Grove, Illinois: InterVarsity Press, 1996), p. 116.
17. Morris Dees, *Gathering Storm* (New York: HarperCollins, 1996), p. 122.
18. John Mintz, "Air Force-German Alliance Draws Right-Wing Flak," *Washington Post* (28 May 1996), p. A-1.

19. Sam Stanton, "Militias Adjust Strategy as Movement Evolves," *The Sacramento Bee* (8 December 1996), p. 1.

11. A National Militia

1. "Ex-Leader of Militia Plans 3-Day 'Congress,'" *The Detroit News* (14 October 1996), p. 1.
2. "Third Continental Congress List of Grievances" (19 November 1997). Internet posting at http://www.eagleflt.com/list.html.
3. Michele Kay, "Smaller Militia Groups Are Seen as Big Threat," *Austin American-Statesman* (7 July 1997), p. 1.
4. "Comments on the Alliance" (12 December 1997). Internet posting at http://www.geocities.com/CapitolHill/Lobby/1076/mm6comnt.html.
5. Internet posting at http://www.pw1.netcom.com/~dan3/alliance.htm.

12. The Power and Influence of Militias

1. Caren Benjamin, "Trial Begins for Tootle Vision Founder," *Las Vegas Review-Journal* (25 March 1997), p. 1.
2. Ed Vogel, "Militia Movement Figure Moves to Las Vegas," *Las Vegas Review-Journal* (17 November 1997), p. 1.
3. Jeff Randall, "What If They Called a Revolution and Nobody Came?" *Modern Militiaman* (June 1996). Internet edition at http://www.mo-net.com/~mlindste/mmmisu1.html.
4. Craig Garrett, "Despite Critics, Canton Lawmaker Says She Stands for 'What's Right,'" *The Detroit News* (28 January 1996), p. 1.
5. Internet posting at http://www.mo-net.com/~mlindste/okc-fund.html.
6. Susan Redden, "Representative: Local Grand Jury Needed," *The Joplin Globe* (21 March 1997), p. 6B.
7. Steve Lipsher, "Right, Left Buzz with Anticipation," *Denver Post* (21 February 1997), p. 1.
8. Internet posting at http://members.aol.com/starkmil.aal.htm.
9. Cynthia H. Craft, "Sen. Don Rogers Finds Favor With Militia Movement," *Los Angeles Times* (30 April 1995), p. A-18.
10. Timothy Egan, "Idaho Freshman Embodies G.O.P.'s Hope and Fear in '96," *The New York Times* (15 January 1996), p. A-12.
11. Sidney Blumenthal, "Her Own Private Idaho," *The New Yorker* (10 July 1995), p. 27.
12. "Friends of the Militias I," *The New Republic* (15 May 1995), p. 10.
13. Blumenthal, p. 28.
14. Janet Hook, "Militias Have Forged Ties to Some Members of Congress," *Los Angeles Times* (28 April 1995), p. A-1.
15. Paul Rauber, "None Dare Call It Reason," *Sierra* (January–February 1997), p. 24.

16. "Gun Control Foe Says Waco Was Planned to Promote Ban," *Miami Herald* (13 May 1995), p. 6A.

13. Militias and the Law

1. Twila Decker, "Jurors Hear Tape of Plot to Kidnap an Orlando Judge," *Orlando Sentinel* (25 June 1997), p. 1.
2. "'Charge' of Treason Rings in Court," *Orlando Sentinel* (6 June 1997), p. 1.
3. Ibid.
4. "Judge Says He Feared Anti-Government Group," *Miami Herald* (12 June 1997), p. 5B.
5. Pat Leisner, "Conspiracy Defendant Hurls Own Charges as Trial Opens," *Miami Herald* (7 June 1997), p. 6B.
6. "'Charge' of Treason Rings in Court," p. 1.
7. "Recording Lets Jury Look inside a Militia," *Orlando Sentinel* (22 June 1997), p. 1.
8. "IRS Agent Infiltrated Renegade Group," *Miami Herald* (22 June 1997), p. 1B.
9. "Tampa Militia Members Convicted," *Miami Herald* (14 August 1997), p. 5B.
10. "Judge Says He Feared Anti-Government Group," p. 5B.
11. Pat Leisner, "Jury Convicts Militia Founder," *Sun-Sentinel* (14 August 1997), p. 1.
12. Davan Maharaj, "O.C. Judges Warned about 'Freemen'-Style Group," *Los Angeles Times* (14 May 1996), p. A-1.
13. Michael Janofsky, "Home-Grown Courts Spring Up as Judicial Arm of the Far Right," *The New York Times* (17 April 1996), p. A-1.
14. Ibid.
15. *Blackstone's Commentaries*, p. 68, as quoted in Rollin M. Perkins, *Perkins on Criminal Law* (Mineola, New York: The Foundation Press, 1969), p. 24.
16. Janofsky, p. A-1.
17. Bruce C. Smith, "Report Stirs Protest from Militia, Panel," *Indianapolis Star* (6 January 1998), p. B-1.
18. Katherine Seligman, "Bay Area Judges in Militias' Sights," *San Francisco Examiner* (19 April 1997), p. A-1.
19. Marsha Ginsburg, "Aim to Disrupt Government Files," *San Francisco Examiner* (31 March 1997), p. A-1.
20. Ibid.
21. Mike McIntire and Rick Hartford, "The Government as Enemy," *The Hartford Courant* (23 November 1997), p. 1.
22. Ibid.
23. "Grassroots Court Activists Create Headaches, Paperwork for Justice System," *The Shawnee News-Star* (15 January 1998), p. 1.
24. Mike Tharp and William J. Holstein, "Mainstreaming the Militia," *U.S. News & World Report* (21 April 1997), p. 24.
25. "Terry Nichols: A Case Study of the Far Right" (1 December 1997). Militia Task Force Internet posting at http://www.splcenter.org/klanwatch/kw-10.html.

26. Joseph P. Shapiro, "An Epidemic of Fear and Loathing," *U.S. News & World Report* (8 May 1995), p. 37.
27. "Virtue, Liberty, and Independence," *The Pennsylvania Minuteman*, Vol. 10, p. 3.
28. Richard Abanes, *American Militias* (Downers Grove, Illinois: InterVarsity Press, 1996), p. 66.
29. George Archibald, "Constitution Scholars Divided over Issues of Self-Defense," *Insight on the News* (29 May 1995), p. 32.
30. Neil A. Hamilton, *Militias in America* (Santa Barbara, California: ABC-CLIO, Inc., 1996), p. 166.

14. State and Local Response to Militias

1. Julie Grace, "Standoff at 'Roby Ridge,'" *Time* (27 October 1997), p. 4.
2. "Urgent Roby Presence Needed" (10 October 1997). Internet posting at http://members.aol.com/starkmil/sa1.htm.
3. "My Full Confession" (10 October 1997). Internet posting at http://members.aol.com/starkmil/sa1.htm.
4. "Shirley Allen of Roby, Illinois" (10 October 1997). Internet posting at http://members.aol.com/starkmil/sa1.htm.
5. Kevin McDermott, "Standoff Raises Questions over Involuntary Commitment," *St. Louis Post Dispatch* (30 September 1997), p. 1.
6. Kevin McDermott, "Ongoing Police Presence in Standoff Wears Thin on Roby, Ill., Residents," *St. Louis Post Dispatch* (12 October 1997), p. 1.
7. Rick Hartford, "The Last Line of Defense," *The Hartford Courant* (24 November 1997), p. 1.
8. "'Roby Ridge' of Illinois Escalates" (28 September 1997). Internet posting at http://members.aol.com/starkmil/sa1.htm.
9. McDermott, "Ongoing Police Presence in Standoff Wears Thin on Roby, Ill., Residents," p. 1.
10. McDermott, "Standoff Raises Questions over Involuntary Commitment," p. 1.
11. Kevin McDermott, "Militia Negotiator Defends Police Actions in Standoff," *St. Louis Post Dispatch* (15 October 1997), p. 1.
12. "My Full Confession."
13. Kevin McDermott, "After Roby Standoff, Woman and System to Face Evaluation," *St. Louis Post Dispatch* (2 November 1997), p. 1.
14. M. W. Guzy, "Victims of Waco: We Ain't Coming Out," *St. Louis Post Dispatch* (6 November 1997), p. 1.
15. "Witnesses Deny That Victim Drew Gun," *Akron Beacon Journal* (30 June 1995), p. B-1.
16. Judy Pasternak, "Roadside Killing Heightens Police-Militia Suspicions," *Los Angeles Times* (8 July 1995), p. A-1.
17. Internet posting at http://members.aol.com/starkmil/mhill.htm.
18. Gary E. McCuen, *The Militia Movement and Hate Groups in America* (GEM Productions, 1996), p. 62.

19. A. M. Rosenthal, "The Traitor Movement," *The New York Times* (20 June 1997), p. A-29.
20. Judy L. Thomas, "Hard-Line Approach Used On Extremists," *The Kansas City Star* (18 August 1997), p. 1.
21. Peter Appledome, "Paramilitary Groups Are Presenting Delicate Legal Choices for the States," *The New York Times* (10 May 1995), p. D-21.
22. "Center Attorneys Craft Model Anti-Militia Law" (3 March 1998). Internet posting at http://www.splcenter.org/klanwatch/kw-6.html.
23. Melvin Claxton and William Gaines, "Under the Gun," *Indianapolis Star* (11 January 1998), p. D-1.
24. Carol Rosenberg, "Gun Laws Blasted by Lawmakers," *Indianapolis Star* (10 April 1997), p. A-6.

15. The Federal Government's Response to Militias

1. James Brooke, "Live Free, Live Off the Fat of the Feds," *The New York Times* (5 May 1996), p. 2.
2. Patrick Dawson, "State of Siege," *Time* (8 April 1996), p. 24.
3. Michael Dorgan, "A Radical Religion Motivates Montana 'Freemen,'" *The Seattle Times* (3 April 1996), p. 1.
4. "Militia Members Converge on FBI Standoff with 'Freemen,'" *The Seattle Times* (28 March 1996), p. 1.
5. Ibid.
6. Jason Anders, "State Militia Prepares for Battle over Montana Freemen," *The Detroit News* (12 April 1996), p. 1.
7. Dorgan, p. 1.
8. Brooke, p. 2.
9. Kim Murphy, "FBI Lets 'Freemen' Talk Themselves Out of Allies," *Los Angeles Times* (5 June 1996), p. A-1.
10. Ibid.
11. Len Iwanski, "Freemen Surrender, Face Charges," *San Francisco Examiner* (14 June 1996), p. A-1.
12. Ibid.
13. Tom Kenworthy and Pierre Thomas, "FBI, Critics Debating Lessons Learned from Freeman Standoff," *Washington Post* (16 June 1996), p. A-3.
14. Internet posting at http://www.alaska.net/~winter/schweitzer_update_9_26.html.
15. Keith W. Strandberg, "The Extreme Right and Militia Groups," *Law Enforcement Technology* (March 1997), p. 43.
16. Mike Chambers, "Militia Leader Sentenced to More Prison Time," *The Evansville Courier* (1 August 1997), p. 1.
17. Rob Wells, "IRS Penalty System Called 'Out of Control,'" *Indianapolis Star* (16 March 1998), p. A-1.
18. Jeri Clausing, "Encryption Tops Wide-Ranging Net Agenda in Congress," *The New York Times* (4 September 1997), p. A-1.

19. Stephen Labaton, "U.S. Is Easing Restrictions on Monitoring Some Groups," *The New York Times* (4 May 1995), p. B-14.
20. Ibid.
21. Bill Wallace, "Citizen Militias Worry Californians," *San Francisco Chronicle* (31 May 1995), p. A-6.
22. Kandace Bender, "Poll: Most Won't Yield Rights for Security," *San Francisco Examiner* (18 May 1995), p. A-1.
23. American Jewish Committee Press Release (9 May 1996). Internet posting at http://ajc.org/press_releases/dees.html.
24. Timothy Egan, "Terrorism Now Going Homespun as Bombings in U.S. Spread," *The New York Times* (25 August 1997), p. A-1.

16. Citizens' Response to Militias

1. Dirk Johnson, "Militia Groups Find New Target: Local Government," *The New York Times* (12 November 1995), p. A-22.
2. Ibid.
3. Kenneth Stern, "Militia Mania: A Growing Concern," *USA Today Magazine* (January 1996), p. 12.
4. Mercedes Brugh, "Good Use of Enforcement Resources," *Indianapolis Star* (14 January 1998), p. A-9.
5. Ian Ith, "Fighting Hate," *Skagit Valley Herald* (25 April 1997), p. 1.
6. Ibid.
7. "Hate Groups Growing In Midwest," *Star Tribune* (4 December 1997), p. 1.
8. Ken Toole, *What to Do When the Militia Comes to Town* (New York: The American Jewish Committee, 1995), p. v.

Final Thoughts about Militias

1. Morris Dees, *Gathering Storm* (New York: HarperCollins, 1996), p. 199.
2. Gary E. McCuen, *The Militia Movement and Hate Groups in America* (GEM Productions, 1996), p. 52.

INDEX